TAKE ME HOME

RASHMI BANSAL

TAKE ME HOME

The inspiring stories of
20 entrepreneurs from small-town India
with big-time dreams

RASHMI BANSAL

BUSHFIRE PUBLISHERS

First published by Westland Ltd in 2014
Reprinted by Bushfire Publishers LLP in 2021 (Venture by Rashmi Bansal)
Core House, Off CG Road, Near Parimal Garden
Ahmedabad 380006

ISBN: 9788193182192

10 9 8 7 6 5 4 3 2 1

BULK ORDERS (over 100 copies) for schools, colleges and institutions.
Send your requirement to enquiry@rashmibansal.in

Typesetting by Ram Das Lal

Printed at Thomson Press (I) Ltd.

DEDICATED TO

My dear brother, Aalok
For all we share

ACKNOWLEDGEMENTS

I am grateful to my Great Big Indian Family spread across the cities and small towns of India whose path to progress inspired me to write this book.

My childhood memories with: Manish, Rakesh, Yogesh(Ujjain), Rakesh (Ratlam), Rekha (Ratlam), Amit, Dipti, Rohit (Indore), Shweta (Ratlam), Aneeta didi (Dhar), Sanju 'The Terror' (Dhar), Sharad, Amit, Dhiren, Mona, Seepi (Jaipur), Ashok, Arvind bhaiyya (Banaras), Meeta, Reetu (Kanpur), Ankit, Akanksha (Nagpur) + The Delhi Gang (Rahul, Rajat, Gaurav, Swati, Mili, Pinky, Preeti).

My family post-marriage: Yatin (Ludhiana), Reeta, Mukul (Ludhiana), Pinky didi, Brij jijaji, Anshu, Akhil (Simla), Vibha didi (Hoshiarpur), Rakesh, Kavita (Chandigarh), Ashwini bhai, Kalpana bhabhi, Vepan, Neera... and everyone else.

To the many institutions who invited me to their campuses from Kakinada to Kanpur, helping me travel across India and collect the material for this book. In particular, IIT Kanpur, IIM Lucknow, IIM Raipur, IIT Jodhpur, IIT Guwahati, XIM Bhubaneshwar, MIT Manipal, BET Global Business School Belgaum, KIET Kakinada, College of Engineering, Chengannur and TIE Nagpur.

To Mr Roshan Babu and his driver, Nisufan, for taking wonderful care of me in Kerala.

To my friend, Madhuri, and driver, Jeetubhai, for a memorable day in Rajkot.

To Sudhanva Jategaonkar of Network 18 for introducing me to Parakrambhai through the LEAP conference, Goa.

Nikhil Manchanda in Kanpur, for his kind assistance with interviews.

To Sunil Handa, who has always encouraged me to be my best. And Divya Handa, for her serenity and hospitality.

My friend, Ravish Kumar, for his online and offline support in everything I do.

My colleague, Niyati Patel, and my cousin, Akanksha, for their help with proofreading.

My transcription team: John B K, Vikash Bakrewal, Dr Athishaya Mamatha, Jagjit Singh, Shweta Gadkari Joshi and Priyanka (Writersmelon). Also Jyoti Arya, Pooja Chakrapani, Priya Naveen and Anchal Patil.

Saurav Roy and Sajith Ansar of Idea Spice Design, for the brilliant new-look cover.

Durgeshbhai at Core House for his help in DTP.

Rupesh Shah for generously lending his Macbook Pro as well as getting my machine repaired.

To Delna and her wonderful staff at The Teapot Café, where I spent many happy days writing on their blue sofa.

My editor, Aradhana Bisht, for bearing with all my quirks and demands. My ever-supportive publishers, Gautam Padmanabhan and Paul Kumar of Westland.

To my dearest daughter, Nivedita, whose presence makes the house a 'home'.

Last but not the least, YB, Mom, Dad and Lata, who all know I go a 'bit crazy' when working on a deadline.

The calm countenance of Swami Vivekananda at my desk gives me strength at such times.

"Country Roads, take me home
To the place I belong..."

– John Denver

AUTHOR'S NOTE

There are some things you can never change in life. One of them is your 'place of birth'. I was born in Ratlam and this was what I had to write on my biodata, on my passport, on the very first page of my school diary.

Why had my parents been so thoughtless?

My brother had the good fortune of being born in Bombay. He would never have to answer the question, "Where is Ratlam?" Uh, it's in Madhya Pradesh. "Really – never heard of it!" And there I would squirm, feel a bit ashamed.

The citizens of Ratlam are proud of two things: their town is an important railway junction, and makes the world's best *namkeen sev*.

To me, it is what we call the 'native place'. It's where I spent summer vacations, with a houseful of aunts, uncles and cousins. Each a colourful character, indelibly etched in my mind.

Like my *chachaji,* Shyam Sunder Agrawal, who never sat at a table, or wore shirt and pant. Dressed in white kurta and pyjama, he cycled to work. There he sat on a thick mattress, with his *bahikhata*, conducting the business of the Agrawal Steel Corporation (Power House Road).

When a child was up to some mischief, chachaji would call them a *benda* or a *bendi*. A special Ratlami word for 'idiot'.

We slept on the veranda and fought over *taash ke patte* (playing cards). I could play *teen-do-paanch* the entire day and still not get bored.

Much as I hated the idea of being born in Ratlam, Ratlam never grudged me.

Looking back I see how snooty I was. Because I lived in Bombay, because I knew English. Because I never oiled my hair, or wore a bindi.

AUTHOR'S NOTE

AUTHOR'S NOTE

An idea of 'coolness' so Western, so shallow. Like the lyrics of 'Careless Whisper', which I once thought was the 'ultimate' song.

Today, I am proud of my Ratlami heritage. Of my cousins and aunts and uncles who have grown and prospered. Some of them still don't speak English, and still oil their hair. But it does not matter anymore.

This is the new India, the 'real India', the consumer every marketer and every soap opera wants to reach. They have overpowered the metros with their numbers, with their hunger. To be something, to do something. Through education, through aspiration, through pursuit of work.

They come to metro cities, in search of opportunity. But how long before the tide turns?

For there is a small revolution taking place in small-town India. A new breed of entrepreneurs who are changing old equations and assumptions. Doing world-class quality work from the city of their birth.

These cities lack the glamour of Bombay, but also the grime. It's a quieter, gentler way of life where time is what people have for each other, not something you chase to 'catch the next train'.

The future is bright, it is beckoning. Close your eyes and remember your roots. You may hear a whisper from that inner voice, "I have seen the world.... Now take me home."

January 2014 **Rashmi Bansal**
Mumbai

CONTENTS

SONS OF THE SOIL

These are the ones who never left for 'greener pastures,' but their vision and ambition expanded far beyond their native towns.

CONTENTS

SONS OF THE SOIL

These are the ones who never left for 'greener pastures', but their vision and ambition expanded far beyond their native towns.

RETURN OF THE NATIVE

They spread their wings and flew to fine institutions and foreign lands. But one day, they returned, with a dream of making a difference.

RETURN OF THE NATIVE

They spread their wings and flew to fine institutions and foreign lands. But one day, they returned, with a dream of making a difference.

CONTENTS

CHHOTI SI ASHA

Where others see problems, they work on solutions. They are agents of change, harbingers of hope for a new generation.

CONTENTS

SONS OF THE SOIL

These are the ones who never left for 'greener pastures,' but their vision and ambition expanded far beyond their native towns.

KHARA NAMAK

(SALT OF THE EARTH)

Chandubhai Virani – Balaji Wafers
Rajkot (Gujarat)

The Virani brothers started their career selling chips at the Astron Cinema in Rajkot. Four decades later, Balaji Wafers and *namkeen* commands a 65% market share in 5 states, a *desi* business holding its own against multinationals.

There is something very down to earth about Chandubhai Virani.

He wears a simple white and green checked shirt. Sits in a brown rexine chair. The walls and tables in the office have pictures of his father, his gurus and Swami Vivekananda.

"1974 se Rajkot mein Astron Cinema ke andar humne pehle naukri ki. Tab se yeh jo namkeen hai, chips hai...yeh bechte hain hum." (From 1974, my brothers and I first worked at Astron Cinema in Rajkot. Since then we have been selling chips and savouries.)

From being salaried employees, the Viranis graduated to running the cinema canteen on a contract basis. In 1982, they set up a *tawa* (wok) in their own home and began making potato chips.

There wasn't much profit in the business but it was growing, and that kept the Viranis going.

In 1992, Chandubhai Virani decided to take a big leap – setting up an automatic plant with a loan of ₹50 lakh. This bet paid off and the company has not looked back since. Today, Balaji Wafers is a ₹1000 crore company with a dominant market share in 5 states of India. And the intent to grow further.

In a corner of Chandubhai's office there is a statue of Lord Hanuman. The background depicts the bridge which the *vaanar sena* built to take Shri Ram to Lanka.

"'74 se aaj tak ek ek patthar dalte gaye, ek din bridge ban gaya, aur sone ki Lanka aa gayi." (Since '74, we put stone after stone, one day it became a bridge. That is the secret of our success.)

With stones of faith you can build bridges across oceans of doubt, and seas of despair.

'Success' is an island in your mind. You can and you will get there.

KHARA NAMAK

(SALT OF THE EARTH)

Chandubhai Virani - Balaji Wafers Rajkot (Gujarat)

Chandubhai Virani was born in Dhun-Dhoraji village in the Kalavad taluk of Jamnagar district.

"Do hazaar ki basti ka gaon hai hamara, wahan mere pitaji farmer the." (The village has a population of 2000, my father was a farmer there.)

Rain was scarce, farming was tough. In 1972, Chandubhai's father sold his ancestral agricultural land and gave his sons ₹20,000.

Popatbhai said to them, *"Jao kuch business shuru karo."* (Go, start a business.)

Coming from a farming family, the Viranis decided to enter the business of fertilisers and farm implements. But due to lack of experience and marketing, the venture failed.

"Someone supplied us with 'duplicate' fertiliser and we lost all our money."

The brothers then shifted to Rajkot and tried to run a boarding and lodging mess for college students. That too failed. But the Viranis did not give up.

At that time Chandubhai was just 17 years old. He had given up school and followed his brothers to the city, to lend a helping hand.

"Humko kuch karna hai, kuch banna hai, waha gaon mein to kuch hai nahi. Ek hi woh maansikta thi hamari." (We have to do something in life, there is nothing for us in the village. That was our attitude.)

In 1974, Astron Cinema was inaugurated in Rajkot. The brothers initially got a job in the canteen but, in fact, they were willing to do anything and everything. From manning the ticket counter to filling in for the doorkeeper, they worked tirelessly – as if the cinema hall was their own.

Seth Govindbhai Khunt was pleased. In 1976, he gave the Viranis a contract to run the cinema canteen on a revenue-sharing basis. Thus, the 4 brothers worked together to sell chips, snacks, namkeen and soft drinks to cinemagoers.

Initially, Chandubhai worked more as a helper, under the direction of his older brothers. But slowly, he developed a sense of responsibility, a sense of ambition. The canteen business was alright, but it wasn't making much progress.

"Toh maine socha, humko karna padega kuch, mehnat karni padegi." (I decided we must do something and work hard to get ahead.)

One of the hot-selling items in the canteen was wafers. The Viranis used to buy readymade packets and sell them. Chandubhai and his elder brother, Bhikabhai, decided to buy loose wafers and packet them. Thus, earning a little more on each sale.

In '76-'77, the Viranis started making sandwiches at home, thus earning more profits. But the turning point came when, in 1982, the Viranis set up a tawa at home to fry potato chips and namkeen. This production was managed mainly by Chandubhai, with support from his brothers.

Again, the idea was to have an item to sell in the cinema canteen but one of the brothers said, "Let's try to sell our wafers to other shops."

The Viranis decided to sell the wafers under the name 'Balaji'.

Initially, one of the brothers would take packets of wafers on his Luna and go from shop to shop. But it was difficult to get anyone to stock the product. And an even bigger task to collect cash after sale. Some shopkeepers would return half-consumed packets and claim the customer had returned it like that. Others would pay in torn and soiled notes.

"Humein lag raha tha ki hum bhikhari hain..." (We felt like beggars.)

Railway canteens and highway restaurants were the worst offenders. They would pay after a month and sometimes, not pay at all. Regardless of whether they received payment, the Balaji policy was to make payment to their own suppliers. For oil, for potato, for plastic bags.

In times of difficulty Chandubhai would personally meet various parties and assure that payment would be made, although with some delay.

"Many competitors were there but *woh aaye, ghaata kiya aur band kar ke chale gaye* (they made a loss and had to shut shop)."

The very fact that one company was still in business, giving delivery of wafers and paying its suppliers became a talking point.

"Jaise-jaise kaam chalta gaya, vishwas badta gaya. (Slowly, we gained trust in the market.) First from 1 shopkeeper, then 10, and in time we had 200 loyal customers."

As business grew, it became difficult to carry wafers on a moped. The Viranis decided to buy a rickshaw but this was easier said than done – they were simply not available.

However, the man who supplied oil to the Viranis happened to own one. And agreed to sell it, as a matter of *vyavhaar* (relationship).

"Jo musibatein aayi thi usme bahut kuch seekhne koh mila* (We learnt a lot from our early difficulties), *that was our 'guru gyaan."

> ***"Chun chun ke hum batata lete the, thoda rate jyada dete the."* (We were very selective in picking the right potatoes, even if it meant paying a little more.)**

The oil merchant said, "You are my big customer, a good customer. *Aapko zaroorat hai, main aapko de dunga (I will help you).*"

In fact, he had taken the vehicle on loan and that loan was transferred to the Viranis. As the business grew further, a tempo was required. This time, Balaji Wafers had no trouble getting a loan from the State Bank of India.

Apart from finance and marketing, at the very core of the business was the golden yellow potato wafer. Balaji Wafers were crisp and tasty, and hence growing in popularity. But how does one get quality on a consistent basis? It's both an art and a science.

Chandubhai found a good cook, who was an expert with wafers. The problem was the cook would bunk 15 days in a month, often without any notice. At these times Chandubhai would take over the tawa himself.

"Starting mein kafi maal humne bigada. Par thode time mein sara mereko practical samajh aa gayi." (Initially I spolit a lot of wafers but in time I understood all the practical aspects of the operation.)

In fact, Chandubhai became so adept at the art of wafer-making that he could simply observe the oil swirling around in the pan and know if the temperature was right for frying.

Another important aspect was the purchase of high-quality raw materials. The ideal potato should be neither too big nor too small. Hence, a lot of effort went into selecting the right-sized potatoes in the *mandi* (market). What's more, Chandubhai insisted on 'quality control' at every step.

Broken and burnt pieces were discarded without a second thought.

Making chips is a laborious process which requires peeling and cutting before frying. A locally made machine was purchased to handle the peeling operation. It was a circular *dabba* (container) with a membrane – as the potatoes rotated inside, the peel came off. However, the machine could handle only 5 kg of potatoes at a time.

"There was no bigger machine available so we got one made."

Being an industrial town, Rajkot had plenty of industrial units. Chandubhai worked with a local supplier to make peeling machines with 10 kg and 20 kg capacity.

Similarly, there was a cutting machine, but it required potatoes to be put inside manually, one at a time. The Viranis fabricated a unit which cut 10 potatoes at once, dramatically increasing the speed of production.

Between 1982 and 1989, business grew, yet profit was marginal. But it was enough to give hope and energy – to keep going. While the eldest brother branched out into other areas, Chandubhai, Bhikabhai and Kanjibhai kept their faith in chips.

"Issko hi aage le jayenge. I thought, we have to do only one business, so why not stick to this one and take it forward."

In 1989, Balaji was selling wafers worth ₹2 lakh every month. That year, the Viranis purchased a 1000 metre plot in the industrial area of Rajkot with a loan of ₹3.6 lakh from Citizen Bank. From 2 tawas at home, they expanded to 8 tawas and added more staff to take care of the production.

By 1992, Balaji Wafers had a respectable turnover of approximately ₹3 crore. But Chandubhai was not satisfied. The struggle was much less but the ambition was to do more.

By this time Chandubhai knew that the 'customer' he had to

"We used to go on bike, in rickshaw to sell our wafers, that gave us practical experience of the market."

> ***"Ek mann mein pagalpan tha ki ghar-baar girvi rakh kar bhi hum business ko zyada kare."* (I had an obsession to increase the business even if it meant mortgaging our house.)**

please was not the shopkeeper but the man on the street who was actually eating chips. And what does that customer want? Better quality, better packaging, better pricing.

"Toh achhi quality ke liye kya chahiye (What do we need for good quality). One thing I knew, we cannot improve further with tawa method."

In 1992, Balaji set up its first automatic wafer-making plant. The investment required was ₹50 lakh – a very large sum of money. The eldest Virani brother objected – why take unnecessary risk?

"Mere toh mann mein tha kuch bhi ho jaye, kitna bhi lagana pade, poora ghar-baar girvi rakh denge lekin humko aage badhna hai." (I felt that no matter what, no matter how much we need to invest, even if we have to mortgage our house, we must move forward.)

Chandubhai, Kanjibhai and Bhikabhai went ahead and purchased the machinery from Mather & Platt, a company based in Pune. However, things did not go smoothly. The Viranis were not engineers, neither did they have technical staff. To make matters worse, the company from which they bought the machine went out of business that very same year.

The first 6 months were sheer hell. The plant had a capacity to produce 1000 kg chips every hour. But there was hardly any production, as the machines constantly broke down. The brothers began bickering over 'who was to blame'.

"Maine socha jhagde se koi achha result nahin aayega. (I realised fighting would take us nowhere, the problem will only increase). We have to focus on moving forward."

Eventually, these issues were solved but there were others which sprung up. In the early '90s, new brands like Uncle Chips and

Binnie's came in the market, with jazzy packaging. At the time, Balaji was selling in transparent plastic bags, with a simple orange, blue and yellow logo.

The Viranis decided to invest in a form-fill-seal packaging machine. These machines use laminated material as well as fill nitrogen which 'puffs' up the packet, keeping chips fresh longer.The cost of importing this machine was ₹60 lakh, while a locally made one cost ₹6 lakh. Balaji opted for the local machine.

"Lekin chali nahin. Technical baare mein humko pata nahi tha, ki dono machine mein bahut farak tha." (It did not work. We did not realise that there was a lot of difference between the two machines.)

After a lot of complaints, follow-ups and, finally, a legal notice, the Baroda-based supplier agreed to take the machine back. But 2-3 years were wasted in the process.

Ultimately, they imported a packaging machine from Japan in 1995. That year, the market had further heated up, with the entry of Frito-Lay from multinational Pepsi. Would a small Indian company be able to survive?

"Hum mar bhi sakte hain lekin hum ladenge, himmat se ladenge." (We can get wiped out but we will fight it out, we will give it our best.)

Making chips is not rocket science. Balaji was already famous for its *karkarapan* (crispness) and *masaledaar* (spicy) taste. Dealers too had strong faith in the company. Thus Balaji Wafers managed to retain its postion in the market, growing year on year at the rate of 20-25%. Yet Chandubhai was far from complacent.

"We will have to improve our product and invest more in technology."

"Jo bhi jiski galtiyan hain...yeh baatein chhod kar humko aage badhna hai."
(Instead of blaming each other we have to focus on moving forward.)

***"Maine kabhi nahin maanga ki bhagwan, mere paas cycle hai, badi car kab hongi. Meri liye cycle ki bhi bahut badi keemat thhi."* (I never asked God, when will I get a big car? Even my cycle was very valuable to me.)**

In 1999, Balaji Wafers went in for further expansion, setting up an automatic plant with a capacity of 2000 kg per day. For this, the company took a loan of ₹2 crore. Demand continued to grow. In 2003, the FMC Potato Processing Machinery (PPM) Chips Line was set up in Rajkot, to process 5000 kg of potatoes per hour.

By this time, Balaji Wafers had crossed ₹20 crore in revenues and day-to-day operations were smooth. Chandubhai got a moment to pause and to think – what next?

"Humne namkeen ke baare mein sochna shuru kiya." (We started thinking about Indian savoury snacks.)

Balaji had been manufacturing *bhujiya* in small quantities – the problem was how to scale up production. After all, namkeen is a thoroughly Indian product. Unlike chips – where automatic plants could simply be imported from Germany or America – there was no readymade 'machine' for namkeen.

"We started with tawas but side by side we were trying to develop automatic system."

An Australian company took up this challenge. Their engineers came to the Balaji factory to observe how *sing bhujia* is made. This required them to stand for hours, next to red-hot tawas.

"Woh foreign wale ekdum laal-laal ho gaye, woh log research mein jaan gawa dete hain!" (Those foreigners used to become flushed but remained sincere to their research!)

There were many technical issues such as how to handle the *chiknapan* (oiliness) of *besan* (chana flour). But the team was determined to crack the problem and, ultimately, they did.

"There is no secret, we did a lot of hard work. It took us 2-3 years to make the machine."

However, all this effort also made perfect business sense. For 20 years, Balaji Wafers had been obsessed with potato chips. A great product but one which was complex to produce. Raw potato must be washed, peeled and cut before it is fried. Small and broken chips must be discarded.

"100 kg of potato gives 25 kg of chips. Rest is all wastage."

Namkeen is also economical in other ways. A locally made machine costing as little as ₹50,000 can be used for packaging *sev-bhujiya*. And while only 2 tons of puffy potato chips packets can be loaded into a truck, up to 8 tons of namkeen can be fit into the same vehicle.

"Sab jagah easy namkeen hai, musibat wali chips hai. (Namkeen is easier than chips in every way.) We started making different namkeens, one by one."

In fact, expansion was also dictated by the need of the market. Initially, Balaji was supplying *chane ki dal* and several varieties of peas, but no sing bhujiya. The supplier of sing bhujiya was holding the dealer ransom by saying, "If you take Balaji namkeen, I will stop giving you my product."

Balaji then added bhujiya in its own portfolio, breaking the other party's stranglehold.

"We realised that the shopkeeper should get entire range of namkeen from us. It is easier for him also, to deal with one company."

Equally important was getting the right taste. And here, Balaji has taken a different approach. The focus is not only on taste but the effect the item has on the stomach.

Take the example of the famous *Ratlami sev*. The traditional recipe is super oily, super spicy. But Balaji has re-engineered the taste, for a wider palate. Today, Balaji's Ratlami sev is outselling all other brands in a traditional state like Rajasthan. And this formula has been successfully applied by Balaji across all its namkeens.

"Thoda sweetpana hona chahiye, thoda teekha hona chahiye,

***Jeevan mein kabhi bageecha green aayega, to kabhi sookha hua aayega.... yehi zindagi hai."* (Sometimes you will experience good, sometimes bad – that's life!)**

thoda khatta hona chahiye. Aur logon ko swadisht lagta hai." (A little sweet, a little spicy, a little sour – that's what people like.)

These kind of insights come to Chandubhai out of long experience of directly dealing with customers and shopkeepers. Apart from taste and quality, Balaji's *brahmastra** is economical pricing. The company sells 50-55 gm of chips at Rs 10, which is double the quantity provided by multinational brands.

"When we started, we sold 50 gm of chips for 50 paise. Even now, you can buy our namkeens in 5 rupee pouches."

While Lays is synonymous with chips and Haldiram with namkeen, Balaji has been able to dominate both categories in the 5 states where it is available. Across Gujarat, Maharashtra, Goa, Madhya Pradesh and Rajasthan, Balaji commands over 65% of the market**.

The company has 8 large dealers who supply the goods to 500 distributors, from there it goes to 7 lakh shops.

To achieve this reach, Balaji Wafers has never advertised on radio or television. Or even put up a publicity board. In fact, the company does not even use bulk discount schemes. Chandubhai believes that the smallest panwallah is as important as the biggest Reliance Fresh.

"Hum chhote the, toh jo chhota aadmi hai hamare liye zyada maine rakhta hai." (We were once small, we do not judge our retailers by their size.)

The same applies to workers. Today, Balaji Wafers employs over

* The most powerful weapon in Hindu mythology, used by Lord Brahma.

** The all-India market share of Balaji Wafers despite being in just 5 states is 14%.

1800 employees in its Rajkot and Valsad factories. Apart from decent wages and good working conditions, the company takes care of transport and medical needs of its workers.

"We don't send our employees to a government hospital, because they are 'workers'. We take them to our own family doctor, a good doctor."

This is what makes the people who work with Balaji '*vishwas ke saathi*' (trusted partners).

Sitting in Rajkot today, the Viranis can procure the best of raw material, the best of technology – from anywhere in the world. Company officials are sent to countries like Israel to learn about the latest methods of potato cultivation. Farmers in Banaskantha district are now cultivating varieties like 'Lady Rosetta' on contract for Balaji Wafers.

"Sab mehnat kar rahe hain, sab ke saath se yeh business badha hai." (Everyone works hard, and together we have built this business empire.)

In March 2013, Balaji crossed ₹1000 crore, with wafers and namkeen contributing 50:50. While Chandubhai is the MD of the company, Bhikabhai is Chairman and Kanubhai its Technical Director. However, Bhikabhai's sons, Keyur (33) and Mihir (29), and Chandubhai's son, Pranay (29), are now leading the day-to-day operations as well as the strategy for the future.

Generation Next feels it is important to raise outside capital to expand further. In August 2013, Balaji Wafers announced the appointment of Ernst & Young to lead talks with potential investors, including Pepsisco. According to *The Economic Times**, the sale of a 25% stake is expected to bring in $100-125 million (₹600-750 crore). But Chandubhai himself is ambivalent.

"Main samajhta hoon jo hum achha kar sakenge utna hi karna chahiye." (I feel we should grow as much as we can handle, and do the business well.)

It's hard to say whether slow and steady can continue to win the race. Certainly, Chandubhai believes in the strength of the tortoise

* At the time of going to print no deal had been finalised.

over the hare. And looks at his 40 years in business, in a very different way.

"Business hamare liye passion hai, business hamare liye aadat hai. Yeh sab humne paise ke liye toh nahin kiya hai..." (Business is a passion for us, it is a habit. We have not done all this for money.)

He fondly recalls the days spent at Astron Cinema. Even small details like the espresso coffee machine at the canteen – the only one of its kind in Rajkot city. When the owner of the cinema had a special guest, he would call for coffee from the Balaji canteen. Chandubhai's job was to deliver it.

"I don't remember seth's bungalow but I remember every single seat in the cinema, I was so passionate about my work."

Every morning Chandubhai spends one minute in prayer at home, one minute at the temple in the factory complex and one minute with Hanumanji in his own office. In this daily communion with God, he has never 'asked' for success, for money, for more material goods.

"Bhagwan se mangta hoon ki sabko sadbudhi dena. Itna hi mangta hoon." (I ask God to give wisdom to everyone, that's all I ask.)

Chandubhai believes there is much to learn from every person you meet. The worst human being will have some good qualities within him. The Viranis are Vaishnavites (worshippers of Vishnu in all his forms) but they are expansive in matters of faith.

"Hum sabke bhakt hain. Jaha sab jagah chhaya milegi... Thoda thoda sabse lena hai bas." (Worship all, for there is some shade to be found under every tree... just take a little from each source.)

Chandubhai considers Pujya Pramukhwami, spiritual head of the Swaminarayan faith, as a living guru. And that there is much to be learnt from this sect when it comes to management skills.

"If you do *sewa* (service) with the Swaminarayans for one year, you will learn a lot."

Small things, from the ingenious manner in which the organisers handle parking of hundreds of cars at events, to the dignity with which all disciples are treated – whether they are ordinary or 'VIPs'.

On a visit to America, Chandubhai could not engage a driver. But when he visited a Swaminarayan function in the US, there were 15-20 volunteers to park the cars of guests.

"Toh woh unke management ki shakti hai, sambandh ki shakti hai." (That is the strength of the organisation, the strength of its relationships.)

The strength you need to sell anything from a humble potato chip to a crazy new idea in this big, bad, mad world.

ADVICE TO YOUNG ENTREPRENEURS

Naujawano koh ye nahin sochna chahiye ke hum dukhi hain, hum sukhi hain. Bhagwan ne humko insaan banaya hai, isse jyada humko kya sukh hona chahiye. (Young people should not think about pleasure and pain. The fact that you are born a human being is the biggest boon… what more can you ask God for.)

Hamari mansikta yeh honi chahiye ke sukhi rahein. Aur samay ka sadupyog karein. (Your mentality should be to stay happy, and to make correct use of your time.)

Kuch karna hai, kuch banna hai, kuch pehchan banani hai, to ban jayegi. To kuch paane ki apeksha kam rakhenge, kuch karne ki koshish jyada rakhenge to ek din success hoga hi hoga. (If you want to do something, be someone, create your own identity, it will happen. You have to have that desire and keep trying to achieve your goal, one day you will definitely be successful.)

Lekin hamare aadmi ko satisfy nahin hota, aur sukhi hona hai, aur hona hai. Rasta change karte rehte hain. Sukhi hone ki daud mein aaj jo 80% jawaan hain, dukhi ho jate hain. (But most of us only want more pleasure and keep looking for it in different things. In this race for comforts, 80% of our young people become frustrated.)

Sukh aur dukh zindagi ka ek-ek part hota hai. Koi duniya mein sukhi, sukhi, sukhi nahin hota, koi dukhi, dukhi, dukhi nahin hota. Bas, mann se aadmi tootna nahi chahiye. (Pleasure and pain are part of life. No one is perpetually happy or perpetually sad. It's all about keeping your mind stable.)

A FEW GOOD MEN

Nand Kishore Chaudhary – Jaipur Rugs
Jaipur (Rajasthan)

In 1978, a young graduate went into the carpet business in Churu, Rajasthan. Today, Jaipur Rugs is India's biggest exporter of hand-knotted carpets, employing 40,000 weavers in villages across India.

It is a universally acknowledged fact that a young Marwari must be in search of a business. Generations of Marwaris found their fortunes in Bombay, in Calcutta and distant lands beyond.

Nand Kishore Chaudhary is different. He started his *dhandha* from Churu, in the heart of Marwar. Starting with 2 carpet looms and a few weavers, all from the 'untouchable' caste.

"Parivar aur aas pados ke log mujhe samajh nahi paaye – meri soch kuch alag thi." (My family and neighbours could not understand my way of thinking.)

But Nand Kishore never wavered in his beliefs – in himself, in his business.

Over the next 20 years, Nand Kishore created a huge network of weavers, working from their own homes in villages and tribal areas. From a contractor, he became an exporter in his own right.

From one among hundreds of exporters, he became a globally acclaimed 'case study' in social entrepreneurship.

"*Maine likhne laayak kuch aisa kiya hi nahin* (I haven't done anything worth writing about)," he protested when C K Prahalad first approached him.

And surely, Nand Kishore did not set out to *create* a social enterprise. Every action he took – from reducing the role of middlemen to improving the lives of his weavers – came from a simple line of thought.

"If my weavers are happy, they will do good work. Good work is good for business."

And being good to people is in *itself* important. No matter what their caste, class or social status.

At the company headquarters in Jaipur's Mansarovar industrial area, Nand Kishore dazzles me with world-class designs. From jute carpets which retail for $250 to finest quality silks which fetch $10,000 a piece.

From the poorest hands to the richest feet – Jaipur Rugs is a bridge. A bridge built on humanity, strengthened by the sweat of family. Connecting villages to the world.

A FEW GOOD MEN

Nand Kishore Chaudhary - Jaipur Rugs
Jaipur (Rajasthan)

Nand Kishore Chaudhary was born in Churu, a district town in Rajasthan.

"I did my BCom from Lohia College in Churu and joined my father's business."

The business was a *chhoti si dukaan* (small shop) which sold branded shoes. At the age of 22, Nand Kishore secured a permanent job as a cashier at the United Bank of India. To everyone's surprise and dismay, he refused the job.

"I decided not to join service because I knew I wanted to do business. *Mujhe apna kuch karna hai aur kuch badaa karne hai*." (I wanted to do something on my own, something big.)

The shoe shop did not have much of a future. Churu was a small town where people didn't have much money to spend on fashion. So what was a young man to do?

Around this time, Nand Kishore got acquainted with Ilay Cooper, a young writer and photographer from England. Cooper's obsession at the time was the study of Shekhawati paintings. The two young men shared a love for the villages and the deserts – they quickly became good friends.

Meanwhile Nand Kishore spent long hours contemplating the meaning of life and work. He read Osho, the Bhagvad Gita, the writings of Mahatma Gandhi and Tagore. And spent long hours in discussion and introspection with the Englishman.

"I thought about it deeply, that what kind of person am I? What business should I get into?"

In the course of his research he heard about the carpet business. A friend who was in the transport line remarked, "The demand for carpets is very high but supply is less... Why don't you set up a loom?"

The idea appealed to Nand Kishore – he went to Jaipur to find out more. The facts were startling: Rajasthan produced 45% of India's raw wool but the majority of carpets were produced in UP. With its blend of economic and aesthetic appeal, Nand Kishore decided the carpet business was the right business for him.

The year was 1978. The young man borrowed ₹5000 from his father and set up 2 carpet looms in the courtyard of his house.

"I employed 9 people who had been trained by the government but had no work."

The weavers belonged to the '*chamar*' community – the so-called untouchables. The family was aghast.

"My father, my mother, my neighbours, all used to say, '*Yeh kya shuru kar diya hai tumne*?' " (What is this useless thing you have started?)

"The people we do not mingle with, do not allow in our homes, are working with you? They are even visiting your house!"

Nand Kishore was immune to these taunts.

"From childhood, I could see that our society is full of hypocrisy. *Main jaat-paat nahin maanta*." (I do not believe in the caste system.)

The weavers were nimble and worked hard. Initially, Nand Kishore also employed a 'master' from Benaras to supervise the work. But the master was also an *ustad* (expert) in money matters – his main interest in life was getting 'advance'.

"One day, he misbehaved. I told him, 'You can go now, I have learnt everything you know.'"

Quietly observing the ustad, spending day and night with the weavers, Nand Kishore had picked up the nuances of the trade. The quality of a carpet rests chiefly on its knots.

"*Funde ki nau barabar ho, lachche ki jod barabar thuke, taadi ka tension barabar ho. Yehi basic cheezein mujhe samajh mein aa gayi.*" (The shape of the knot, the joint of the loop and the tension of the thread – these are the basic things you need to get right.)

But the single most important aspect is the number of knots per square inch. The more the knots, the more the detail, the more valuable is the carpet.

Nand Kishore also forged a close relationship with the weavers. He would sit with them, talk to them, eat with them.

"*Unke upar mera vishwas badta gaya.*" (My trust in their abilities kept increasing.)

And that trust was rewarded when the very first carpet was completed. It was made to order for a large Jaipur-based exporter. The buyer was so delighted by the quality, he called his own *karigars* (artisans) to inspect it.

"This boy is new in the carpet business but look at the fantastic piece he has produced!"

In September 1980, an article written by Ilay Cooper appeared in the prestigious *Inside Outside* magazine. Titled, 'More than a Revival' it featured a full-page photograph of Nand Kishore's first carpet. The article also talked about the bright future of the handmade carpet industry and why it needed young men like Nand Kishore.

***"Meri soch hamesha se hi alag thi. Parivaar wale kabhi mujhe samajh nahin paaye."* (My thinking was always different, my family could not understand me.)**

***"Ustad ko dekh dekh kar main khud ustad ban gaya."* (Observing the master at work, I too became a master.)**

"I got a lot of confidence and decided to expand."

In addition to acclaim, the first sale netted Nand Kishore ₹4000 and more jobwork. In 2 years' time, with 6 additional looms, the business was thriving. The contractor supplied raw material, Nand Kishore supplied finished carpets. After accounting for labour and transport, he was making ₹30–40,000 per month – a big sum in 1980.

"I reinvested what I was earning into buying more looms*."

However, this time he went outside Churu, to nearby villages like Ratangad, Sujangad, Laxmangad and Jodhpur. The main challenge was identifying and training good weavers. People were desperate for work, yet Nand Kishore was careful in his selection.

"I wanted those who have a passion for this work, some discipline. *Achha aadmi hona bhi zaroori hai.*" (He must also be a good person.)

Good weaving requires team effort. 4 weavers working on a single 8 x 10** high-quality carpet would take 3-4 months to complete the job.

As the number of workers and sites grew, Nand Kishore created a rudimentary management system. One of the weavers was upgraded to 'quality supervisor'. The man was given a motorcycle and his job was to go from loom to loom, checking the work. His job was to compile a PPR, or Production Progress Report.

This supervisor noted the square feet of weaving per artisan. He also made payments to the workers, accordingly.

---

* A loom cost approximately ₹3000 in 1980.

** The quality of a carpet is determined by the number of knots per sq inch.

After 8 years of working as a contractor, the business had touched ₹15 lakh with more than 300 weavers and 100 looms. But something was missing.

"*Mere andar aur badiya kaam karne ki ichcha thi. Magar exporter ke liye paisa hi bhagwan tha.*" (I had a desire to excel in my work. But the exporter cared only for money.)

And Nand Kishore's entire business rested on his greedy shoulders. This disturbed the somewhat idealistic Nand Kishore. In 1986, he parted ways with the exporter and decided to enter the export business himself. A new company was formed in partnership with his brother.

Nand Kishore shifted to Jaipur, where he took a house on rent. He set up additional looms as well as invested in raw materials. But it wasn't that simple to start exporting.

"Initially, I supplied to other exporters in Jaipur and Delhi. After 3 years, we got our first direct order, from a German customer."

The first order was worth ₹10 lakh and more followed. Clearly, there was a big opportunity. But could handmade carpets be produced on a large scale?

"Iss kaam ko bade roop main kaise karein?" How is one to grow big?

Around this time, Ilay Cooper was commissioned by INTACH to document the monuments of Diu, a former Portuguese enclave on the coast of Gujarat. He also travelled extensively across Gujarat, including the tribal belt.

"Can I get weavers in Gujarat?" Nand Kishore asked his friend.

Ilay replied, "Yes – why not. Tribals are artistic as well as loyal, if you treat them with respect and love."

***"Weavers ke saath mera itna lagaav ho gaya ki dopahar ka khaana bhi loom par baith kar hi khata tha."* (I bonded so much with the weavers that I would eat my lunch with them.)**

"My interest of living in villages and close to nature made it easier to connect with the tribals."

He added that Gujarat was also a very safe state for women.

"Women have a lot more freedom – it will be a good environment for your daughters and wife."

What's more, the state government had schemes to train tribals in carpet weaving. The district administration had even formed co-operative societies and provided free looms. But when Nand Kishore went from village to village, he sensed a problem. The tribals were good weavers but poor managers.

This was an opportunity for an entrepreneur like Nand Kishore.

"In 1990, I decided to make Gujarat my big production base."

Leaving his 200 looms in Rajasthan in the hands of trusted lieutenants, Nand Kishore shifted, bag and baggage, to Valsad. His 3 daughters and 2 sons enrolled in the local school. Work took Nand Kishore to distant villages, where the tribals lived. But, initially, it was not easy.

"Tribals are not very friendly towards outsiders. But I remembered Ilay's words and I knew, slowly, I will be able to win them over."

It took 3 years to develop a rapport, to become a mentor and '*bhaisaheb*' to them. Nand Kishore began training tribals, with a focus on quality of weaving. He was especially impressed by the women.

"I saw the tribal women manage home, food, children, budget and still find time to weave carpets. They are probably some of the best managers in the world!"

Working in far-flung villages also brought practical problems. Without a phone, fax or Internet, how do you keep track of production? The solution came in the form of a wireless set which Nand Kishore spotted at an exhibition in Ahmedabad.

"We installed one repeater (tower) on top of a hill called Sapatura and 15 wireless and fixed stations were set up, costing approximately ₹6 lakh."

To carry quality inspectors over rocky terrain, he invested in 2 jeeps and 20 motorcycles. As in Rajasthan, the supervisors went from loom to loom, delivering raw material and payment to weavers.

Gradually, production scaled up, with a truckful of carpets being despatched to Jaipur every week for inspection, prior to export. But now, there was another problem. Nand Kishore's success in working directly with weavers was slowly eliminating the role of the middleman.

One morning, a politically powerful contractor came to his office, waving a gun.

"You better leave Gujarat!"

Nand Kishore did not take the threat seriously.

"I knew it was the frustration of his failure… I was doing good work and had support of the tribal community."

By 1999, Nand Kishore had trained 10,000 tribal weavers with over 2000 looms in Gujarat. That same year, Nand Kishore and his brother decided to go separate ways.

"*Phir shuru hua jo main bolta hoon*…University of Hard Rocks of life (*laughs*)." (That's when I entered a phase which I call as University of Hard Rocks of life.)

Nand Kishore started a new firm by the name 'Jaipur Carpets'. The trouble was he had spent his whole life working with the weavers at the grassroot level. He had little idea about how to run the business. All he had were some looms in Jaipur, the looms in Gujarat and 20 years of goodwill.

"There are 60 processes in carpet-making, right from buying raw wool to the final delivery... we have a quality control at each level."

> ***"Jo bina padhe-likhe hain unke andar ek alag talent, ek alag wisdom, ek alag experience hai."* (Uneducated people have a different kind of talent, wisdom and experience.)**

"Mera weaving ke kshetra mein bahut naam raha...uska market mein kuch fayda mila." (I enjoyed a lot of respect in the field of weaving and that helped me.)

From a blank slate, Nand Kishore was able to take the exports to ₹4 crore in the first year itself. But then, problems began piling up. Finance and HR were Nand Kishore's two biggest bugbears. To handle these aspects, he hired professional managers. But handling their expectations and egos was another new headache.

"The business suffered, we started making losses."

At one point it seemed like the company would have to be shut down.

Once again, Nand Kishore turned inwards – reading the scriptures, attending *satsangs* and communing with nature. In this process, the alchemist within the man discovered one simple truth: "You can blame other people but, ultimately, all limitations are within yourself."

"*Mujhe ek baat samajh mein aa gayi – ki dhande ko badalna hai to apni soch badalni hogi.*"(I understood one thing...to change my business, I need to change my thinking.)

The 'philosophy' that Nand Kishore adopted was "finding yourself through losing yourself".

Take a cube of ice – hard and unyielding. Compare it with water – which flows freely and naturally. Taking the shape the situation requires.

"To grow my business, I need to become free-flowing and flexible like water."

In practical terms, what this meant was losing one's ego. Seeing *more* in other people.

"*Mujhe log dikhai dene lage...unki capability dikhai dene lag gayi.*" (I became more sensitive to the capabilities of my people.)

Nand Kishore realised that his professional managers and those who had risen from the ranks needed to develop respect for each other. This led to an initiative called the 'Higher School of Unlearning' where the MBAs and CAs worked with the older, uneducated managers in different departments. To truly and deeply *understand* the carpet business.

Not everyone was a right 'fit' with the company and those employees left.

"I used to read books...lots of books. I realised I need to recruit 'A-class' people – who think differently and who are smarter than me."

One of the smartest decisions Nand Kishore made was to recruit his eldest daughter into the business. Asha graduated from Emory University, Atlanta, in 2001, with a BBA. The 23-year-old returned to Jaipur with new ideas and new vigour. Her entry raised the bar in 2 imporant areas – product design and marketing.

Sending Asha to America to study was a very unusual step for a Marwari family.

"It is true," admits Nand Kishore. "In Marwari families, girls get less priority than boys. But from the beginning, my wife and I treated all our children equally."

When Asha expressed a desire to study abroad, Nand Kishore agreed.

"Quality ka shauk pehle se tha mujhe, carpet ki quality ka aur aadmi ki quality."
(I am fond of quality, quality of carpets and of people.)

> ***"Kisi bhi NGO wale ne mujhe milne ka samay nahi diya...kyunki woh samajhte the business is exploitation."* (NGOs refused to meet me because they thought business means exploitation.)**

He said to her, "*Beti, main to kabhi plane mein baitha nahin hoon, maine duniya nahin dekhi.* (Daughter, I have never sat in a plane, nor seen the world.) You become my eyes and ears. Study America, and especially the American housewives. *They* buy our carpets."

Asha had grown up seeing her father's struggles with buyers and merchandisers. They would find fault, claim that colours and designs were not perfect. Then ask for a discount.

"When my father was treated badly...he used to come home and pray to God!" says Asha.

The prayers were answered as, one by one, his children joined the business. Archana, who completed her BA in Textile Chemistry from North Carolina University in 2004, followed by Kavita who graduated from the Art Institute of Chicago in 2006. The same year, son Yogesh dropped out of Boston College to work full-time with his father.

Each entry created a visible impact on the business.

Asha expanded the customer base in the US from speciality rug stores to mass retail and interior designers. She began the process of modernising carpet designs to suit current trends and taste. Archana's focus was quality – setting up checks and balances at every step of production.

"We start with inspection of raw material, then at each stage – spinning, dyeing, weaving and finishing."

Field workers known as 'area commanders'* are skilled weavers

---

* An area commander is responsible for between 50-200 looms in a given area.

and, hence, can identify and help correct mistakes while work is in progress. Even then, a small, randomly selected number of unfinished rugs is sent for checking to headquarters.

"We go into every detail – like measuring the rug length and width in 3 different places!"

Obsession with quality increases costs but it is the very foundation of the company. And its loyal customer base.

As orders increased, there were other challenges. How do you produce 200 identical rugs on looms spread across the country? The hand-drawn design process had to be converted into a computerised one. Asha developed graph-based 'maps' and trained the traditional designers to use them.

"The maps have easy instructions, such as where to start weaving. This goes to weavers along with a Raw Material card and the required bundles of yarn."

This system allows the company to introduce new designs quickly without retraining weavers. The design department is now headed by Kavita Chaudhary.

Adoption of ERP was another milestone, where son Yogesh played a key role. The Microsoft Dynamix software was purchased in 2005 although implementation took almost 4 years. It allows the company to track sales and inventory, in India and the US.

"Our customers can also check the status of their order in real time."

In the year 2006, the company underwent major restructuring, with a name change from 'Jaipur Carpets' to 'Jaipur Rugs'. However, operations are handled by different legal entities, each handled by specific family members.

Jaipur Rugs Company, headquartered in Jaipur, is run by Nand Kishore (CMD), and son Yogesh (Director). This company and its 22 branch offices take care of all aspects of production from procurement to export. Jaipur Rugs Incorporated in Atlanta is run by daughters Asha (CEO) and Archana (COO) – this company manages sales and distribution of carpets in the US, which is Jaipur Rugs' biggest market.

"Agar business mein loss ho jaye toh bhi, usse mujhe seekhne ko kya mila, us cheez par dhyaan do." **(Even if you suffer a loss, focus on what lesson that experience taught you.)**

Nand Kishore's brother-in-law, Navratan Saraf, manages the entire wool-procurement process and its 7 warehouses in Bikaner. The majority of the work is outsourced to local partners with carding and spinning machines.

"We use hand-carded and hand-spun wool which is of superior quality," says Nand Kishore.

This work is done on per-kg basis by women in the villages in and around Bikaner.

A third and important pillar of the organisation is the 'Jaipur Rugs Foundation'. Established in 2004, the foundation receives a percentage of profits from the Jaipur Rugs Company. These funds are employed towards the welfare and training of weavers.

"We came to know that weavers can benefit from many government schemes if they have an 'artisan' card. So, we helped them obtain these cards."

Benefits of the artisan card include group health insurance and bank loans. The foundation also conducts medical camps and literacy classes for weavers and their families. But, it was only in 2008 that Nand Kishore realised – this is 'CSR' (Corporate Social Responsibility).

It started with a telephone call from America.

"This is C K Prahalad," said the voice at the other end.

"I know who you are," surprised, Nand Kishore replied but wondered – why is this management guru calling me?

Prahalad explained that he wanted to do a case study on Jaipur Rugs.

"I am a simple man doing a simple business. If you ask my neighbour, he probably has no idea what I do. Who will read about me?"

Prahalad explained that he was interested in Jaipur Rugs for its complex grassroots-to-global supply chain.

"You are connecting the poorest with the richest…there is a lot to learn from you."

Prahalad's students came to India and studied Jaipur Rugs. In September 2009, a case on Jaipur Rugs was published by the Ross School of Business, University of Michigan. This was a turning point for Nand Kishore. The work he had been doing all along had a 'name' and definition – 'social entrepreneur'.

"*Maine toh bas yeh socha tha ki agar mere saath kaam karne waale khush hain to zyada mehnat karenge. Customer ke liye achha kaam karenge aur hamara profit achha hoga.*" (I thought that if the people who work with me are happy, they will work hard. They will make good products for customers and the business will profit.)

What Nand Kishore did differently from others was simple: he treated weavers with respect. As equals and human beings.

The second, equally important, thing he did was improve their incomes. By employing weavers directly he eliminated the middlemen who gobbled up 30-40% of their daily wages. In addition, they did not need to travel to the city to work, to get raw material or payment.

"*Ghar baithe unko sab kuch mil jaata tha.*" (Sitting at home, they got everything.)

"I consider myself a weaver and I tell my children that weaving has been the greatest enjoyment of my life. They must never forget this."

"In Marwari families, girls get less priority than boys. But from the beginning, my wife and I treated all our children equally."

Over time, weavers also got upward mobility. Take the example of Sawarmal who has been working with Jaipur Rugs in Gujarat and Rajasthan since 20 years. From weaver he rose to map reader, then area commander and is now a branch manager, earning ₹30,000 per month. Many others have been helped and encouraged to become entrepreneurs, undertaking jobwork for Jaipur Rugs.

These homegrown practices were lauded by the C K Prahalad case study and, suddenly, Jaipur Rugs was in the limelight. In 2009, Nand Kishore was invited to speak at the University of Michigan, as well as Wharton Business School.

"*Mujhe thoda jhijhak thi kyunki main angrezi itni achhi nahin bol sakta.*" (I was a bit hesitant as I don't speak English well.)

But the lectures were extremely well-received.

"*Pehle koi suited-booted aadmi milta tha to main naak neeche karke baithta tha. Magar dheere dheere mujhe confidence aaya.*" (Earlier I used to feel small in front of people in suit and tie. But slowly I have become confident.)

Addressing the annual session of CII, interacting with CEOS across the board, Nand Kishore realised he was on the right path.

"*Pata chala ki jo main sochta hoon woh mera 'vision' hai.*" (I came to know that I too have a vision.)

With a turnover of ₹104 crore in March 2013, Jaipur Rugs is India's largest exporter of hand-knotted rugs. The company employs over 400 people directly and 40,000 indirectly, including 28,000 weavers.

"My vision is to have 1,00,000 people working with me by 2020."

Most of the weavers are currently concentrated in Gujarat, Uttar Pradesh and Rajasthan. But Jaipur Rugs Foundation 'Motivators' are identifying and recruiting weavers in new territories, such as Nagaland, Jharkhand, Orissa and Bihar.

"Jahan gareebi zyada hai, road nahin hai, school nahin hai – wahan ham kaam shuru kar rahe hain." (Where there is extreme poverty, no roads, no schools – we are entering such areas.)

In Orissa, Jaipur Rugs works with Muslim women who aren't allowed to leave their homes.

Earlier, these women made *beedis* and earned ₹10-15 per day. As weavers, they can earn ₹100-150 per day and the work is not seasonal.

"We have big orders and we need more weavers to complete them... *Ek rug loom se utarta hai, doosre lag jaata hai*!" (One rug gets off the loom and the next one is ready to work on.)

Between 2005-08, Jaipur Rugs grew at a scorching 38% year on year. When recession hit the world market, the company was not spared. But it managed to hold its own, nevertheless.

"Mandi ki wajah se hamari soch mein bahut jyada parivartan aaya." (We had to change our strategy drastically during the slowdown.)

Nand Kishore realised that customers wanted the same look but would not pay the same prices. The company decided to focus on more affordable wool carpets and styles such Indo-Tibetan, which are quick and easy to weave. The strategy worked.

"Silk earns better margins but 8 X 8 wool carpets are our bread and butter*," admits Nand Kishore.

The Jaipur Rugs model is robust but challenges remain. The company strives hard to work directly with weavers but 20% of its work is still routed through middlemen. On the issue of child labour, it has been more successful.

"We only employ weavers of minimum working age. All our looms are registered with the Rug Mark Foundation and open to inspection at any time."

---

* Margin on silk rugs is up to 18%, while overall net margin is 6-7%.

> ***"Aur aage badhne ke liye kya kya skills chahiye, yeh main hamesha khojta rehta hoon."* (I keep searching for the skills I need to move forward.)**

Going forward, Nand Kishore wants the weavers to get a greater share of the wealth they produce. By making them stakeholders, along the lines of Fabindia. He also sees a future where end-users of rugs are directly connected with those who make them.

"Ek emotional connection hona bahut jaruri hai – ki yeh carpet kahan se aaya hai, kis ke haath se aaya hai." (An emotional connection is very necessary – to know where the carpet comes from, whose hands have created it.)

In the near future, every loom will have a barcode making this dream a reality.

Another Big Idea is to move from supplier to selling under the 'Jaipur Rugs' brand. Not only rugs but curtains, furniture – complete interior-decor solutions.

"Aur aage badhne ke liye kya kya skills chahiye, yeh main hamesha khojta rehta hoon. Subah uth ke aadha-pauna ghanta padhta hoon. Jab main office aata hoon toh ekdum majboot hoke aata hoon!" (I keep searching for the skills I need to move forward. Every morning I spend 30-45 minutes reading and come to office highly motivated.)

But no matter how many management books he reads, Nand Kishore is clear about 2 things: the joy of weaving and the joy of family. In particular, he acknowledges the role of his wife, Sulochana, since 1977.

"She not only gave me moral support but used to serve tea and food to my workers."

Despite pressures of business, Nand Kishore never neglected his role as a father. Sundays were always spent at home, with the kids. Working together, there has been little conflict.

From weaver to owner, it's one big family. Threads of love and respect, woven by deft hands and deep hearts, bind them together.

ADVICE TO YOUNG ENTREPRENEURS

Kuch bhi shuru karne se pehle apne aap ko jaaniye. Ki bhai mujhe kya achha lagta hai, kis kaam mein anand aata hai. Aur jo mujhe achha lagta hain kya uski logon ko zarurat bhi hai. Agar haan, toh uska enterprise ban sakta hai. (Before you start anything, understand yourself. What kind of work do you enjoy and is that kind of work needed by others? If yes, you can start that enterprise.)

Kisi aur ki dekha dekhi ya jealousy ya bada banney ki ichcha nahi karein. Jo successful log hai unhe dekh kar apne aap mein khojein ki mere andar kya hai. (Do not compare with others, be jealous or indulge in one upmanship. Study successful people but use that to discover yourself.)

Padhai likhai se knowledge jyaada badh jaati hai, lekin practical reality bhi jaanne ki koshish karein. Padhe likhe hone ka ghamand nahin hona chahiye. (Higher education gives you knowledge but you must also be aware of practical realities. Do not be too proud of your degrees.)

Kam padhe likhe logon se bhi seekhne ko bahut kuch hai. Unke paas jayein, unko prem karein, unsey duniyadaari seekhein. (There is much to learn from less-educated people also. Go to them, be loving and respectful and you will learn the true lessons of life.)

Main bahut bade CEOs se milta hoon. Jab bhi unko nayi skill ki zaroorat padi toh they started learning…yeh kaam toh main bhi kar sakta hoon, aap bhi kar sakte hain. (I have met many big CEOs and found that when they need new skills, they learn them. You and I can also do that.)

Sabhi ke jeevan mein utaar chadav aatey hain, patience rakhenge toh utaar chadav paar ho jayega. (Everyone's life has ups and downs, you need patience to overcome such times.)

Jis cheez mei mein believe karta hoon, jo values hain, us cheez ko kabhi nahi khoya maine. (The only thing you must never lose are your values.)

Kirit Joshi

Vivek Deshpande

PEHLA NASHA

(First Love)

Vivek Deshpande & Kirit Joshi – Spacewood
Nagpur (Maharashtra)

In 1994, best buddies and engineering college batchmates, Vivek Deshpande and Kirit Joshi, set up a small workshop to make office furniture. Spacewood Furnishers went on to pioneer modular kitchens and is now a ₹200 crore business.

"*Yeh dosti, hum nahin todenge...*" sang Jai and Veeru in the iconic film, *Sholay*.

That's the feeling I got when I met Vivek Deshpande and Kirit Joshi. Only, they're not speeding down a country road in a scooter with a sidecar. These two friends are speeding down the highway of life.

They first met in engineering college and hit it off – both as buddies and business partners. Selling study-material to students, they soon had a flourishing publishing company.

"We earned a handsome amount and even invested in shares of Essar Steel and Essar Shipping," recalls Vivek.

After graduation, they took up a job in the same company so that they could continue the business side by side. But, even while working with VIP, the two young men were always looking for a good opportunity. That came in the form of modular furniture.

"We started by doing jobwork for VIP, then other big companies like Godrej."

Along the way they discovered an exciting new technology and brought it to India. If you've installed a modular kitchen in your home, there's a high chance it's been manufactured by Spacewood in Nagpur. A central location from where you can efficiently supply anywhere in India.

In the last 2 years, Vivek and Kirit have raised the bar further, by launching exclusive showrooms under the 'Spacewood' brand. And there is much more to come.

"Kirit is basically a visionary and I am an executor," says Vivek. "He dreams and I try to make it a reality!"

It is a partnership – like Jai and Veeru. Built on love, respect and abiding friendship.

"People say that once you get married, you may have problems," adds Kirit. "But for us both, factory is the first wife."

Todenge dam magar, tera saath na chhodenge.

PEHLA NASHA

(First Love)

Vivek Deshpande & Kirit Joshi - Spacewood Nagpur (Maharashtra)

Vivek Deshpande and Kirit Joshi are Nagpur boys.

"My father was with the irrigation department while Kirit's father was with ORG-MARG. But his grandfather and my grandfather, both were farmers."

Yet, for some reason, both Vivek and Kirit had a common interest – to do something on their own.

"I had that in my mind, *ki job mein jyaada kuch padha nahi hai* (there is no great future in a job)," says Vivek.

For Kirit, it was vacations spent in Dhamangaon with his grandfather which created an interest in commerce.

"Farming is not a 'business' as such but I saw him buying, selling, calculating profit. It was a kind of learning for me."

However, both Vivek and Kirit went to traditional Marathi-medium schools where there was little stimulus apart from studies.

"There were no Sindhi or Marwari children coming to school in a car *jinko dekhkar you feel ki, arre*, I want to be like them, I want to do business."

At that time there were two respectable professions – medicine or engineering. Both Vivek and Kirit chose the engineering stream.

Like many business partners, they first met in college. In fact, the two friends started their first business while they were studying Mechanical Engineering at VNIT Nagpur. The opportunity came in the second year, when they used the 'solutions' for engineering mechanics prepared by seniors.

"It was a very helpful study material. We thought many other students would also like to use it!"

At that time, a number of private engineering colleges had just come up in Nagpur. Students paid a 'donation' and got admission, but found it difficult to pass the semester exams.

"We took the *jimma* of selling the material on a commission basis, earning ₹25 per sale."

Going from college to college, hostel to hostel, on a friend's scooter, the duo sold 100 copies in a jiffy. That's when Vivek and Kirit decided to become 'V K Publishers'.

"We got our classmates from other branches to write solutions of the last 5 years' exam papers, in all the tough subjects."

V K Publishers typeset the material, published and sold it in book form. By the time they were in final year, Vivek and Kirit had 20 books in the market which were getting distributed as far as Pune and Bangalore. The business was generating a topline of ₹5 lakh per year.

"After the second year, we never took money from our parents, not even for fees. But we really didn't do this business for money," says Vivek.

At the time he had a sports bicycle and every time he rode it, he would look down at the road and say to himself, *"Issi raste par main ek din gaadi lekar chalunga."* (I will drive my car on this very road one day.)

Both Vivek and Kirit wanted this car to come out of their own business, not working for someone else.

"Once a lion tastes human blood, he becomes a maneater. Same way, once you taste a small success, there is no looking back, you want more!"

The publishing business was a good start but they wanted to do something bigger. So, they searched high and low for an 'idea'. Visited different DICs (District Industry Centres), pored through project reports and met different people.

"From agro industry to hotel industry, you name it and we had thought of doing it. But somehow nothing clicked!"

However, their families objected.

"While we were studying, we used to say – *first class ke upar hi aayega* (we will get a First Class), you don't worry. But in final year, they pressurised us – go for a job, get some experience."

So Vivek and Kirit appeared for campus interviews. The plan was to get a job in Nagpur and continue the business. As luck would have it, Vivek was selected by Kirloskar, Glaxo and VIP Industries while Kirit was placed on the waiting list for VIP. Vivek turned down the VIP offer, as they were posting him out of station.

One week later, he bumped into a batchmate who had joined VIP and, in fact, been posted in Nagpur.

"Main to bewakoof ban gaya (I lost an opportunity). So then I sent a letter and a telegram saying that I was unable to join, but would like a second chance."

The company replied by telegram, "Join on 21st."

Kirit was still on the waiting list. By 20th evening, when there was no news for Kirit, Vivek once again decided to forgo the offer.

"We thought it's better we both join the same company, it will be more conducive for our business."

On 22nd morning, Kirit received a confirmation from VIP Industries.

> **"*Typical Maharashtrian middle class mentality kya hai, rozchi aadhi bhaakar, woh mil gaya toh khush hai.* (Typical middle class Maharashtrian mentality is: if I get my chapati every day, I am happy.) That mindset never appealed to me."**

"Once you start a business, you taste blood. Then you have to succeed any how, *boss karna hi karna hai...*"

"Join immediately."

Now, Vivek was really upset – how could this happen? To his surprise, exactly 5 days later, there was a letter from VIP saying, "Join on 27th."

Call it a miracle or a mix-up, the two friends finally ended up together – in the luggage division of VIP. While Vivek was on the manufacturing side, Kirit was in the purchase department.

"Kirit is more into commercials and I am into technical – *shuru se yehi hamara combo raha hai.*" (This has been our combination from the start.)

Along with their jobs, Vivek and Kirit continued the publishing business. Even while on tour, they would spend the evenings poring over proofs.

"The manager at the company guest-house used to think we are studying for competitive exams!"

Since Wednesday was their weekly 'off', Vivek would head back to Nagpur on Tuesday night with all the material. Printing would be completed on Wednesday and binding by the next morning. That evening Kirit would pick up the books and begin distribution.

But soon, a new opportunity presented itself.

VIP Industries started an office-furniture division in collaboration with a Canadian company. The big challenge was finding good suppliers. In India, a sofa-set or dining table was never made according to exact specifications. One inch more or less was no big deal. However, this was a modular system with a 'tolerance limit' in millimetres.

"We were failing miserably as no supplier could do the job. So we thought – why can't we start on our own?"

When they approached the general manager, one Mr Kulkarni, he said, "You want to do it, fine. But you will have to quit the job."

No problem, they said.

"*Dekhna baad mein mat bolna galti ho gayi, waapas le lo.*" (Don't come back later and ask me to take you back.)

"Sir, don't worry, *uska koi chance nahi!*" (That won't happen.)

They had been working not for salary but for exposure. The ultimate goal had always been to get into a good business. Thus, in March 1994, after one and a half years in service, the two friends took a loan of ₹65,000 to buy 2 locally made wood-working machines. And began operating from a rented shed of 1500 sq ft.

"Using simple circular saw, we managed to achieve precision up to the last millemetre, as they wanted," says Vivek. "Here our engineering background came handy."

Some months later, VIP bought old wood-working machines from its collaborator's plant in Canada. However, instead of setting up their own unit, they wanted to lease out the machines. Naturally, Vivek and Kirit were keen to do so.

But there was one condition: "You need to have your own shed in MIDC (Maharashtra Industrial Development Corporation)."

The cost of a shed was a princely ₹12 lakh. Where would the money come from?

"We went to a chartered accountant and he said, *'Haan, sab jama denge.'* "(I will get you a bank loan.)

With this assurance, the young entrepreneurs went to VIP and said, "Our shed is ready, show us photos of the machines."

The GM retorted, "First show me pictures of your shed!"

And thus it went back and forth but ultimately a deal was struck. General Manager Kulkarni promised that the lease would be for a minimum of 3 years and there would be a steady order-flow from VIP.

On 1 January 1995, Vivek and Kirit moved into the new premises. The machines had arrived but nobody had a clue how to assemble them.

> **"Last 18 years, every year, we are importing machines. *Koi bhi saal mera aisa nahi gaya ki maine machines nahi li.*" (There was not a single year that we did not add machines.)**

"We had to use a photograph from the catalogue and figure it out! Like that, even how to operate the machines, we learnt through trial and error."

Finally, production started but another problem reared its ugly head.

"The CA was unable to arrange our loan. Already we had given a down payment of ₹1 lakh from our own pocket...so we were stuck!"

The landlord was breathing fire.

"*Mera paisa do ya khaali karo".* (Pay up or move out.)

Finally, Vivek and Kirit went to him and admitted, "*Hum toh fail ho gaye."* (We have failed.)

Being a shrewd businessman, the landlord said, "You were going to pay interest to bank. Instead, why don't you pay me!"

Thus an 'EMI' scheme was worked out and the young company acquired its shed. After this, there was no looking back. Business grew day by day. So much so, that after just 9 months, VIP decided to start its own wood-working unit. Now, they wanted their machines back.

"We had a contract but this was a decision taken by the top management...we had no choice."

It was a setback, but Vivek and Kirit decided – the show must go on. By this time, they had exited the publishing business as well, mainly due to piracy issues.

"We ran both ventures concurrently for about a year but found it difficult to sustain publishing. There were too many duplicates flooding the market!"

The wood-working business definitely had more future – the first-year turnover had touched ₹19 lakh. But how to continue working without equipment? For some time, the young entrepreneurs had to revert to their old *desi* machines. By and by, they scraped together funds to import a second-hand machine from Germany.

"Our first imported machine arrived in October 1996, costing ₹5.5 lakh."

Now, the challenge was where to get business.

"We learnt an important lesson – you cannot depend only on one buyer. You have to reach out to the market."

Kirit recalls how he used to go from office to office, looking for orders. Many people would make him wait endlessly, or even refuse to meet.

"I used to convince them by saying – give me one trial order, see our quality. That way we gradually built their confidence."

One important point was that, despite being treated unfairly by VIP Industries, the young men did not become bitter towards the company. The other vendor who had leased machines from VIP immediately made a lookalike product and became a competitor. Vivek and Kirit did not take that route.

"VIP's business multiplied and they could not meet the demand. Within a year, they came back to us with jobwork!"

Thus Spacewood* got a captive buyer and a steady income stream. Whatever profit the company made was ploughed into importing more machines.

"Every 6-8 months we used to buy one machine – at that time the cost was ₹3 lakh."

With more machines came a need for workers to handle them. Vivek would take his bike to the big factories like Mahindra and Mahindra where workers hung around looking for *dehadi* (daily-wage work).

---

* The company was started as Nutech Systems, but is now known as Spacewood Furnishers. For ease of understanding, the company is referred to as Spacewood throughout the chapter.

"To do business, *sirf character dabbang hona chahiye." (You need to be bold and fearless to do business.)*

"*Tumko kaam chahiye? Aao mere sath.*" (You need work? Come with me.)

The worker would actually hop on to the bike. At the workshop, Vivek would painstakingly train these men on how to operate the machine. The factory operated from 7 am to 7 pm.

"I would come in the morning and open the factory," says Vivek. "Kirit came later with a tiffin, we had lunch together and he would stay back late, to close the factory."

The primary responsibility on the manufacturing side was Vivek's, while Kirit looked after commericals. This resulted in high quality, at the lowest possible cost.

"*Hamara combo bahut achha tha.*" (We made a wonderful combination.)

In a short span of 3 years, Spacewood clocked revenues of ₹5 crore. Apart from VIP, the company was supplying office furniture components to the likes of Shapoorji Pallonji and Godrej.

In 1997, the two partners travelled to Europe for the first time, to attend the famous Interzum-Ligna furniture exhibition at Cologne and Hanover respectively. That's where they stumbled upon 'membrane-press technology'. A technology which can create 'wood' which is not actually wood.

"It's actually PVC foil on top of MDF – so you get the look of wood. However, the material is 5 times cheaper as well as water-proof!"

This made it ideal for use in the kitchen and was already used widely in Europe. While Vivek was fascinated by the technology, Kirit felt it made sound commercial sense.

"We liked the idea of pioneering a new product, of creating our own niche."

At that time, modular kitchens were unheard of in India. Anyone they talked to, was discouraging.

"Such a product won't have market in India," they said.

But Vivek and Kirit had a gut feeling – this *can* work. They went ahead and imported a machine costing ₹50 lakh from Germany. As the existing space was too small, Spacewood bought the plot next door. For this, they had to take a loan from the State Bank of India.

The bank insisted on collateral, which the company did not have.

"I convinced my father to give our house as the security," says Vivek.

Thus, after great lengths, the machine was finally installed in plot N-7 at MIDC. The first few months were extremely slow. The technology was new, so there was hardly any demand. The machine was running for one week in a month, at best. But Vivek and Kirit did not lose faith.

A seed, once planted, takes time to take root. In the meanwhile you water the pot, keep it in the sun.

"We used to send small samples to architects to tell them – look, here is something new!"

The product Spacewood chose to propogate was kitchen shutters. It took some time, but the idea clicked. From the second year onwards, the company started reaping benefits. By the year 2000, turnover jumped to ₹35 crore.

Naturally, people took notice and decided to invest in the same technology. With more suppliers, there was pressure on costs.

"We thought, how do we grow further, despite competition. Actually we took advantage of the situation!"

Kirit realised that if more vendors take up membrane technology, they will need the basic raw material. Which is prelaminated particle-board. Hence, the company went in for backward integration and set up a plant to manufacture prelam and MDF (medium density fibreboard).

To set up such a unit, more space would be required. Hence, in 2003, Spacewood acquired a 6-acre plot in MIDC and started the new factory.

"If you think that 'this problem is mine' and I am not going pass it on to somebody, then and only then can you solve it!"

"*Uske baad hamara koi competitor nahi bacha.* (After this, we had no competition). Everybody was either buying raw material from me or buying our components."

Yet, challenges remained. In India, the readymade furniture market has always been relatively small. Carpenters are cheaply available, so most people prefer to get it made.

"*Typically hamare andar ek designer chhupa hota hai* (Each of us thinks I am a designer). We show some Fevicol books and tell the carpenter to make the piece, but with minor modification. Then, we like to show off!"

This mindset is difficult to change. More so, for a company based in Nagpur, which was essentially a manufacturing unit.

"Our focus was never on sales and marketing to the end-consumer, we always tried to look for big buyers like Godrej for our office furniture."

In the kitchen segment, Spacewood had tie-ups with dealers across the country, including specialist chains such as 'Sleek Kitchen'. But the real turning point for this segment came when Spacewood aligned with Future Group.

In 2007, Kishore Biyani launched a new retail format called Hometown. This store provided everything one could possibly need to turn a house into a 'home'. The vendor they chose for modular kitchens was Spacewood.

"I would give the credit for our company's growth to organised retail," says Vivek.

Schemes like Big Bazaar's *'sabse sasta din'* (lowest price day) on 26 January every year brought over 1000 orders in just 5 days.

"Of course, the margin we get on such bulk orders is low but it is good for our factory," says Kirit.

After all, manufacturing is a productivity game. The more orders you have, less the idle time.

"We don't keep finished goods' inventory, we keep only raw material," adds Vivek.

At any given time, Spacewood would have an inventory of particleboard – up to 150 containers. Every kitchen needs to be customised. Hence, once the order comes in, the board is laminated and cut into required shapes and sizes.

By 2010, customers in metro cities like Mumbai, Bangalore and Hyderabad were showing increased preference for buying furniture off the shelf. Spacewood had thus entered into bedroom furniture, as well. The company now had office and home components and raw material verticals and was working as a 'core partner' with its clients.

"We don't just supply products as per specifications. We contribute in the area of strategy and design, we come up with new concepts."

The Spacewood 'success formula' is simple: European looks with Indian functionality. Indian buyers have peculiar needs such as 'storage' inside beds and 'lockers' inside wardrobes.

"We look into minute details, like Indian wardrobes need more shelves. Why? Because we give our clothes to the dhobi and they come back folded."

It is the understanding of the Indian psyche that gives Spacewood an edge over Chinese vendors. And this extends to the retailers as well.

"If you want to import from China, you have to buy an entire container. We supply even 20 pieces and at an unbeatable price."

Spacewood has set up a small factory in China – to understand best practices and draw inspiration.

"Actually, I have this habit of learning from observing others, how they do things, what they are doing better than us," says Kirit.

One early inspiration was a company called Amit Polyseats in Kanpur, which Kirit often visited when he was working with VIP. This company's style of operations, their commercials, the factory and even the owner's bungalow was clearly imprinted on the young engineer's mind.

"Looking at a lot of people who are retired, I am sure we can never stop working!"

"*Paise kamaane ka* inspiration (the desire to earn money) and industry *ka* inspiration – I got both from Amit Polyseats."

By March 2010, a company started with a loan of ₹65,000 had crossed a turnover of ₹125 crore. Yet, the partners were restless. On a scale of 1 to 10, they rated themselves as reaching '4' or maximum '5'.

"The important factor is that we made a lot of money and we were never afraid to invest it back into the business. That is one of the crucial factors in growth."

But being a vendor, or even a 'partner' to other retailers was now a limitation. At the same time, launching the 'Spacewood' brand could create a conflict of interest. Vivek and Kirit grappled with this dilemma and ultimately decided to go the Style Spa way and launch their own exclusive showrooms.

To do this, the company would need to start thinking differently.

"One key decision we took is to move from being an owner-driven company to a professionally managed one."

The first step in this direction was the appointment of Mr Sudhame – Kirit's former boss at VIP – as executive director. This made it easier to attract professional talent in areas like marketing and design.

An expansion also requires careful commercial planning – an area where Kirit excels. His love affair with balance sheets started when he was a student.

"That time we used to invest the money we earned in our business in the share market. So I used to study a lot of balance sheets!"

Vivek believes Kirit knows more than any chartered accountant.

"See, probably chartered accountant knows more but my perspective is totally different…from a business angle."

While the CA is trained to be conservative and avoid risk, the entrepreneur is always looking for growth. This is a fundamental difference in outlook.

"Actually, we are both lower middle class, the more poor you are, the more daring you can be," chuckles Kirit.

You have to get on to the field and just start hitting the ball.

"When Sehwag starts batting, he doesn't know how many runs he will make. *Jaise ball aaya, maarta gaya.* (Each ball which came, he hit it by instinct). Our first 15 years were like that."

While a batsman may not plan the initial hundred runs, to reach the next hundred takes strategy and planning. It's the same with a business. Spacewood is now operating in a structured manner, with concrete goals and targets to reach.

In March 2013, Spacewood's group turnover stood at ₹210 crore. The company now operates 12 stand-alone showrooms in different cities across India. The target is to open more than 50 showrooms in the next 3 years.

The workers who came to a makeshift factory started by two young engineers are still with the company. The total staff strength is over 1000, with 80% in the factory and the rest in the management cadre. In the factory, there is a mix of permanent and contract workers.

"All permanent workers are paid at least double, triple the minimum wage. Happy to say, we have not faced any situation of worker unrest or strike in the past 18 years!"

The secret is not just money, but a sense of belonging and mutual respect.

"Both of us are hands-on, day in and day out we work with the juniormost workers. It's not like *yeh director hai, yeh owner hai* (there is no rigid hierarchy), even they take many decisions at their level."

The same cordiality marks Vivek and Kirit's dealings with clients. When Godrej bought a particleboard manufacturing

"When Sehwag starts batting, he doesn't know how many runs he will make. *Jaise ball aaya, maarta gaya.* (Each ball which came, he hit it by instinct.) Our first 15 years were like that."

plant in Pune, the company asked if Spacewood could act as a technical consultant.

"We readily agreed because we can never forget how they supported us when we were starting our business."

While they have got many offers from private-equity firms, Vivek and Kirit have not taken in any major outside investment. The company has been built on internal accruals and bank debt. However, in April 2013, Spacewood struck a deal with Bennett, Coleman & Co (publishers of *The Times of India*). BCCL acquired a 4% stake and, in exchange, will provide advertising and brand visibility.

The company is also in talks with strategic overseas investors, but the partners have no plans to sell out completely.

"We are still passionate about this business. The day we feel we've stopped contributing to the organisation, now we are just an investor here...we will bow out."

While both founders remain intensely committed to the venture, the pace of life is a little more balanced now. From 24X7, 365 days a year for the first 12 years, they now enjoy a 6-day week with more time for the family.

"In the beginning, we did a lot of physical work – production, dispatches, invoices, everything. Now it's more of a management work," says Kirit.

Like the judge who 'works' for very few hours, but must spend a great deal of time understanding the law – to make the right decision.

"Same way, if I am here, I have to be in a very right state of mind. We still have a long way to go."

Keep your eyes on the road and your hand upon the wheel! Let it roll, baby, roll…from Nagpur, the heart of India, to anywhere at all.

ADVICE TO YOUNG ENTREPRENEURS

Kirit

My advice would be, work with passion – whatever work you do, whether in a job or as an entrepreneur.

If you are passionate about your work, then don't chase money. Money will automatically chase you.

Work hard, be focused, just don't look here and there. Focus gives you depth, it gives you mastery. In the short term you will find that someone else is making more money by doing many things. But, in the long run, focus gives a much bigger payoff.

In today's scenario, one can start a business and earn lot of money by using one's brain...you don't need anything more. But yes, you must be fearless.

Once you get into the military, you never fear for death. When you come into business, never fear for money. If you fear for money, then you start losing from Day One.

Remember that the buck stops with you. Say to yourself, "I am the last person in the organisation. If I am not able to do it, nobody will do it." Then be it technical or commercial, you will solve the problem. Once you make a habit of this, you can take on the entire world.

Vivek

My mantra is *karmanye vadhikaraste, ma phaleshu kada chana*, from the Bhagvad Gita. (Do your duty, be detached from the outcome.) Whatever you do, you have to put yourself completely into it. Don't expect instant results... have patience.

If you are putting full effort, ultimately you will get success.

SPICE ROUTE

C V Jacob – Synthite
Kadayiruppu (Kerala)

At an expo in Japan, C V Jacob came across 'oleoresins', a technically challenging industry but one ideally suited for his native state. Four decades later, the ₹1000 crore Synthite is the world's largest company in value-added spices.

Kerala is the land of coconuts, lagoons and spice villages, rest and rejuvenation. A place which you never associate with the word 'work'.

This is 'God's Own Country' from where god's own children go to *other* countries. In search of work.

Therefore, it is really a surprise to find a company like Synthite in the sleepy little village of Kadayiruppu. Not far from the lazy backwaters, a company which is the world leader in oleoresin manufacturing and export.

This amazing story begins in the 1950s, around the same time that Karl Marx was gaining a hold in the state. As young C V Jacob was learning the ropes of business, Kerala elected the world's first communist government.

But somehow, this capitalist dream survived.

"I left school after matriculation and joined my family business which was in construction."

Not very remarkable you might say but, in 1970, Jacob took a daring leap into the unknown. At an expo in Japan, he saw spices being used in liquid form – as 'oleoresins'. He put two and two together.

"Kerala is famous for pepper and cardamom, the raw material was freely available. It seemed like a good business to enter."

Of course, there was no market in India and it was a risky new product. But Jacob was convinced that this was the future. And he was right.

Today, this ₹1000 crore company is the largest oleoresin extractor – not just in India but in the world.

At 80, C V Jacob is active and still at the helm of affairs. As the genial old man relates his story, it all seems to be 'a long time ago'. But in a larger sense it is relevant – even today.

There are many opportunities in God's Own Country.

Spicy new ideas – waiting to be extracted.

SPICE ROUTE

C V Jacob - Synthite
Kadayiruppu (Kerala)

C V Jacob was born in Kolenchery, a small hamlet near Cochin.

"My father was a civil engineering contractor and he also owned the St Peter's High School, Kolenchery, where I studied."

Jacob was a smart boy but always more interested in sports than studies. He was also fascinated by the family construction business. During vacations, Jacob would go up to worksites and hang around. Two such projects he observed were the construction of the Kundala and Mattupetty Dams in Idukki district.

"First my father wanted me to complete studies, then after matriculation he allowed me to go for business."

Jacob was first sent to look after the family's 50-acre cardamom estate in Kallar, The cardamom (*elaichi*) trade is a peculiar one with many different varieties of the spice being grown. The farmer would supply cardamom in lots with 1 kg sample for the purpose of auction.

"50 farmers means 50 lots of cardamom… Merchants from Tamil Nadu used to come to Kallar every Wednesday and the cardamom samples would be circulated in 2 trays."

Based on the quality, a merchant would call out the price he was willing to pay. A deal would be struck anywhere between ₹6 to 8 per kg. Since the tray passed through many hands, some of the cardamom spilled on the floor.

"Whatever quantity was on the floor would be our commission!"

Jacob's brother-in-law, E J Paulose, used to handle the auction, and acted as the young man's mentor and guide. Jacob spent a year learning the ins and outs of the cardamom trade but his heart still lay in construction. With his father's blessings, he joined the family business, looking after small roadworks and construction of family quarters for the staff of the Kerala State Electricity Board.

In 1954, Jacob bagged his first major contract – the Kalarkutty hydroelectric project and bridge. Subsequently, he won the tender for the Anayirangal tunnel and Upper Kallar tunnel.

These projects were technically and financially challenging. More so for a young man who had only attended a few evening classes in engineering. But Jacob had complete confidence.

"I did not have a degree but I had some idea of construction business watching my elder brother, C V John. I had worked with him on Chenkulam Dam in tunneling work up to the power station."

Jacob's father, C U Varkey, was a big name in construction and this certainly helped him win contracts.

"My father had been helpful to many of the engineers when they started their careers. So they gave me very good consideration."

However, the old man did not back his son financially, it was his uncles and brother-in-law who gave that support. Nevertheless, when Jacob founded a firm, he named it 'Varkisons Engineers'.

"I was the managing partner, there were others partners but the day-to-day work was managed by me."

Doing a construction business in the 1950s was very different from today. At that time, there was no culture of giving or taking bribes. What mattered most was the quality of your work. And contractors like Jacob put in far more effort than they were officially required to. This is evident in the case of the complex Pamba Dam project.

"In Pamba, there is a dam and there is a reservoir. The original proposal from the Government of India was to make 2 power stations."

Jacob's favourite Chief Engineer, V Ranganathan, proposed an ingenious solution. Since both reservoirs were at the same height with a single hill in between, he recommended a single power station.

"We had to make a 1 km long inter-connecting tunnel but in this way a lot of money was saved and the state electricity board got a power station with bigger production capacity."

Tunneling work was started in 1961 and completed in 1964. Subsequently, Jacob was involved with the Idukki Dam – a 168.91 metre tall mega-structure. This too was a unique project where the Canadians designed the powerhouse inside a rocky hill. Jacob's company was given the task of creating a 24 ft wide and 20 ft high tunnel with length of 3000 ft – such that 2 trucks could pass through freely.

This was completed in 1965-66 and was, in fact, his last major contract.

"After that I changed my industry because in construction I have to be on-site from Monday morning till Saturday night. I did not have any family life, no time for my wife and children."

Being in construction, Jacob had blasting and drilling equipment, as well as trolleys and trucks to transport debris. A good way of putting it all to use was 'stone crushing'. Jacob went on to pioneer a mechanised quarry and granite-crushing unit, the first of its kind in Kerala.

Around the same time, he also set up a company called 'Arborites Pvt Ltd' which manufactured urea-formaldehyde resin – a low-cost industrial adhesive. Jacob got the idea when he visited a factory in Calcutta and realised there was good demand for this product in Kerala.

"I started a unit in Poonithura, in partnership with Ram Mohan from Calcutta. Later I invited my brother, C V Paul, to join the business."

The modus operandi was to take urea and formalin, heat it and add a special material to make the adhesive. The product

"Education is required for anything but I am telling you education alone will not make you successful."

was packed in 200 kg drums and supplied to the local plywood industry. In 1969, due to shortage in India, the government allowed formalin to be imported. Jacob found a supplier in Japan. This company invited Jacob and his partner to attend 'Expo Japan' in Osaka, in 1970. The world's biggest industrial exhibition at that time.

"It was my first visit abroad and at this expo I got exposure to whole new type of industries, new ideas."

One such idea was that of 'oleoresin' – spice extracted in liquid form. The extraction consists of 'oleo' (the oil which gives intensity of flavour) and 'resin' (which gives colour and bite).

Jacob realised that this idea was 'made for 'Kerala', a land laden with spice. But it was a highly technical business for which he did not have the expertise.

As luck would have it, the Central Food Technology Research Institute (CFTRI), Mysore, developed this technology indigenously. In 1972, CFTRI invited applications from entrepreneurs interested in starting an oleoresin business.

"We went to CFTRI and were able to get all the designs of the plant and the know-how. In return, we gave a royalty of 1.5% of our turnover to the institute."

The technology worked but not without glitches. Oleoresin production is a 2-stage process where flavour is taken out as 'essential oil', while the 'resinous fraction' is obtained through solvent extraction. If it is not cooled properly, the resin becomes too viscous and solid.

"Our first product was from pepper and in the second year we started extracting from ginger. Ginger we managed but pepper we had lot of problem."

The first 2 years were difficult, with various trial and error methods failing to yield the desired pepper oleoresin. But in late 1973, an American gentleman arrived in Cochin. And this changed everything.

In fact, Jacob had requested his cousin in the US to look around for buyers of oleoresin. And one such party was a Jewish firm in New York called J Mannheimer & Co. One of the partners – Arnold Mannheimer – expressed an interest in meeting Jacob and made arrangements to visit India.

"I received him here, showed him everything, he was very happy."

At the end of the visit, Mannheimer said, "I will give you all the technical know-how you need for the US market and any other help you require."

He had only one condition – the oleoresins exported by Jacob to the US must be routed through his company. It was a win-win situation for both parties. The United States Food and Drug Administration (USFDA) has strict regulations regarding standards, consistency and even packaging. Without a local partner, it would have been impossible to navigate.

"You know in Kerala, if you go to the market and buy some chilli from a shop and the next day you go again and buy from the same shop – you make a curry, you see different results!"

The amount of chilli used would be exactly the same but one curry might be mild and the second one very hot. Such a situation will never occur with use of oleoresin. Whether you make a food product in hundreds, thousands or millions, the flavour and 'heat' of the chilli across all batches will be the same.

Every spice contains an 'active molecule' – in case of chilli it is capsaicin, in case of pepper 'piperine'. The standard pepper oleoresin consists of 40% piperine and 20% essential oil. What's more, oleoresin is highly concentrated.

"A 25% concentrate means 1 kg of oleoresin must be blended with 25 kg of carrier (such as oil) for cooking purpose. It is mainly used by big companies in the processed food industry."

Oleoresins also require special packaging in HM high-density containers, to prevent breakage and chemical reaction. This material was not available in India at that time – it had to be imported. Crossing all these hurdles, Synthite secured its first

"When we started in India nobody else was doing this industry...by the grace of God we achieved it."

order from the US through J Mannheimer and Co. An order worth ₹70 lakh.

Jacob did not have the money to execute such a large order, so he went to the Union Bank of India in Cochin. The manager refused to advance any money.

"Can I use your telephone?" requested Jacob.

From the manager's desk he placed a call to Mr K P Menon at Union Bank of India in Madras. Mr Menon had earlier been looking after the Cochin branch and when Synthite started operations, he had promised 'all possible support'.

"I explained all the matter to him – that I had got an order for ₹70 lakh but I need to buy the raw material as well as working capital. For that I need ₹30 lakh urgently."

Without hesitation, Menon replied, "We will do it. Hand over the phone to the manager..."

There was only one condition – raw material would be stored under a 'double key' system. The bank would unlock the godown as and when it was required, thus keeping track of the stock. In this manner, the bank extended to Jacob the full amount he had asked for.

"You know that was 40 years ago. ₹30 lakh was a very big amount then.... I think it might be equal to ₹30 crore today!"

With Mannheimer's technical support, the first order went off smoothly and there was no looking back. Having mastered the product, Synthite was able to create a good market not just in the US but in Europe and Japan as well.

To communicate with all these buyers, Synthite set up an office in Cochin where telex, telegram and trunk call facility was available.

"My nephew, George Paul, joined the company in 1976 and he was in charge of the Cochin office. He speaks English very well which was a big advantage."

Another big advantage for Synthite was the system of 'dollar advance'. Initially, Citibank offered dollars to the company at 1.5% interest pa. The condition being that if you take $1 crore today, it has to be paid back within 6 months.

"Almost all the money we were taking like that, it was very effective and cheaper than the normal bank rate."

As demand grew, Synthite set up a second processing plant in Kolenchery where everything from design to fabrication was done in-house. This included stainless steel vessels with capacity up to several tons. A tremendous effort was required, yet the team was able to commission these plants in time.

"We got some ideas from good people and so many literatures also. If you get a design you can make anything."

In 1984-85, Synthite bagged the national award from the President of India for outstanding export performance. By this time, the company had embarked on a major expansion drive.

First, Synthite set up a unit to manufacture dehydrated pepper and 'pepper in brine'. Second, it adopted a new strategy.

"Instead of transporting to Kolenchery, we will start a plant where raw material is abundant."

The first such plant outside Kerala was set up in Madurai, Tamil Nadu, to extract essential oil and fragrance from flowers like jasmine, tuberose and mimosa. Jacob's son, Viju, had joined the company and took responsibility for the new plant, even as Jacob continued to seek out opportunities.

"I am always searching for some new ideas…that is my principle."

On a visit to New York in 1987, Jacob asked one of the Mannheimer brothers, "Steve, do you have anything new and interesting for me?"

Steve asked him to wait for half and hour and, finally, emerged with a file. He file contained a write-up on mustard. This spice contains a special property – when heated in the presence of water, mustard seeds give out a strong, piercing odour. In chemical terms, it is

"We have good designs available in India, we pay the royalty and get the design."

known as 'Allyl Isiothiocyanate' (AITC) and this had never been captured through traditional methods of extraction.

"In case of most spices we can isolate the essential oil by steam distillation. But for mustard we can obtain the active molecule only after hydrolysis."

To source the special equipment required for mustard, Jacob flew to Australia with his son, Aju, and chief engineer. A company in Melbourne agreed to supply custom-built distillation assembly on an exclusive basis, on the condition that their designs would not reproduced. Jacob agreed and purchased the equipment at a cost of ₹2.5 crore.

"Also we had to import a special variety of mustard from Canada and special 'seamless' drums from Japan for the packing!"

But the efforts yielded excellent results. Mustard oleoresin is widely used in condiments like mayonnaise and also in sushi. In 1994, Synthite became the first Indian company in the food sector to receive ISO 9002 certification from BSI UK. The company continued to add new products and new markets, but it was facing one major problem – the lack of an international airport in Cochin.

"Every day we used to load one truck of our finished product and send to Trivandrum… It will take 5-6 days to reach the destination."

When the Civil Aviation ministry proposed the Cochin International Airport (CIAL) in March 1993, many dismissed it as a pipe dream. But the CIAL project found a champion in Ernakulam district collector, V J Kurien, and Jacob was the first to come forward and offer his support. Not only did he contribute ₹25 lakh to the project*, on Kurien's insistence, Jacob agreed to guide the airport construction work.

---

* Cochin International Airport is India's first airport built under PPP (Public-Private Partnership).

"I am a director in CIAL from 1994 and I am proud to say this airport has transformed our city. It has also helped our business in its growth."

The Cochin International Airport began functioning in the year 1996. That same year, Synthite and the Mannheimers parted ways.

"23 years I worked with them…! Then they sold that company and advised that you can send anyone to the United States to continue your business."

Thus, a business relationship between gentlemen came to a gentle end.

By 1997-98, Synthite crossed ₹100 crore in revenues. Over the next few years, Synthite continued to grow rapidly and, in 2001, set up a separate unit for processing of chillies in Harihar (Karnataka). By this time, the company was a dominant player – one with whom the Americans were finding it difficult to compete! When you cannot keep up, you try to create hurdles.

An oleoresin extractor called Rezolex, based in New Mexico, filed a case with the International Trade Commission, alleging that Synthite was 'dumping' its product in the US. The petitioner alleged:

"… imports of oleoresin paprika from India are being, or are likely to be, sold in the United States at less than fair value within the meaning of section 731 of the Act and that such imports are materially injuring and threaten to injure an industry in the United States."

Jacob's nephew, George Paul, recalls that challenge.

"We engaged an attorney, fought the case and got a verdict in India's favour."

While paprika is mostly extracted from the 'Capsicum annum' (sweet pepper), Synthite was using 'Capsicum frutescens' (Indian red chillies). Sweet pepper yields only colour extract while Indian chillies also have a mild pungent property. This gives Synthite 2 products – double the economic value.

"Paprika was one of our money-spinners," says George Paul. "But still, we were facing lot of problem because productivity of chillies in India is very low."

The company tried to incentivise farmers to grow high-yielding varieties, but with limited success. Demand had to be met by importing crude oleoresin. However, in 2012, Synthite took the bold step of setting up a processing unit in the People's Republic of China. This project was led by Aju Jacob.

The plant is located at Hejing city in Xinjiang province where paprika is abundantly produced.

"It is a remote area where the crops are grown with snow water, with the help of Chinese troops!"

The Hejing unit processes 3,00,000 tons of locally produced paprika. The company plans to start growing lavender and tomatoes in the area and making the facility a 'major export hub'.

"Working in China we had some cultural issues, especially language barrier," admits Paul, "But we have been able to adapt."

In March 2013, Synthite's revenues crossed ₹1000 crore, with 8 processing units and over 2000 employees. The company has no trade union and has never had any labour unrest. Jacob attributes this to the 'human touch'.

"See, anybody from sweeper to top manager knows I care about them and they can approach me."

The company also provides facilities like interest-free housing loans (up to 50%), education allowance and health insurance.

Despite its global reach, the enterprise remains close to his roots. The company head office, also known as 'Synthite Taste Park', is situated at Kadayiruppu, a small village near Kolenchery town.

Synthite's portfolio now includes 500 products and 90% of its business still comes from oleoresins. But the future may be different. The company also has 2 joint ventures – one with seasonings company, Omega, from Austria, the other with confectionary flavour-maker, Aromco, from the UK. The idea being to supply value-added spice products to snack food, dairy and bakery manufacturers.

"We are also supplying crushed and steam-sterilised spices to the big hotels and caterers. Now we want to enter the retail market."

Synthite has launched *sambar*, *garam*, chicken and meat *masalas* under the brand name 'Kitchen Treasures'. The company also plans to enter the gourmet foods market with a range of natural colours, soups and sauces. In due course, there may also be an oleoresin 'spray' for use in home cooking. The target is to reach ₹3000 crore – by the year 2020.

Jacob's zest for life and for growth can be seen, not just in company initiatives, but in his love of badminton. Even at age 80, he spends an hour and a half each morning on the court, against opponents half his age. Does he play to win?

"Naturally." (*Laughs*)

Now more of a 'chairman emeritus', Jacob still attends office everyday from 8.30 am to 5.30 pm. He is also responsible for a number of educational institutions in Kolenchery – the school, arts and science college and the Malankara Orthodox Syrian Church Medical College.

"If you love God, you contribute to the poor people, to education, it is for Him only."

Every morning, before having his tea, Jacob reads the Bible according to a 'system'. He has a box filled with 'cards', each card indicates a verse from the Bible.

"I take 3 cards every morning and I read the verse mentioned… from that I get a message. That is what advice God is giving, what is required for any problem."

Problems come and go, Jacob remembers only one situation which rendered him helpless. That was in his early days, in the construction business. At that time his brother-in-law, E J Paulose, was his partner and mentor, as well as handling the firm's accounts and finance. One Sunday he made a rare visit to the tunneling site, to attend to an emergency.

What nobody noticed was the 'weak zone' of the tunnel, which collapsed all of a sudden.

"One worker and my brother died on the spot…that was the only thing in my life…most painful thing to remember even today."

Bitter, sweet, sour and spicy – those are the many flavours of life. All you can do is keep savouring it, until your last breath.

ADVICE FOR YOUNG ENTREPRENEURS

Secret of success is the idea and the planning.

Select the right industry according to your interest.

Never copy somebody, be the first to do something new. Some risk is there but once you come through, you are happy.

Work hard, work sincerely, do your best and leave the rest to God's grace.

ANGRY YOUNG MAN

Parakramsinh Jadeja – Jyoti CNC
Rajkot (Gujarat)

In 1989, a young man started a jobshop in Rajkot, one of thousands in the city. In the last decade, Jyoti CNC has grown from an SSI unit of ₹7 crore to a ₹1000 crore company, the largest machine tool manufacturer in India.

Rajkot is a city with a rich royal past, ruled for over 300 years by Jadeja Rajputs. A fiery, martial race known for winning on the battlefield.

Royalty is no more, but a Jadeja continues to rule in Rajkot. A fiery young man, fighting on a whole new battlefield – the cutthroat world of global business.

Parakramsinh Jadeja charged into the machine tool industry in the year 1989. After dropping out of school to pursue chess, Parakram realised that sports was a luxury his family could ill-afford.

"Since I had learnt to use a lathe machine in Class 9 and 10, I thought of starting a jobshop."

Hot blood and a hot head worked in the young man's favour. A quarrel with the only 'apron' manufacturer in the city became the motivation to start making aprons. When the Japanese company, Fanuc, treated him badly, Parakram decided to never work with them again. This led to a long and valuable association with Siemens.

There are hundreds of small manufacturers in Rajkot, but none with the hunger, the passion or the determination of Jyoti CNC. In 2003, this company with revenues of ₹7 crore chose an audacious mission and vision – to be a ₹1000 crore company in 8 short years.

"*Hum do saal late ho gaye* (We were late by 2 years) but we have achieved it."

This is the story of a bold conquest, across new markets and new territories. A battle won not by brute force but with strategic thinking and inspired execution.

Like a grandmaster, playing his pieces to perfection.

ANGRY YOUNG MAN

Parakramsinh Jadeja - Jyoti CNC
Rajkot (Gujarat)

Parakramsinh Jadeja was born and brought up in Rajkot.

"My father was a municipal corporation employee. I grew up in a notorious area of Lakshmiwadi."

The neighbourhood was infamous for gambling and *desi daru* (illicit liquor). But it also boasted one of the best *garbis* (Navratri dances) in Rajkot city.

"Every day there used to be 2000-3000 coming to see the garba dance. We used to sell a ticket of ₹2 and make a good income from that."

As a student of the Gujarati-medium Virani High School, Parakram was also an active sportsman. National-level cricketers like Karan Ghavri and Yajuvendra Singh were products of the school, inspiring students to follow in their footsteps. Like everyone else, Parakram was fond of playing cricket.

"But one sport where I was excellent is chess."

As one of the top 3 chess players in Gujarat state, Parakram was selected to play in the National Tournament 'B' division. However, the dates of the tournament were clashing with his Class 12 exams. This happened because, in 1985, there was a statewide *'Anamat Andolan'* (agitation for reservation) in Gujarat.

"It was similar to Mandal. *Woh time pe hum log ka exam March mein tha* (our board exam was in March). It was shifted to October. In between, *meri padhai chhuut gayi* (I dropped out of studies)."

The young man chose to play chess, without a thought about 'future', 'career', '*kal kya hoga*', etc. And his family did not argue or object to it.

"*Woh time par pappa ne poochha bhi nahin ki bhaiyya tu 12th class mein padh raha hai – issko chhod kar tu aage jaakar kya karega*." (My father never questioned my decision, what is my future plan, etc.)

From 1985 to 1988, Parakram lived the life of a sportsman and enjoyed it thoroughly. In 1989, he was selected to play for the under-19 side of an English county cricket team. Parakram was excited – all he needed was ₹25,000 for his air ticket and other small expenses.

"*Pappa mane paisa ni jaroorat chhe…* " (Pappa, I need money from you.)

"Okay," said his father.

One week later, he handed his son ₹10,000. The following week, he gave ₹5000. After a few more days, he brought another ₹5000. This irked the young sportsman.

"Pappa, yeh hafte hafte kya de rahe ho…ek saath de do, abhi mera teen din baaki hai jaane ko?" (Pappa, why are you giving me installments, give me all the money, I am leaving in 3 days.)

His father replied, "*Kuch provident fund se loan mila, kuch credit society se…friend se poocha hai, aa raha hai*." (I got a loan from provident fund, from credit society, rest I am borrowing, it will come soon.)

Parakram was stunned. Till that day he had been oblivious to the financial hardship in his family. The lengths his father was going to, so he could pursue sports.

"It was a turning point in my life. I left my game and I entered into a new game…to do something in life, in business."

But what kind of business? In Parakram's school, there was a subject in Class 9 and 10 called 'workshop technology'. He knew how to use a lathe machine and it seemed like a good line of work.

The lathe* is a metal-cutting machine – it rotates an object on its axis producing a desired shape.

But the machine was expensive, Parakram could not afford it. So, then what?

As luck would have it, a friend's uncle manufactured lathe machines. Praful *mama* agreed to give Parakram one machine, under 'barter system'.

"*Woh humko kaam denge, aur us jobwork se main unko hafta doonga. Aisa agreement tha.*" (He will give me jobwork and that way I will repay him weekly. That was the agreement.)

Parakram roped in his cousin, Sahdevsinh Jadeja, and a 10 X 15 jobshop came into being. True to his word, Praful mama would send parts and the young entrepreneurs undertook the 'machining work'. Mama was also happy to take the boys under his wing and train them on the job.

"We called the workshop as 'Jyoti' which is the name of my younger sister."

In those days, the government was promoting the 'Jawahar Rozgar Yojana' for educated, self-employed youth. Parakram received an interest-free loan of ₹35,000 under this scheme. With this money he bought the lathe machine as well as a small shop right next to Praful mama's factory.

"*Hum logon ne ek saal mein itna achha business kiya* (we did such good business) that we were able to pay the entire loan in the next year."

By this time, the young entrepreneurs had started manufacturing parts for Praful mama, using raw material supplied by him. One morning, mama complained about the 'apron**' manufacturer. The fellow had taken advance weeks ago but wasn't delivering the goods.

Mama said, "*Tu us taraf ja raha hai, Jadhvani mistry ko pooch kya situation hai.*" (You are going that way, enquire with Jadhvani carpenter what is the situation.)

* Another way to cut metal is to keep the job stationary and rotate the tool – this is known as milling.

** Apron is a part inside the lathe holding the clutches and gears.

> ***"Jab business shuru kiya aisa kuch 'dream' nahi tha, yeh to ek zarurat aa padi aur karna pada."* (When I started the business there was no dream or vision as such, it was a need to survive.)**

Parakram set off on his cycle and stopped by at Jadhvani's workshop. The mistry assured, "*Yeh paanch apron jo ban rahe hain, Prafulbhai ke hain. Waapsi mein le lena*." (These 5 aprons being made are for Prafulbhai. You can take them on your way back.)

In the evening, when Parakram returned to pick up the aprons, he got a rude shock. A 'cash' customer walked in, agreed to pay ₹50 extra per apron and the mistry gave him the goods.

"*Mama ko bolna ek hafte ke baad de doonga*," said the mistry. (Tell mama he can take his aprons next week.)

Parakram's hot Rajput blood boiled over. He roughed up the mistry, snatched mama's money back and went to his factory.

"*Mama yeh rakkho, woh aapko ullu bana raha hai...kuch dene wala nahin hai!*" (Uncle, that man is making a fool of you; he is not going to give you anything.)

Mama was aghast. He said, "*Paagal – yeh tu kya kar aaya*!" (Mad boy, what have you done!)

Jadhvani mistry was the sole supplier of aprons in Rajkot city. Where would Praful mama get the component from now?

"*Main bana ke doonga*," declared Parakram. (I will make it.)

Mama was not convinced – apron was not a simple thing to make. But Parakram took it as a challenge. He went to his workshop, opened up his own lathe machine and inspected the apron. Surely, there was a way to replicate it! Working day and night, the team 'cracked' drawing, design and assembly.

"We promised mama that he would get 5 aprons in 20 days...and we kept that promise."

Very soon, Parakram was supplying aprons all over Rajkot, driving Jadhvani mistry right out of business.

Impressed by its performance, the bank recommended the young company for an IDBI scheme – a loan of ₹5 lakh at 1% interest p.a.

In 1991, Parakram heard about something called AutoCAD and decided to buy a computer. At that time, a 486 PC cost ₹1.6 lakh – a huge sum of money. But Parakram was convinced – this is needed.

"I bought scooter much later..." he laughs.

AutoCAD was indeed very useful, to make engineering drawings and designs. It was tedious to operate, using arrow keys. But gave the young company an 'edge'.

In 1992, Parakram purchased a plot in Aji GIDC, an upcoming industrial area. The workshop was now a factory, supplying aprons and 'Norton' gearboxes to almost all lathe manufacturers, including companies like Kirloskar. In addition, there was an HMT plant in Bhavnagar called Gujarat State Machine Tools and Corporation (GSMTC) which manufactured 'vikram lathe'.

The most precise part of this lathe is its 'head' – this was supplied by Parakram. Unfortunately, the HMT plant closed down in 1993 leaving Parakram with unsold inventory. He tried to sell these gearheads to machine tool builders in Rajkot. But, they were not interested.

"In Rajkot, everyone was using the older 'belt' technology. Only big companies like Kirloskar and HMT made gear-driven machines back then."

Parakram's pitch was simple: today machines made in Rajkot sell for ₹15-25,000 while Kirloskar machines sell for ₹1-1.25 lakh. If you add a gearhead (costing ₹20,000), you can compete with them and sell your machine for ₹60-70,000. Bringing in more sales, more profits.

Unable to convince a single manufacturer, Parakram took a bold decision – he would start making lathe machines himself.

"I am not an engineer...never passed through any institute or college but *sikhte sikhte '93 mein hamne lathe machine ki pehli design banayi* (in '93, we made the first lathe machine design)."

"I took a challenge, *mama aisa kuch hota nahi hai duniya mein jo nahin ho sakta hai."* (Uncle, there is nothing in this world that is not possible.)

Now, began the task of marketing. In those days, all manufacturers in Rajkot supplied through dealers based in big cities. Parakram went on tour – first to Bangalore, then Coimbatore and, finally, Chennai. In Chennai, one of the dealers had given him an appointment for 2 pm.

At precisely 1 o'clock, Parakram reached the dealer's office.

"*Uske office mein koi nahin tha lekin usne mujhe teen ghante tak bitha kar rakha*." (There was no one else he had to meet yet he kept me waiting for 3 hours.)

When he was finally called in, Parakram could not contain himself.

"*Aapne enquiry bheji, mujhe samay diya, phir aisa kyun kiya mere saath?"* (You sent an enquiry, you gave the time, now why are you treating me like this?)

He said, "*Theek hai, theek hai. Rajkot mein jab mein flight se utarta hoon to aapke jaise pachaas machine tool wale mere peechey ghoomte hain."* (Okay, okay, when I come to Rajkot, 50 machine tool fellows like you try to get my attention.)

The dealer emphasised that he bought only in large volumes, at low prices. Then, he remarked, "*Rajkot mein all-geared lathe ban sakti hai*?" (Are you sure you can make all-geared lathes in Rajkot?)

Parakram got up, folded his hands and said, "*Aapse dhandha nahin karna hai*. Thank you very much!" (I have no desire to do business with you.)

The young man was shaken – the only thought in his mind was how to get home quickly.

"That day I took a flight ticket from Chennai to Ahmedabad via Bangalore…for the first time in my life."

By the time he reached Rajkot, Parakram took a momentous decision. His company was a small one, with 16 employees and ₹25 lakh turnover. But it would not be bullied – by anyone.

"*Maine decision liya ki hum dealer ke through marketing nahin karenge, direct customer ko bechenge*". (I decided we won't sell through dealers, we will go directly to our customers.)

At an industrial exhibition in Rajkot, Parakram's company bagged its first major customer – Bhikabai Parmar from Surendranagar, a manufacturer of textile spindles. Bhikabhai placed an order for 9 machines but he had a special requirement.

"Can you fit a hydraulic cylinder and a high-speed spindle?" he wanted to know.

Parakram said, "We have never done that but if you guide me, surely it's possible."

The period from '93 to '98 was a growth phase for Jyoti, also packed with learning. The company developed an expertise in 'special purpose machines' with a high degree of automation. Based on what the customer needs.

While sales of basic aprons and gearboxes continued, these customised machines fetched a handsome premium – selling for ₹2 lakh each.

"We never gave any advertisement, it was only through word of mouth."

Orders came in from all over Gujarat and even from Mumbai. During this period, Parakram and his team also learnt a lot in terms of machining and manufacturing practices.

In 1998, a new technology called 'CNC' was emerging and only one company in Rajkot possessed such a machine. When Parakram asked to see it, the owner haughtily replied, "*Isme TV laga hai, computer laga hai, yeh tere bas ki baat nahin hai.*" (It has a TV and a computer, this machine is beyond you.)

Later that year, Parakram attended the IMTEX exhibition in New Delhi, organised by IMTMA (Indian Machine Tool Manufacturers' Association). There, he realised that the days of mechanical lathes were numbered. But how to enter this new world of CNC?

> ***"Hum baaki sab toh banate hi the, ab puri machine bana lenge."* (We were already making the parts, we decided to make the entire machine.)**

Help came in the form of a seminar called 'First time CNC' held in Rajkot. This was organised by IMTMA and UNIDO (United Nations Industrial Development Organisation).

"This kind of a seminar is sometime changing the life of people, in my case this happened also."

CNC stands for 'Computerised Numerical Control'. The cutting operation is driven by a computerised command system, making high precision output possible. These controllers were manufactured only by 2 companies – Fanuc (from Japan) and Siemens (from Germany). Both companies made presentations at the seminar.

At the end of two days, Parakram was all charged up about CNC. He invited the Fanuc representative to visit his factory so that he could place an order.

The Fanuc man said, "First fill out this form. How many engineers do you have, what is your turnover?"

Parakram was surprised – this was no way to treat a potential customer.

"*Aapko mera turnover jaanne ki kya zaroorat hai*?" he asked. (Why do you need to know my turnover?)

"Can you afford our machine?" said the Fanuc man, quite bluntly. "Our machine is ₹20 lakh."

Jyoti was indeed a small company but Parakram's ambition was not.

"*Mujhe gussa aaya* (I was angry) – I told, thank you very much, I don't want to work with you!!"

He went straight to Siemens and started discussions. At 2 am, Parakram placed an order for his first CNC machine costing ₹20 lakh. At that time, the turnover of the company was indeed just ₹60 lakh. But 'affordability' was not the issue. Parakram was more worried about how he would operate the CNC.

He said to the Siemens salesman, "I don't know A, B, C of this technology. Your engineers will have to help me, train me."

Indeed, the impulsive decision to work with Siemens instead of Fanuc paid rich dividends. Fanuc was a Japanese company, very closed and secretive with its technology. On the other hand, Siemens was open and willing to share its trade secrets.

"We learnt a lot from the Germans and quickly moved ahead of others in our industry!"

Parakram also realised that to expand the CNC business, he would need professionals. The first person he asked was his cousin brother, Hiren, an electronics engineer and MBA, working with IBM. He declined. Some weeks later, Hiren's college batchmate, Hitesh Patel, came to Parakram's office to sell a fax machine.

"*Maine usko poocha ki bhai tu Hiren ke saath padhta tha* (I asked him that you studied with my brother, Hiren), why are you wasting time selling fax machine?"

Hitesh replied, "There is no job available for an electronics engineer in Rajkot... Can you give me a job?"

Soon after, he joined Jyoti, becoming the first engineer on the company rolls. With a lot of trial and error, with help from Siemens, Parakram and team managed to build a CNC lathe machine. In the first year, they sold 6 such machines in and around Rajkot.

In 1999, Siemens sponsored 3 of its customers to visit the EMO (World Machine Tool Exposition) in Paris, the world's largest trade fair for machine tools. It was Parakram's first trip abroad and it opened his eyes as well as his thinking. He was particularly fascinated by a lathe machine using 'linear motor technology', made by a company called DMG. It was the 'fastest' machine in the world at that time.

On the last day, all the others in Parakram's group were going to Disneyland. But, he did not join them.

"*Mujhe bura laga ki kisine hamare upar paisa kharch karke yahan bheja hai aur hum ghoomne ke liye jaa rahe hain.*" (I felt bad

"*Destination ka jo picturisation hona chahiye puri team ko pataa hone chahiye.*" (You must be able to picture your destination and share that picture with your team.)

that someone spent money to send me here and I am going for sightseeing.)

Parakram stayed back at EMO and something magical happened. As the exhibition was ending, stall owners started dismantling their machines. Parakram sat there, all through Saturday and Sunday, and got to see his dream machine in an 'open' condition.

Once he saw the mechanism he realised, "*Yeh to hum bana sakte hain*!" (We can make this.)

On returning to India, he asked Siemens to supply him with the necessary motor. They warned him – it would be difficult.

"*I says theek hai, jo bhi hota hai humein karna hai...*" (I said it's okay – we are going to do it anyway.)

When the motor arrived, it was held up by Customs. Being linear, it had no ball bearings and did not rotate. The officer insisted it was not a motor at all – it took 3 months to convince him otherwise.

The purpose of importing the motor was to build a world-class machine to display at IMTEX 2001. Even though Parakram knew that there would be no customers for an ultra-fast, ultra-sophisticated lathe costing ₹1 crore. The effort was part of a larger strategy.

"*Log aisa kehte the ki Rajkot wale quality nahi dete hai, to hamein unko aisa ek jerk dena tha.*" (People believed that companies in Rajkot did not deliver quality, we wanted to change that perception.)

At that time Jyoti was a company with a turnover of ₹1.3 crore. Yet, with the support of his bankers, Parakram invested ₹2.8 crore for the IMTEX exhibition. It was a leap of faith but not a flight of fancy.

"*Humne rakkhi ek crore ki machine magar humein bechni thi 15 lakh wali CNC machine.*" (We displayed the ₹1 crore machine although our real objective was to sell ₹15 lakh CNC machines.)

The linear motor machine created excitement and awe – it was a turning point.

"*Kisine mujhe poocha nahi ke aap kahan se ho* (No one asked me where are you from). And from that day we were growing every year by 100%."

In 2002, Parakram purchased a plot for a new factory in Metoda, an upcoming industrial area. As per GIDC rules, the company which owned the land did not have the right to transfer it.

"We went ahead and bought that company – AMB Bearings. Later we changed the name to Jyoti CNC."

The following year, Parakram decided to participate in the EMO in Milan. Exhibition space at such events is very precious, very expensive. To encourage Indian companies to participate in larger numbers, IMTMA and UNIDO reserved 100 sq m for SSIs. Each SSI was eligible to apply for 15 sq mt of 'free' space.

Parakram bent the rules a little – he applied under 2 names – Jyoti (his old partnership firm) and Jyoti CNC Ltd (formerly AMB Bearings Ltd). He wanted 100 sq m in total, to display the linear motor machine, as well as 4 other lathes.

"*Jab exhibition mein jaana hai to no more cost cutting. Hum log full energy ke saath jayenge.*" (When we are going to an exhibition we want to go with full energy, no more cost cutting.)

Parakram's 2 companies got 30 sq m, and he was all set to pay for 70 sq m. But, he was in for a pleasant surprise. As there were no other SSI applicants, the entire 100 sq m reserved by UNIDO was allotted to Jyoti.

"My stall was the biggest by an Indian company. And I got the booth without giving money. This was the big boost."

Parakram attended EMO with his 15-member strong team. The idea was to expose them to 'what is happening in the world'. To raise their confidence, their ambition. A few months after EMO, IMTMA organised a 3-day seminar called 'Vision Exercise' conducted by industry veteran, Shaileshbhai Sheth.

At the end of it, Parakram was shaken to the core.

> **"We were always a debt company. *Aisa kabhi nahi hua ki hum log pehle kamaa lein aur phir spend kare.* We always spent more than we earned in order to grow."**

"*Tab mujhe laga ki yaar aaj tak kya kar rahe the* (I asked myself – what have we been doing so far). Where is our vision, what is our mission?"

A 'vision' is more than an outcome, it is an idea. Which inspires people to work towards an outcome. A classic example quoted at the seminar was the 1942 'Quit India' movement.

On his return to Rajkot, Parakram called his entire team and said, "Let's put our vision on paper."

Every morning there was intense introspection, discussion, soul-searching. This exercise took 8-9 months. At the end of it, Jyoti CNC had its vision and mission: to be the No 1 Machine Tool company in India by the year 2011. And not just by turnover.

"We took a decision that we want to be No 1 in technology, in quality and in volume. Figurewise we were at ₹7 crore, we put a target that we need to be ₹1000 crore."

Along with the statement, there was a plan. Taking the ₹1000 crore figure, the team worked backward and put down 'engineering details'. How much equipment, finance and manpower they would need to make this vision a reality. The entire plan was made without an outside consultant.

"Actually, we tried to take 2-3 consultants but they all told us, you will fail, you are being too ambitious."

And possibly, it was. In making 'risky' moves, Parakram's training as a chess player was very useful. When taking decisions, he could visualise 5-6 scenarios and the permutation-combination which might play out.

"*Doosron ko nahin dikh raha hai jo mujhe dikh raha hai* (Others could not see it, what I could see). So I find it that I am not gambling...behind my plan something is there."

Another important thing he learnt in chess is the value of patience. Even the best tactic will take time to produce a result. This was certainly the case with Jyoti CNC's entry into the export market. When the company put up a stall at EMO in 2003, it won acclaim and attention, but not a single order. Yet, Parakram did not hesitate to participate in EMO 2005.

"Actually we did not get any order even in 2005. We got our first foreign customer after EMO 2007."

The machine tool industry is an old one, and extremely quality conscious. A new player is not accepted easily. Only when customers saw Jyoti CNC return, again and again, were they convinced. This company is serious, it is here to stay.

"After EMO 2007, many dealers and OEMs (Original Equipment Manufacturers) came to Rajkot to see our factory. They were impressed and gave us good orders."

This was also the time when Parakram gave up his *zid* (adamant stand) and Jyoti CNC established relations with Fanuc.

"We are working closely and excellently with Fanuc since last 5-6 years."

True to its plan and promise, Jyoti CNC had managed to achieve its ambitious growth targets. From ₹7 crore in 2003, the company had crossed ₹150 crore by 2008. With such pace and performace, the company had no problems at all in raising whatever funds it required from the bank. At times, it was difficult to fund interest payments. But Parakram had a simple rule of thumb.

"*Installment ek bhi din late nahi bharna hai, uske liye dusra loan bhi lena pade to manzoor hai.*" (We will not pay an installment even a day late. If necessary, I will take another loan.)

Thus, Jyoti CNC maintained a very clean credit history with the bank. Allowing it to borrow more funds and grow even faster. As per the vision plan of 2003, in 2008, Jyoti CNC was to acquire another company. The company Parakram identified was a major competitor. But the management refused to sell out.

One morning Parakram and his colleagues were sitting in his office, discussing this. At that time, a French gentleman happened to be present in the room. He was the general

"The word 'method' was invented by the French people. We have learnt a lot from them."

manager of a company called Huron and had spent many years working in India.

"We were discussing in a Hindi-English mixture about our takeover, why it failed and all that."

Suddenly the Frenchman spoke up, in perfect Hindi, "*Khareedni hai to meri company khareed sakte ho*." (Why don't you buy my company.)

The owner of Huron had crossed the age of 70 and wished to exit from the business. But Parakram was doubtful. Huron was two and a half times the size of Jyoti CNC. How would a buyout be structured, where would the funds come from?

At that time the State Bank of India (SBI) was aggressively helping Indian companies acquire foreign companies. Parakram was already an SBI customer.

"We visited the SBI branch in Paris. The DGM from forex department came, inspected our factory and gave an in-principle sanction from the MD."

With this commitment, Jyoti CNC bid for Huron in March 2008 and a sale was concluded. Parakram requested 3 months' time to secure the funds and complete the transaction.

Initially, SBI agreed to extend a 100% loan against the security of the Jyoti SNC factory premises. But sometime later, the DMD (Deputy Managing Director) raised objections. Doubting Jyoti CNC's experience in managing a company twice its size, the DMD cancelled the deal.

This put Parakram in a tight spot.

"*Humne waha contract sign kar liya tha, humne commitment de diya tha*."(We had signed the contract and given our commitment.)

Finally, Jyoti CNC agreed to put up 15% of the funds required from internal sources and Madam DMD softened. But, in the final meeting, she raised the issue of 'integration plan'.

"Without seeing integration plan I will not release your file!" she warned.

The trouble was, Jyoti CNC had not made any such plan yet. The payment deadline was fast approaching and SBI was not budging.

At this difficult time, one day Parakram got a call from Mr K R Kamath*, Executive Director, Bank of India. It was an invitation for a dinner the bank was hosting in Rajkot. Mr Kamath was, in fact, the banker who disbursed the very first loan of ₹35,000 to Parakram, when he was a manager at Corporation Bank.

"We have a very close relation, like a family. I told him *kya sab chal raha hai* (what is happening)."

If funds did not come in very soon, Parakram would have to go back to Huron and say the deal was off.

"If I back out now it is not just Jyoti, but a loss of face for India!"

Mr Kamath offered to organise a meeting with his forex department as well as Bank of India's Paris branch. Two days later, Parakram and his chartered accountant were on their way to the French capital. 20 days later, Jyoti CNC received a 70% loan to buy Huron. The company put together the balance 30%.

Jyoti CNC took possession of Huron on 1 January 2008. The combined turnover of the two companies was over ₹500 crore – the target of ₹1000 crore by 2011 looked well within sight. But all of a sudden, the market crashed.

"In 2009-10, our India operations went flat, no growth. And Huron suffered a big loss."

Despite that, not a single employee at Huron was laid off. The team did introspect – was the buyout a correct decision? The conclusion was 'yes'. The crash was an external event affecting every business, the company was still a valuable asset.

"A Chinese buyer was ready to buy the company from us but we took a long-term view and refused him."

* K R Kamath is currently Chairman of Punjab National Bank.

"When I entered the Huron plant, the owner had put up the Indian tricolour at the front gate. It was the proudest moment of my life."

As Jyoti CNC's topline fell by 50%, there was a cash crunch. While other companies might have gone for restructuring, Parakram opted to sell his family's agricultural land to keep his commitment to the bank.

"Luckily *woh time pe* land price had gone very high. I sold everything and put money here."

At this difficult time, Parakram realised that the company would have to change its strategy. Instead of targeting the industry alone, Jyoti CNC decided to seek business from the government. Defence, ISRO and Indian Railways were major buyers of machine tools. However, they mostly relied on imports.

Jyoti set an ambitious target – to generate 30% of its business from these buyers.

"To work with Indian government with your ethics and idealism is most difficult. But we have to grow, and we have managed to do it."

The company closed its books in March 2011, with revenues of ₹650 crore. Huron was now growing by 30% and contributing to Jyoti CNC's success, in many different ways.

"We learnt a lot from them – how to design better, how to make high-speed machines."

Huron had highly experienced employees who brought in a different way of thinking, and doing. The French are extremely method-oriented, hence more efficient.

"They will work only 35 hours a week but that is equal to 50 hours put in India."

Unlike Arcelor-Mittal, the integration of Huron with Jyoti CNC has been quite smooth. The downturn was instrumental in making this happen. The buyout was a 'lifeline' – it saved jobs in France. But they too had much to learn from the Indians, in order to survive and thrive.

"The French company was lacking in costing... They did not have a good commercial sense."

For more than 150 years, Huron had been a supplier to large companies such as Alstom and Fiat. The Italians split up the company and sold it to various buyers. The aerospace division was bought by the plant's general manager and ultimately sold to Jyoti CNC. The Indians made 2 important changes.

"We revived many of the old product lines – automotive, power, general engineering. Because these designs were still with the company."

Secondly, high-quality need not be seen only in 'high-end' machines. Huron shifted its focus from the 'Rolls Royce' end of the market to a wider customer base.

"Initially, we thought of shifting the production to India and only marketing under their brand name. But we realised for that the European factory had its own merits."

So much so that Jyoti CNC bought another company in France and expanded its factory in Strasbourg. With French expertise, the Indian operations were also able to start manufacturing high-end machines. Thus, capturing the 'import substitution' market.

"70% of the machine tools used in India are imported from Europe and Japan. We want to capture that market and grow our company."

In March 2013, Jyoti CNC finally achieved its ₹1000 crore target. The next goal is to become a 'top 10' player in the world by the year 2020. The company is also planning a public issue in the near future.

Jyoti CNC has 1200 employees in India and 150 in France. Each one can be seen in office wearing the same grey T-shirt bearing the company logo. A symbol of pride, of equality.

"It is also the most practical and comfortable dress to wear in a factory!"

"Government buyers are not affected by economic cycles...hence we decided to target them."

The majority of employees in the Rajkot factory are young engineers from the Saurashtra belt. An interesting new initiative is the intake of fifth semester BTech students – they attend college during the week and work at Jyoti CNC on weekends.

"We are finding that with this experience, the engineers are ready for industry by the time they graduate. In fact, their entire body language changes!"

As the CEO, Parakram maintains an 8 am to 7 pm schedule in office. He does make time for badminton and table tennis at the office sports complex and an annual vacation either to the Himalayas or the Alps, with wife Rajashree and 13-year-old daughter, Prarthana.

After 24 years in business, there is much to take pride in, and much to reflect. Behind every success lie moments of doubt and deep despair. Parakram recalls the year 1995, when he was struggling and one day it all seemed 'too much'. He went to his friend and confidante – his father – and burst out.

"*Pappa jab main chess khelne gaya, aapne mujhe kyun nahin kaha ki abhi tu padh le, engineering kar le* (When I went to play chess why did you allow me, you should have told me to continue my studies). It means you are least bothered about me!"

Pappa replied, "You know I am a follower of Bhagwan Osho Rajneesh. *Bhagwan batate the ki hamare jo bachche hain, woh hum se aate hain lekin woh hamari property nahi hain.*" (Bhagwan always said that our children come from us but they do not belong to us.)

A child is not born to fulfil the dreams of his parents or of society. He is free to choose his own path.

"*Bas iss liye, maine socha jo tu karega, woh theek karega.*" (Whatever you choose to do it is fine with me.)

Subsequently, Parakram himself became a follower of Osho. His ultimate dream is to build a 'commune' or ashram for orphans.

"I will train them in sports and give more opportunity. *Company bhi saath saath chalti rahegi."* (Company will also continue alongside.)

Live in awareness, work with enthusiasm – for then, life itself is a sport. Go out on that field and give it your best. Team India needs more players.

ADVICE FOR YOUNG ENTREPRENEURS

Main aisa youngsters ke liye bolna chahoonga, logon ko mann mein jo aata hai woh kare. (I always say to youngsters, you should do what you are really passionate about.)

God has given everybody an equal opportunity. Stop listening to others, look inside yourself.

Take up one idea and start implementing it. You have nothing to lose.

Entrepreneurship does not just only mean starting a business. You can also work for a company with the mindset of an entrepreneur.

BEE POSITIVE

Jagjit Singh Kapoor – Kashmir Apiaries
Doraha (Punjab)

Starting with 10 boxes of bees, Jagjit Singh Kapoor popularised beekeeping, across the length and breadth of India. Today, Kashmir Apiaries is the largest exporter of honey from India with revenues of over ₹100 crore.

In life, often we stand at a crossroad. There is the choice of doing what has been done before, and that of going down a new path. Such a crossroad is called '*doraha*'.

It is therefore apt that a young man stood at a doraha, *in* Doraha. An unremarkable little town situated on the Grand Trunk (GT) Road to Ludhiana in Punjab.

As a small-time *thekedar,* he earned a living – like any ordinary businessman. But then, he stumbled upon something new, something which had never been done before. Jagjit Singh Kapoor found a way to make money, from beekeeping.

The credit for bringing the 'European bee' to this country goes to the Punjab Agricultural University. But the credit for spreading the Apis Mellifera across the length and breadth of India goes to this enterprising *sardar*.

"Jab maine shuru kiya, Doraha ke aas paas kul paanch sau bakse the." (When I started this business there were just 500 boxes of bees in and around Doraha.)

Jagjit Singh was the first beekeeper to go beyond keeping bees. He saw himself as a salesman, who would find a market for his honey – whether it was his own or sourced from other farmers.

In 1995, when he met the Union Agriculture Secretary, M S Gill, Jagjit Singh made an offer: "I will buy the entire honey produced in the country."

Deeng nahin haank rahe the, serious the sardarji. It was no empty boast.

The venture Jagjit Singh set up with 10 bee boxes in 1978 has grown into India's largest honey exporter. I meet 'Honey King', as he is fondly called, at the Kashmir Apiaries head office in Doraha. Now, a sprawling, modern, world-class facility, with its own R&D unit.

When I ask Jagjit Singh for a picture in his office, he smiles wide and says, "Bee…eeee…eeees!"

Indeed, the humble bee has given him much to smile about. Much to be proud about. And he is willing to share that honey and spread the money, to every farmer in India.

BEE POSITIVE

Jagjit Singh Kapoor - Kashmir Apiaries Doraha (Punjab)

Sardar Jagjit Singh Kapoor was born in Doraha, a small town near Ludhiana in Punjab.

"My father came to India after Partition and settled here. He was a school headmaster and a very honest man... *school ka ek chalk tak ghar nahin laate the*." (He never even brought a piece of chalk home.)

Jagjit Singh attended a government school in Doraha till Class 9. He continued his studies in Jammu and Chandigarh, finally graduating from Arya College in Ludhiana with a BSc degree. Educating 3 sons and 2 daughters wasn't easy for a schoolteacher with a modest salary.

"My father used to get ₹300 per month. *Usi mein ham sab ko padhaya likhaya, kaabil banaya*." (With that small salary he raised us and educated us.)

Although a schoolteacher, Jagjit Singh's father helped many family members set up a business. Like him, they had fled Pakistan after Partition.

"Mere mama ko kitabon ki dukaan khulwakar di. Phir ek photography ki dukaan khol ke di. Phir cycle ki dukaan, phir tenthouse." (He set up a bookshop for my uncle, then a photography shop, a cycle shop and a tenthouse.)

Every business was small and none of them helped the schoolmaster and his family. Ultimately, *masterji* opened an 'academy' to give tuitions and supplement his income. In 1970, when Jagjit Singh was about to graduate from college, the family took up a wine shop on *thheka* (tender basis).

"*Sharaab peete nahin the...aaj tak nahin pi hai...sirf bechte zaroor the.*" (We never drank alcohol...not to this day...we only did it as a business.)

Over the next decade, one shop grew into 8 shops. But the wine business never made fantastic money, nor did it give a real sense of satisfaction. In 1978, Jagjit Singh attended a bee-keeping course at Punjab Agricultural University (PAU) in Ludhiana.

"I heard about some experiments with bees in Doraha and was fascinated to know more."

Under the guidance of Dr A S Atwal, PAU had introduced the Italian honeybee, Apis Mellifera, to India in 1962. The first colonies were established in Himachal Pradesh in 1962 and later brought down to the plains of Punjab. PAU conducted breeding experiments with farmers in and around Doraha. When these experiments concluded in 1978, they offered the farmers the hives – free of cost.

"When I did the beekeeping course, the University offered me 2 free hives."

Jagjit Singh refused.

"*Agar free mein loonga toh meri aadat kharab ho jayegi.*" (It is against my principles to take anything for free.)

The young businessman bought 5 hives of Apis Mellifera from a farmer for the princely sum of ₹1000. The very first extraction yielded 50 kg honey. Far more than what the farmers produced. The farmers merely kept the bees – it was researchers from PAU who extracted the honey and even sold it for them.

"*Sarkaari kaam tha. Ghar baithe unko paise mil jaate the. Beekeeper toh nikamma reh gaya.*" (It was government work. The beekeepers got money for doing nothing. They had no motivation to learn or do more.)

Applying techniques he learnt at PAU, the hungry new beekeeper was able to raise production. The problem was where to sell the honey. So far, farmers had been producing small quantities, which was sold in PAU itself. The price was ₹20 per kg and payment came on time.

"*Par aage agar badhna tha, toh woh kahaan bikega...yeh sabse bada sawaal tha."* (To go forward, I needed to sell more…that was my main problem.)

The search for new markets led Jagjit Singh to Khadi Ashram in Amritsar. They agreed to take honey from the young businessman. Jagjit Singh used a simple technique to 'process' his honey: a muslin cloth. After filtration, the honey was packed into glass jars with the label 'Kashmir Honey'. Why? Because Jagjit Singh's father was originally from Mirpur in Pakistan-occupied Kashmir. But the name was more than sentimental.

"World's best honey is from Kashmir. So I thought this is the best name."

In its very first year Jagjit Singh earned just ₹5000, from a meagre 50 kg of honey. As demand for 'Kashmir Honey' grew, Jagjit Singh began purchasing more beehives or *baksas* (boxes). Unlike Indian bees, the Apis Mellifera can create hives in a beekeeper's box. Each box consists of a moveable wooden frame on which bees make their honeycombs. This makes Apis Mellifera attractive for agriculture – production can quickly be scaled up.

"Yeh Italian bees baxein mein hi rehti hain, jo jungly bees hai woh jungle mein hi rehti hain." (Italian bees live only in boxes while jungle bees stay only in jungles, they cannot be put in a box.)

What's more, traditional methods of extracting honey destroy the honeycomb. In the box method, the frame is removed and honey is extracted from it, without affecting the bees. Apis Mellifera is also relatively easy for humans to handle.

"Thodi bohot hi kaatati hai…agar aap tang karoge, otherwise nahin." (They don't sting unless you trouble them.)

The *malai* on the lassi was that you could grow this business, without borrowing money. By the law of nature, bees multiply – and they do it quickly. More bees equals more honey.

"Beshak hamare pass paise nahi the… par free ki aadat nahi thi." (I did not have the money but I did not believe in taking anything for free.)

"*Koi bhi kaam karna hai toh kadar aur mehnat se karna chahiye.*" (Anything you do, needs respect and hard work to succeed.)

"If you invest ₹1 lakh in beekeeping it pays for itself in 2 years and after that, yields ₹1 lakh a year in income."

Jagjit Singh kept reinvesting his money to buy more boxes. To increase supply further, he began purchasing honey from other beekeepers in the area.

"*Main shehed leta gaya, shehed deta gaya, aisa mera kaam badhta gaya.*" (I bought honey, I sold honey, the work just kept increasing.)

A salesman cannot succeed without wearing out his *chappals*. Jagjit Singh travelled across Punjab, then Haryana, Rajasthan and Uttar Pradesh in search of honey. Eventually, he reached as far as Bihar, Bengal and Tamil Nadu. On many of the trips, he was accompanied by his wife, Parvinder Kaur. Their mission was to collect as much raw honey as possible. And more and more orders, for the bottles.

Farmers realised there was money to be made from honey.

"*Jab logon ne dekha ki shehed bik raha hai, unhone beekeeping shuru kar di.*" (When people saw that there is a market for honey, more people started keeping bees.)

The government also came out with schemes to incentivise beekeepers. People from across India came to Doraha to procure bees.

Like a bee which unwittingly carries seeds of flowers, Jagjit Singh carried the idea of beekeeping across India. Pollinating many a new business, increasing income for farmers. In the course of his travels, Jagjit Singh was struck by another opportunity. To produce more and better quality honey, bees need to feast on the nectar of flowers like leechi, sunflower and cotton. These flowers bloom in different parts of India at different times of the year. Therefore, it made sense to 'migrate' the beekeeping boxes. Moving from one area to another – bees chasing flowers, so to speak.

Initially, boxes were sent to Sriganganagar in Rajasthan, to be kept near the mustard fields. Then they were brought back to Punjab, in sunflower season. In the summer, the bees went to Kashmir, where *kikar and acacia* flowers abound.

"Kam bakson se hum zyada shehed nikalne lage." (This way we could get more honey from a small number of boxes.)

Every box has a small opening at the bottom. Bees fly out as far as 3 km, in search of flowers. They return to the hive, to deposit the nectar in the honeycomb. This is ultimately transformed into honey. Beekeepers can extract 5-6 kg of honey every 15-25 days, if there is ample flora. The life of a honeycomb is approximately 3 years, so each box can yield 40-80 kg of honey – depending on the number of migrations.

"We don't own the farms, we take permission from farmers to keep our boxes."

Of course, when first approached, farmers did not co-operate. They believed that bees would destroy their crops. In fact, bees are beneficial to farm-yield as they naturally disperse seeds. Jagjit Singh had to befriend farmers, educate and convince them to keep some boxes.

"Thode samay baad woh samajh gaye ki unhi ko fayda hai. Phir har saal khushi khushi rakhne lage." (After some time they understood the benefit of having the bees and welcomed us every year.)

The presence of bees was not an additional hassle for the farmer. Jagjit Singh sent boys from his own village to oversee the boxes.

"Khadi Ashram ne mera shehed becha, mera hausla khul gaya. Main badi market ki sochne laga." **(When Khadi Ashram sold my honey, my confidence grew. I started looking for bigger markets.)**

***"Hindustan bhar mein makkhi mere yahaan se gayi hai."* (I gave bees to farmers all across India.)**

These boys lived in a tent on the field itself and were responsible for both the bees and the honey collection.

"*Jab shehed nikalta tha, woh tin mein shehed dalkar le aate the*." (The honey was brought to us in tin cans.) We employed 3-4 boys for every 250 boxes."

By 1985, Jagjit Singh had 1000 'baksas'. That year, he won a large tender from the Punjab government to supply bees as well as boxes to farmers across the state. The idea was to supply 700 beekeeping boxes in each district, a total of 7000 'baksas.'

"*Magar jab dene ki baari aayi to baksa banane wala mukar gaya*". (When the time came to supply, the carpenter refused, saying I had quoted too low a price in the tender.)

Now what? The situation looked grim until Jagjit Singh's father advised, "*Ghabrao mat*." (Do not panic.)

The elderly man went with his son to the *lakkad bazaar* and bought wood worth ₹10,000. A *mistry* (carpenter) was hired to make the boxes. The boxes were populated with bees. The bees multiplied quickly, boxes were despatched. With the money he received, Jagjit Singh bought more wood for more boxes and, of course, the bees kept multiplying.

"The word spread *ki yeh party achhi hai*." (We acquired a good reputation.) "We started getting wood on credit."

The 'low price' tender ultimately yielded handsome profits. And this contract, along with the honey sales, saved the day for Jagjit Singh. His wine business had shut down in 1980, when the government changed its licensing policy. A subsequent foray into the hotel business was a disaster.

"To start the hotel I had borrowed ₹8 lakh from the bank. But I had no sale at all."

With Punjab reeling under terrorism, there were few customers at roadside dhabas. The loan, with accumulated interest, ballooned to ₹16 lakh. How was a small businessman to pay off such a big debt?

"*Mujhe makkhi ne paisa diya. Itna paisa diya, karja poora kiya, aur bahut kuch kiya. Main aage badh gaya.*" (The honeybees saved me. Honey gave me so much money, I paid my debts and moved forward in life.)

With terrorism ruling the roost, doing *any* kind of business wasn't easy in Punjab. So how did beekeeping flourish? As per tender, Jagjit Singh had to supply bees to Amritsar, Khandusa, Bhor, Bhatinda – all strongholds of the Khalistani camp. But Jagjit Singh refused to lie low. Travelling by a ramshackle jeep and at times on a 407 tempo, he went from village to village handing out the beekeeping boxes. Often, returning home after midnight.

Never once was he attacked.

The simple explanation: *"Jab aap sahi kaam kar rahe ho na, bhagvan aapko dekhta hai..."* When you are doing good work, God looks after you.

The entire business, in fact, seems to rest on childlike faith. Jagjit Singh recounts an incident when he set out with his bottles of honey, to make a sale.

"*Tooti phuti jeep hoti thi. Itna paise nahi hota tha ki hum diesel ka kharch bhi de sake jaane ke liye. Phir bhi, main chala gaya.*" (I had a ramshackle jeep and not enough money to buy diesel for the trip. Still, I decided to go.)

The hope was that the Khadi Ashram in Ambala would make a payment. And with that money, he would fill diesel and go to the next destination. Well, the Khadi Ashram took the honey all right, but they did not pay on the spot.

"*Hamari factory mein makkhiyon ka A to Z kaam hota hai.*" (Our unit is backward and forward integrated.)

"*Ab mere paas technical staff hai, managers hain magar dilchaspi rakhta hoon har ek kaam main...har ek kaam ki samajh hai.*" (Now I have technical staff and managers but I retain an interest in every aspect of work.)

"*Maine kaha chalo Yamunanagar denge, Yamunanagar se milega.*" (I drove to Yamunanagar, thinking I will get payment there.)

But there was no such luck. Now they were neither here nor there, there was very little diesel left.

A relative who had accompanied him blustered, "*Koi baat nahin...gadi chalti rahegi. Hum Dehradun tak jayenge...waapas bhi aayenge.*" (Don't worry, this car will take us to Dehradun and back.)

The jeep picked up a few *sawaaris* (riders). As soon as it crossed the Yamunanagar bridge, it spluttered to a halt. Collecting 5 rupees each from the passengers he had picked up, Jagjit Singh bought a can of diesel from a passing tractor.

In Saharanpur, he finally found a party which made a small payment. That took the jeep till Hardwar and finally, Dehradun. By the time he returned, the honey was all sold and there was some money in the pocket as well.

"*Bas maine kabhi aage ki nahin sochi...chalti ka naam gadi hai... chalte jao, chalte jao, gadi chalti rahi.*" (I never thought too much about the future... I kept going, kept going and the wheels kept turning.)

Another time, Jagjit Singh was bedridden for 3 months after an accident. Business came to a standstill as there was no one to follow up on payments. At that time, Jagjit Singh's eldest son, Shahzada, was in college.

He said, "I will go in the field and get the money."

Accompanied by his mother, Shahzada travelled across India and accomplished the job. However, payments continued to be a bugbear – they were always late. Beekeepers were constantly asking to be paid in advance while 'Kashmir Honey's' policy was payment only after sale. Over and above everything, the profit margin was slim.

Jagjit Singh's frustrations grew. But he never despaired.

"*Dekho agar aap karam thik karo toh bhagvan jo upar baitha hai na, woh aapki baat sunta hai, woh aapko naye naye raaste deta hai.*" (If you perform your duty, God hears your prayers and shows you new paths.)

In the late '80s there was an epidemic in South India which wiped out the bee population. This resulted in a severe shortage of honey. To cater to this demand, Jagjit Singh sent the first full truckload of honey to Kanyakumari. Payment for the first consignment payment was received promptly but the customer refused to pay for the second truckload.

"Bahut ro-dho kar thode paise mile." (After lot of pleading, we got some of our money.)

It was a bitter experience yet Jagjit Singh kept trying to grow his market within India.

Then came the real turning point. In 1990, an exporter approached Kashmir Apiaries with an order for the UK. After sending 3-4 containers, it was the same old story – no payment. To collect their monies, Jagjit Singh and wife Parvinder had to make a trip to the UK. It was their first ever trip abroad and opened their eyes to a whole new world.

"We saw that the market for honey is very big in foreign countries. We must cater to them."

But it was not that simple. Export markets have specific requirements, such as honey with reduced moisture content. Machines were available for this but Jagjit Singh could not afford them.

"*Bahut dekha, bahut dhoondha phir maine apne dimag se ek machine banayi jisse moisture reduce ho gaya.*" (I searched high and low, ultimately I made my own machine and it worked.)

Another issue was the use of pesticide. Beekeepers were mostly illiterate, they would use antibiotic meant for poultry farming as a *'makkhi ki dawai'* (medicine for bees). This left residue in the honey, which was unacceptable in Europe and America*. But what were farmers to do, to protect their bees from mites? Jagjit Singh developed an organic method, using formic acid and oxalic acid to tackle the issue.

"We had to start training the beekeepers. *Achhi quality ka shehed paida karenge to export mein achha daam milega.*" (If we export better quality honey it will fetch a better price.)

Initially, Jagjit Singh found that Indian honey was sold at the lowest rate in the world market.

"*Kehte the ki ye honey itni achhi nahi hai…humein bhi kuch pata nahin tha.*" (They said your honey is of inferior quality and we could not contest that.)

Jagjit Singh then learnt the importance of testing and grading his honey. At first, 'Kashmir Honey' was tested in Delhi, later the company started sending samples to a laboratory in Germany, spending up to ₹40,000 on each lot. These, and many other learnings, came from attending Apimondia (a congress of International Federation of Beekeepers' Associations). The first Apimondia which the Singhs attended was in Antwerp, Belgium, in 1997.

It was an eye-opener.

"At that time we did not even know what is a brochure. *Maine ek page par apni photo laga di, madam ki photo aur beti ki, saath mein company ka naam aur pataa.*" (One a single page I printed my photo, wife and daughters' photo, company name and address.)

Kashmir Apiaries could not afford its own stall. Jagjit Singh, Parvinder and their 11-year-old daughter, Ritu, went from one counter to the next, befriending exhibitors and taking permission to sit at *their* stalls. After the exhibition, they went to the countryside to see what European beekeepers were doing.

"We waited for hours for appointments because our company was very small, I was a nobody."

---

* Honey sold in India does not follow the same standards. As per tests conducted by the Centre for Science & Environment, all domestic brands contain antibiotic residue.

But all these efforts paid off. The Singhs made contacts and secured small orders. But more importantly, they started thinking big.

"*Hum 15 din ghumte rahe, wahan ki badhiya badhiya factory dekhi. Phir socha ki hum kyun nahi aaise ho sakte hain?*" (We spent 15 days visiting the modern factories in Europe, then we thought why can't we become like them?)

At that time, Kashmir Apiaries was a ₹25 lakh company, working like a cottage industry. The 'factory' was a small room where honey was heated and filtred through muslin cloth, then packed into bottles – all by hand. This had to change.

"When you start exporting, customers want to know what is your factory like. What is your office like… Gradually our style of working improved, it became more professional."

With the co-operation of banks, Kashmir Apiaries expanded and modernised its factory. Spread over 12 acres, the premises include a heating/ filtration plant, bee-box and wax-sheet manufacturing facilities, numerous godowns and a cold-storage plant. In 2009, the company set up its own state-of-the-art testing laboratory which can measure impurities up to particles per trillion.

This was followed by the Lee Bee Institute of Beekeeping and Agro-Enterprises headed by entomologist Dr L R Verma. The institute imparts free training to beekeepers across India.

"*Sab kuch PAU ke paanch sau bakson se shuru hua… Makkhi badhti gayi, badhti gayi.*" (It all started with the 500 bee boxes of PAU, those bees multiplied and multiplied.)

There are now more than 1,00,000 beekepeers in India, tending more than 30 lakh boxes of bees*. Of these, more then 50,000 boxes belong to Kashmir Apiaries, but the company also buys huge quantities of honey produced across the country through its procurement channels.

"Our capacity is to process 3,00,000 kg of honey daily. *India mein hamara pehla number hai aur vishwa mein fourth.*" (We are one amongst the largest beekeepers and honey processors in India

* Total annual output of honey in India is 40-50,000 tons per year.

and fourth in the world). Jagjit Singh's dream is to be 'No 1' in the world.

The road to world domination is potholed with trade barriers. In 2010, the European Union banned import of honey from India, alleging it was contaminated with lead. It was a difficult period for the company and the industry as a whole. The Export Inspection Council of India and Kashmir Apiaries worked shoulder to shoulder to get the ban lifted within a year.

"EU delegations visited Doraha facility for spot inspections and they were fully satisfied."

At present, Kashmir Apiaries Group commands a 65% market share in the export market from India, supplying honey to more than 42 countries. The company is now eyeing the domestic market, where Dabur is the market leader. Kashmir Honey sells through organised retailers such as Reliance, Spencer and Bharti Walmart as well as its own 'Little Bee' kiosks in popular malls. 'Little Bee' offers a variety of antibiotic-free honeys as well as honey-based products such as jams, syrups, sauces and tea.

"*India mein abhi bhi shehed dawaai ki tarah dekha jaata hai*[*]." (In India people still think of honey as a medicine.) *Ab unki aadat daalni padegi*." (We need to create the habit of eating more honey.)

Over time, Jagjit Singh's sons and daughter have joined the business. Elder son, Shahzada Singh Kapoor, is in charge of the 'Little Bee' retail business while Raja Singh Kapoor manages overall operations and finance. Daughter, Ritu, is a two-time holder of Apimondia 'World Honey Queen title'. She is attempting to restructure the company using management fundas from the MPWE[**] program she attended at IIM Bangalore. But Jagjit Singh singles out the role played by one person, for a special mention.

"*Meri wife, Parvinder Kaur, hain jiske saath chaalis saal se main yeh business kar raha hoon, shuru se yeh mere saath hain. Bachche to baad mein aaye!*" (My wife, Parvinder Kaur, has been

---

* The per capita consumption in the country is less than 15 gm per person while in Europe, it is over 2 kg per year.

** MPWE = Management Program for Women Entrepreneurs.

with me and with this business for 40 years. Children have come much later!)

Daughter, Ritu, recalls her parents mostly being out of the house, out in the field. Making her a very independent, self-sufficient child.

"I used to feel very proud of their work and everything they have achieved."

The Kashmir group of companies clocked revenues of ₹131 crore in FY 2012-13. Which Jagjit Singh is proud of. The company employs over 1000 staff, who come from nearby villages and from Ludhiana in the company-operated bus. Indirectly, it has helped create thousands of beekeepers and fought for the industry as a whole.

In 2002, Jagjit Singh started the National Bee Board, along with some other exporters. The purpose being to get government support for honey production. The board is now managed by the government and promotes apiculture all over India.

Returns from beekeeping are consistent and keep increasing. Beekeepers have prospered – bought additional land, own tractors and cars.

"Ye sab makkhi ki dein hai, makkhi ki mehnat hai." (It's all due the gift of the bees, hardworking bees.)

Beekeeping also complements and supplements agriculture itself. These humble insects are natural pollinators, increasing crop production by 40-55%.

"*Ye hum ek nation ki sewa bhi kar rahe hai....*" (We beekeepers are serving the country as well.)

The flower lets the bee drink its nectar, so must the entrepreneur allow others to imbibe his wisdom.

"Ab hum chahte hain ki dusre log bhi yeh dhanda apnayein toh woh bhi paisa kamayein, woh bhi humare jaise bane..." (I want many more to join this line of business, earn money, be successful like me.)

For success is the sweetness of the soul that is expressed through work.

ADVICE TO YOUNG ENTREPRENEURS

Jab tak aadmi struggle nahi karta toh banta bhi kuch nahi hai ji. (Unless you struggle, you cannot achieve anything.)

Agar aap ko bada banna hai toh do cheez dhyaan mein rakhni hain: (1) *Mehnat* aur (2) *Imandari*. (If you want to become big, keep 2 things in mind: (1) Hardwork and (2) Honesty.)

Agar imandari nahi hoti har samay yeh dhyan mein rehta hai ki kis tarah kisi ke paise chura loon, kisi se rishwat le loon…toh usi cheez ko woh sochta reh jayega. Aage development nahi hoti iss tarah. (If you are dishonest, your attention will always be on how to make a quick buck, how to take a bribe…you will get stuck and not develop yourself further.)

*Kabhi free ki cheez milti hai toh mat lein, apni mehnat ki kamaai karein. Paisa kharch ke kamayien tabhi kaam chalega. Mere saath makkhiyon ka jisne shuru kiya tha, jinko government ne makkhi free mein de di, sab khatam ho gaye. (*Do not take free handouts, invest your hard-earned money in your project. Anything you get free has no value. All those who started with me but got free bee boxes from the government, are no longer in business.)

Jis kaam ko lagan se karo, kaam ban jayega. Rasta apne aap aage nikalta jaata hai... (Whatever you do, do it diligently. The path will unfold before you...)

Pehle hi sochne lag pade ki kaise hoga, mere paas paise nahin hai, yahan kaise jaunga, vahaan kaise jaunga... toh kaam hi nahi hota. Kaam start kar do, gadi chalti gayi, na. Dheere dheere speed aa jayegi. (If you worry about money, you cannot start at all. Start the work, it will gradually take off.)

Aaj bhi main field pe, office mein, factory mein ghumta rehta hun...saal ke 365 din bhi mein factory mein jaata hoon. (Even today I am deeply involved with my work… in the field, in the factory, in office – 365 days.)

Aap sahi karam karte jao, phal uparwala deta hai. (You keep doing your work, your duty, result and reward come from God.)

POT OF GOLD

Mukhtarul Amin – Superhouse Group
Unnao (Uttar Pradesh)

Mukhtarul Amin dropped out of college to join the family business, then left that business to start his own. Today, his Superhouse Group, with a ₹900 crore in turnover, is India's largest leather exporter.

Unnao is a small, sleepy town in Uttar Pradesh. A town which is, all of a sudden, in the news. The Archaeological Survey of India is digging there, in the hope of finding 1000 tons of gold.

All because a godman called Shobhan Sarkar saw this treasure, in a dream.

Almost 30 years ago, an ordinary man also had a dream. A dream with his eyes wide open.

In 1985, Mukhtarul Amin left his family business, to start on his own. The young man could not afford to set up a tannery in Kanpur – the traditional hub for leatherwork. So, he purchased land in underdeveloped, unheard-of Unnao, at ₹10 per metre.

"Tab wahan koi facility nahin thi, telephone nahin, road bhi nahin." (That time there were no facilities, no telephone, no road.)

With passion and perseverance, he embarked on the task of conquering Europe. With superior quality at low manufacturing cost. And a management philosophy rarely seen in small towns – that of empowering employees and allowing them to work professionally.

"*Company aaj jo hai, jo grow kar rahi hai* (what the company is today, the way it is growing), it is because of the people we have."

In fact, Mukhtarul Amin's Superhouse Group is now India's largest exporter of leather goods, with an annual turnover of over ₹900 crore. A treasure built above the ground. With head, hands and heart.

Dream of the future, instead of digging up the past.

There is a pot of gold waiting, at the end of your very own rainbow.

POT OF GOLD

Mukhtarul Amin - Superhouse Group
Unnao (Uttar Pradesh)

Mukhtarul Amin was born in the industrial town of Kanpur.

"My early education was in a government school – Shri Bahudushan Awasthi Rajakiya Uddeshi Ucch Madhyamik Vidyalaya. That was up to Class 12."

Mukhtarul then joined Christchurch College, Kanpur, for his BSc. But he never actually completed the degree.

"*College mein shararatein zyada thi* (I was up to a lot of mischief in college) so Father thought I better leave that and join the family leather business."

The business had actually been started by Mukhtarul's grandfather – Chaudhary Mohammed Amin. He used to manufacture saddles for the Scindias of Gwalior. After Independence, Mukhtarul's father, Chaudhary Ehsan Karim, diversified into leather for shoes and *chappals*.

When Mukhtarul joined 'Super Tannery' in 1975, at the age of 19, the turnover of the business was ₹40 lakh. The tannery was one of many, located in Jajmau, on the banks of the Ganga.

"At that time we used to make leather only for soles – this leather is thick and made from vegetable tanning. We supplied the soles to manufacturers in Delhi and Agra."

Soon after Mukhtarul joined the business, there was an order from Iran which opened the door for exports. At the time, Iran was still ruled by the Shah and was a progressive, fashion-conscious country. Then came the revolution led by Ayatollah Khomeini in 1979.

"We continued our exports from Bandar Abbas Port in Mumbai but then due to currency problems in Iran, we had to stop."

In fact, war broke out between Iran and Iraq in 1980. At that time a shipment from Super Tannery was stuck at the Tehran port. Even though some goods were damaged, the party paid the full amount.

"Fortunately, Iranians *ke saath kabhi payment ka problem nahi hua* (we never had any payment problem with the Iranians). They were very good business people."

Encouraged by this experience, Super Tannery began exporting to countries like UK and Germany. But it was not easy.

"*Ek shipment ke baad bank ko hi nahi pata tha ki kis tarah ke documents chahiye, kya terms negotiate karenge, kis tarah hoga.*" (The bank itself did not know what documents were required, what terms would be negotiated, etc.)

Although there were many hassles, it was a good learning period.

Around this time, PU (polyurethane foam) was becoming popular, hence demand for sole leather started falling. Hence, father and son decided to enter the market for 'uppers'.

"*Joote ke upar ka chamda hota hai 'upper', jo alag technique se banta hai.*" (The leather used to make the top of a shoe is called 'upper' and it is made with a different technique.)

Until the late '70s, upper leather was made only in Calcutta. As luck would have it, the Amins met a Chinese tanner who was visiting Kanpur, just for a holiday.

"Chinese were good at that time for making upper leather. *Toh us se phir baat ki*, 'Can you stay with us here?' "

The tanner agreed and thus Super Tannery entered the 'upper' business. People were sceptical as upper leather had never been made in Kanpur before.

"Fortunately, *hamara chal gaya* (it worked). Now, we can say very proudly that Kanpur upper leather is much more popular, *usne Calcutta ko peechey kar diya* (Calcutta has been left behind)."

This bold step helped Super Tannery grow rapidly. From ₹40 lakh in 1975, the company turnover leaped to ₹6 crore and then ₹14 crore. But, in 1985, there was a dispute within the family.

"*Mere chhote bhaiyon ne business join kiya. Company itni badi nahi thi ki sab log usmein kuch kar sake, kuch kar dikhane ka mauka milta.*" (My younger brothers joined the business. But it was not big enough for all of us to play a big role.)

Mukhtarul's father said, "Better *hoga ki tum apna khud dekh lo.*" (It will be better for you to branch out on your own.)

As a dutiful son, he agreed to abide by this advice and resigned from Super Tannery. And start from scratch.

"*Mujhe settlement mein sirf upper banane ki machine mili aur ek kasai ki factory – sab mila kar kuch pandrah lakh.*" (As part of the settlement I got some machines to make uppers and one bone factory– altogether worth ₹15 lakh.)

Mukhtarul Amin thought long and hard about 'what to do'. Where to start? At Super Tannery, his main job was marketing and his interest lay more in exports. But he did not want to directly compete with his own brothers. So, he chose an all-new category – industrial footwear.

Workers in factories require special shoes for safety purposes. These shoes were manufactured outside India but the 'upper' required a lot of labour input.

"*Toh isiliye they prefer to import from developing countries, ki yahan pe cost kam aaye. Yaheen se phir maine shuruat ki.*" (They prefer to import in order to reduce cost. This was a fresh start for me.)

Mukhtarul adopted the name 'Superhouse', took a place on rent and hired workers. The problem was where to procure leather. As he was no longer with Super Tannery, people were not sure about his ability to pay.

"I did not have cash to pay upfront and sellers were hesitating to give credit. *Kisi tarah convince kiya* (Somehow I convinced them)."

"*Aaj kehte hain ki aadmi ki personality aap samajh lete hain* (Today people say they can know the personality of a man) from which type of footwear the person is wearing."

Mukhtarul knew he would have to set up his own tannery but the traditional location was out of question. Land prices in Jajmau were much too high. So, he took a leap of faith.

"*Maine us time mein UPSIDC se Unnao mein zameen li.*" (I bought land in Unnao from UP State Industrial Development Corporation.)

There was no tannery, no bridge, no proper road or telephone line. In fact, it was also not very safe. But fortune favours the brave. The cost of land was only ₹10 per metre.

Mukhtarul Amin now had land, but not enough money to build a tannery. So he decided to go to Bombay and look for a financier.

"I met one Mr Vohra who suggested, 'Why don't you go for a public issue?' "

Mukhtarul was astounded – how is possible?

"*Meri company bahut choti thi. Aur tab tak koi leather ki company ne public issue nahi kiya tha.*" (My company was very small and until then no leather company had floated a public issue.)

Mr Vohra said, "Don't worry, I will manage it."

The man was true to his word. He made the projections, prospectus and took care of all other formalities. A small public issue of ₹1 crore was floated in the year 1990 and fully subscribed.

"Of course *woh ek crore ke public issue laane mein bhi hamare das-pandrah lakh rupaye lag gaye* (to raise ₹1 crore we spent ₹10-15 lakh), which the merchant bankers agreed to take after the money came in."

This was a turning point for Mukhtarul Amin's Superhouse Group. The money was not enough to build a very modern tannery at the time. But with some new machines, some second-hand machines, he was able to create a decent infrastructure. To handle the new business and to expand it.

"Phir toh hua ye ke Europe mein cost of labour kaafi badhne laga. Logon ko safety footwear banana viable nahi ho raha tha." (Soon after, the cost of labour went up in Europe and making safety footwear there was becoming unviable.)

UK Safety was the company to whom Superhouse was supplying 'uppers'. They came up with an out-of-the-box idea.

"We will give you our machine and know-how, you make complete footwear for us."

Thus, Superhouse got machines free of cost, as well as a captive buyer. Other companies heard about this arrangement and approached Superhouse. They too were willing to provide machines and buy 100% of the output.

"Is tarah hamari phir turnover aur profitability ko jump mila." (This way our turnover and profitability jumped.)

After 10 years in business, Superhouse turnover had crossed ₹41 crore, with modest profits of ₹1.80 crore. Now, the company spread its wings further.

Until the mid-'90s, Superhouse was making footwear with rubber-vulcanised soles and its main market was UK. But other countries in Europe used safety shoes made by 'direct injection', a more complex technology.

"We got the confidence *ki hum ye bana sakta hain toh humne pehli DESMA machine Kanpur mein import ki*." (We were confident about making these shoes hence we imported the first DESMA machine in Kanpur.)

DESMA is the 'Mercedes Benz' of the shoemaking industry. These sophisticated German machines enable direct injection of the sole into the rubber or PU shoe upper.

At that time the Europeans said, "PU technology is not easy, even for us! You will have sleepless nights."

Mukhtarul Amin said, "That's okay, but we will try. We will do it."

It was a big step because the machine itself was very expensive (₹4 crore). But by this time the company had internal accruals as well as the full support of Punjab National Bank.

> **"*Ek jo aapki quality hai aur doosri jo delivery ki reputation hai* (Your quality and reputation for timely delivery) is the most important."**

"I was very fortunate *ki PNB ke jo bhi log the, unhone jab workings dekhi* (when the PNB managers saw our workings), they were very positive."

In fact, Punjab National Bank has played an important role in the success of Superhouse. Initially, the company was banking with SBI. Then, the Punjab National Bank GM, Mr Gupta, called Mukhtarul Amin to his office.

He said, "*Batao kya karna hai*?" (Tell me, what are your plans?)

The young entrepreneur said, "Sir, *kar toh raha hoon kuch*, *aur karna chahta hoon* (I am doing something and am keen to do more), but I can't put up any collateral."

Mr Gupta said, "*Requirement batao tumhari kya hai?"* (What is your requirement?)

Mukhtarul replied, "*Chaalis lakh rupaye agar mil jaye toh mere kuch orders confirm ho sakte hain. Kaam badh sakta hai*." (With ₹40 lakh working capital I can confirm some orders and grow my business.)

The GM called his manager and said, "Give him ₹40 lakh."

Mukhtarul Amin was speechless.

"I don't know why he had that sort of confidence in me… But *woh ho gaya aur upar wale ki karam se kabhi banking waalon ka confidence hilne nahi paaya*."(It happened and, with God's grace, we have retained our bankers' confidence throughout.)

The man with a mission is always looking for a new target. In the late '90s, Mukhtarul Amin turned his focus on fashion footwear. The first market Superhouse entered was the UK, a market it knew well. But the initial period was tough.

"UK was importing high-end shoes from Italy, Spain and Portugal, and cheaper footwear from China or Vietnam. India was nowhere in the picture."

Consumer footwear is completely different from industrial footwear. Hence, Mukhtarul Amin decided to initially go for the 'basic' shoe, nothing fancy. Slowly, the company got the hang of the market.

"*Pehle yeh tha ki joota mazboot hona chahiye* (Earlier people wanted long-lasting shoes)...but now people want to keep changing with the season and the fashion."

From functional and durable industrial footwear to comfort and style-based consumer footwear was a giant leap for Superhouse. The company set up a marketing office in Leicester and, over time, employed designers based in France and Italy.

"In this line we have to offer something new every time, every season."

The business had crossed ₹120 crore, when Mukhtarul Amin decided to diversify into leather goods. The company was already in the riding shoes and accessories market. Now, it entered ladies bags, travel goods, business cases and belts.

"I was more keen in using my tanning leather in my own factories than supplying to others."

Mukhtarul Amin's strategy was to go to existing clients – the departmental store chains in UK and France. Since they were already selling fashion footwear from Superhouse, they were open to the idea of leather goods from the same company.

"*Woh jo reliability jo shuru se rakhi* (the reliability we maintained right from the beginning), in terms of delivery, in terms of quality, helped us in introducing our new products to the same company."

More business with the same client is also easier because you know their needs, their way of thinking and working. And taking this idea one step further, Superhouse acquired a German company in 2007.

"That was a bankrupt company, so we took the plant, we took the sales force, we took the back office. Only manufacturing we shifted to India."

> ***"Maine hamesha freshers lekar unko train kiya hai apne hi sab se. Unka commitment aur involvement hamari strength hai."*** **(I always believe in recruiting and training freshers. They have more commitment and involvement.)**

With cost coming down, the company began making profits. Using the same strategy, Superhouse bought and turned around a company in UK in 2011. And recently, Mukhtarul Amin acquired a manufacturing unit in Spain. Both companies are giving regular business to Indian factories.

"The buyout helped our Indian company, as well as the European company. We did not fire a single employee."

The overall employee strength of Superhouse is now over 7000, with 5000 workers and remaining staff in administrative, supervisory and R&D roles. The company's manufacturing units are in Kanpur, Agra and Noida and the policy is clear – always hire local talent.

"*Aaj bhi Superhouse ki jo strength hai, backbone hai, zyadatar woh log hain jinhone as a fresher Superhouse ko join kiya.*" (The backbone of Superhouse are those who joined me as freshers.)

This includes those who put faith in Mukhtarul Amin at the time that he shifted from Super Tannery, to start his own business. Money is one incentive, but more than that it's the professional working atmosphere – rarely seen in smaller towns.

Each of Superhouse's 20 factories is a separate profit centre, with a management team in charge.

"For every factory I take yearly projection, *ki* this will be the sale, this will be the profit. Then I let them work their own way."

There are monthly meetings and reviews but no day-to-day interference.

"So they get the feeling *ki* this is their own company. *Aur usi commitment level se, whatever I dream, they make sure ki woh dream success ho."*

At times, an employee gets an excellent offer from outside and, as a well-wisher, Mukhtarul Amin will encourage – go for it.

"*Jab jaate hain aisa lagta ki family se koi bichad raha hai* (When someone leaves it's like a family member going away). *Kaafi aisa bhi hua hai ki* (Often it happens that) they came back to Superhouse."

Going beyond family members means going beyond limitations. The rise of Superhouse is living proof of that. In March 2013, the annual turnover of the group crossed ₹900 crore, making the company the largest exporter of leather goods in India.

"Now we are slowly pushing our own brand also in UK and France. We have also entered the domestic footwear business."

Superhouse has also diversified into riding garments and industrial uniforms. In both cases, the idea was to take advantage of the existing client base to whom Superhouse was supplying riding accessories and industrial footwear.

And what about the China factor? That threat, in Mukhtarul Amin's estimation, is reducing. Labour cost in China is rising, making products like footwear less viable.

"*Achha, aur dusri cheez*, China *mein* workers prefer to work in a high-tech industry where they get better pay. *Toh isliye unko workers milna mushkil hota hai.* (They find it difficult to find leather workers)."

Yet, difficulty is inevitable, no matter where you are. Mukhtarul Amin is no stranger to ups and downs in business.

***"Har problem ka solution hota hai magar solution sukoon se nikalta hai, tension se nahi nikalta."*(Every problem has a solution but you will find it only when you are calm.)**

"It gives a very good feeling when I go to our schools and children say, 'Good morning, Sir'."

"In between *recession aaya, thodi problem aayi* (there was recession). I had invested all my money in the machines and factory floor, the working capital was a little short so I really had a tough time."

Naysayers took the opportunity to spread rumours about the company's viability. Will it have enough sales, enough profit?

"*Hamare 'chahne' walon ne yeh kehna shuru kiya ki* (our detractors started saying), 'They are gone, they're gone. Bank is going to take over the factories.'"

The negative talk created some issues with suppliers but only temporarily. Mukhtarul Amin was able to tide over the crisis with the support of the bank as well as some customers who agreed to pay in advance.

"I don't get distracted by all the negative messages and all these things. Think positive *ki theek hai, isse nikla kaise jaaye* (how does one solve the problem) and you will definitely find a solution."

And there is no substitute for hard work. Almost 40 years since he began working, Mukhtarul Amin still puts in long hours, travels to visit clients, spends time at his factories.

"*Mere ko ek hi shauk hai, movies dekhne ka* (I have only one hobby, which is watching films). *Time milta hai kabhi-kabar toh books padh lete hain* (sometimes I read books), that I do when I'm travelling."

Mukhtarul Amin married young – at the age of 20 – and has 4 children. Eldest son, Zafarul Amin, joined Superhouse after completing a 3-year course in leather tanning in the UK. That's helping, in many ways. He is working on different types of leather, different kinds of finishing.

"Customers always want to see something new – new design, new colour, new feel, so that helps our business to grow."

While his younger son is still studying in Class 12, daughters, Nausheen and Shadah, are married. Along with Mrs Shahina Mukhtar and daughter-in-law, Firdaus Amin, they are involved with the 10 schools which Superhouse Group is running in Uttar Pradesh.

It all began in early 2000, when someone with the idea of starting a school approached Mukhtarul Amin to finance the project. He decided it was something worth getting into.

"It was the need of the city, *tab achhe schools the nahi* (we had few good schools). I had a big problem in getting my own children admitted in good schools."

This initiative resulted in the first-ever franchise of Delhi Public School (DPS) in the private sector. Today, Mukhtarul Amin is running 3 branches of DPS in Kanpur city as well as under his own brand name 'Allenhouse Public School'. These schools are not only in Kanpur but Lucknow, Saharanpur, Bareilly and Ghaziabad. All the schools are rated among the top 200* in India.

"We started Allenhouse Engineering College 4 years ago. That is also doing really well."

Mukhtarul Amin does not view the foray into education as a business. It is a means of moulding minds, making futures.

"*Bachche sahi cheezein padhenge toh aage bhi us hisab se kuch achha karenge.*"(With the right education, the child can go places.)

That place is a point within you, which can expand infinitely. In any direction you choose.

---

* As per survey by Education World Magazine 2013.

ADVICE TO YOUNG ENTREPRENEURS

We are lucky that we are in a country where there are enough opportunities. Even if you want to start your own business with a small investment, that's a possibility, it can be done.

There's an opportunity in every sector. You have to think *kya karna hai*, dream big, *sochiye kya karna hai aur uske upar work kijiye* (think what you want to do and start working on it). You have the *confidence in yourself, haan yeh humein karna hai aur yeh haasil karna hai, woh hota hai aur woh ho jayega.* (You decide to do it and set your goals, it happens and you get success.)

Aisi koi baat nahi hai ki Bombay, Delhi, ya bade cities mein hi opportunities hai. Chhote cities mein bhi hai. (It's not that opportunities exist only in metro cities like Bombay and Delhi. They exist in small towns also). *Har sheher ki apni specialty hoti hai, wahan ka ek core business hota hai, usse shuru kiya jaata hai.* (Every town has its specialty, some core business which you can start in.)

Aur wahan se grow karke (Once you grow) if you want to move to the bigger cities that's a possibility, but *shuru se* (to start), probably, *bade shehron mein* (in big cities) things are more difficult. The cost is higher.

Sabse important cheez jo hai, koi bhi company successful banana ke liye (The most important thing to make a company successful is) you have to have the right people, a motivated team. Today you can raise money from banks, schemes *bhi hai, sab kuch hai*, you can build a big factory, you can build a nice office, but if you don't have the people to run that then you can't do anything.

WELL BRED

Bahadur Ali - Indian Broiler Group
Rajnandgaon (Chhattisgarh)

In 1984, Bahadur Ali and his brother Sultan Ali set up a small poultry farm with 100 chicks. Today, the ₹2200 crore IB group is in the business of chicken and soya, with a vision of making protein affordable to all Indians.

Raipur is a 'newly arrived' city. Once a sleepy town of the vast state of Madhya Pradesh, it is now a state capital as well as home to an IIM.

The airport has multiple direct flights from Mumbai and Delhi, at horrendously expensive prices. Thickset businessmen wearing flashy gold chains are constantly chattering on their cellphones. Perhaps laying the groundwork for yet another coal scam.

But even in such a state, success need not be based on illegal tenders and political contacts. The Indian Broiler group is living proof of that.

Started in 1984 by brothers Sultan Ali and Bahadur Ali as a small poultry farm, the venture has grown into a ₹2200 crore company with multiple agriculture-based businesses.

"*Bas, hum aage badhtey chale gaye aur isi ka parinaam hai hum iss mukaam pe pahuch gaye*," is what the soft-spoken Bahadur Ali said. (We kept moving forward until we reached our goal.)

But what was special about this poultry farm – one among a thousand others? Quite simply – *inki soch* (their way of thinking).

Keep costs low and quality high – do *whatever* it takes to achieve that. On the advice of an American expert, Bahadur Ali took a leap of faith and invested heavily in technology. And what MBAs will recognise as 'backward' and 'forward' integration.

To the Ali brothers, it was a matter of common sense. And a larger purpose.

"*Kisi ko achha protein khaate dekhte hain toh khushi hoti hai...kisi family ko aap enjoy karte huye dekhte hain toh khushi hoti hai...*"(When I see someone getting good protein and enjoying good food it brings me joy.)

For the blessings of this land are not just in its coal mines. The bounty of nature lies in every piece of earth, just waiting to be discovered.

WELL BRED

Bahadur Ali - Indian Broiler Group
Rajnandgaon (Chhattisgarh)

Bahadur Ali was born in Rajnandgaon district of Madhya Pradesh.

"*Mere pitaji ki chhoti-moti naukri thi phir unhone khud ki cycle ki dukaan kholi.*" (My father had a very ordinary job, then he opened his own cycle shop.)

Subsequently, he got into *haddi-chamri* business – collecting and trading the skin and bones of dead animals. Despite these efforts, the family barely eked out its existence in a small hut.

All of a sudden, in 1978, Bahadur Ali's father passed away.

"At that time, we brothers were all young – 18, 20, 22. *Achanak hamare upar parivaar ki zimmedari aa gayi.*" (The responsibility of the family fell on us.)

Eldest brother, Sultan Ali, took over the cycle shop while others took up whatever odd jobs they could get. One day, Sultan Ali happened to meet a veterinary doctor who made a suggestion.

"Why don't you get into the poultry business? You can make good money there." Sultan Ali thought, why not.

Scraping together a little money, he started a small poultry farm with 100 chicks.

"This was in 1984. *Yaheen se hamara poultry mein pravesh hua*!" (This is how we entered the poultry business.)

Breeding chickens is one thing, selling them another. That part of the job fell on Bahadur Ali. He went to the wholesaler, as was the practice. The price the wholesaler offered did not even cover the cost of production – let alone profit! What kind of business was this?

But Bahadur Ali was not one to give up so easily.

"*Un sau murgiyon ko bechne mein jo kathinayi mehsoos hui, maine usse ek challenge liya...ki kyun na main khud marketing karoon*." (The troubles I experienced in selling those first 100 chickens, I took as a challenge to do my own marketing.)

At that time, people bought chicken either from the mutton market or directly from farmers. Bahadur Ali decided to set up his own retail outlet in Rajnandgaon. The shop sold live chicken, which was 'dressed' for the customer on the spot. This is a delicate job where the feathers, head and internal organs are removed. Bahadur Ali himself was an expert in this task.

Butchers routinely cheat the customer by cutting off a little more than necessary. But not at Bahadur Ali's shop.

"*Hamare usool tha ki customer ko poora chicken milna chahiye, iss maamle mein koi cheating nahin honi chahiye*."(It was my principle that the customer should get the full chicken he was paying for. There should no cheating from our side.)

When the owner sets an example, the employees follow. Bahadur Ali's chicken shop became well known and soon he started another in nearby Bhilai. But, sales were relatively small.

Bahadur Ali conducted a survey of the market – where do people buy chicken, how do those shops function. And he discovered one important thing: people in the local area preferred *desi murgi* (traditionally bred chicken). Whereas the Alis were breeding 'broiler chicken'.

Broiler chicken* looks different and tastes different from desi

---

* Broiler chickens are genetically different and grow very fast – upto 1 kg a month. This chicken is sold in the market after 4-5 weeks.

chicken. The market for broiler chicken was in big cities and the closest such city was Nagpur.

"*Wahan log broiler chicken jaante the, samajhte the, aur achha maante the.*" (People there knew what is broiler chicken and considered it to be a delicacy.)

Thus, in 1985, Bahadur Ali decided to open a small shop in Nagpur. The target he set was modest: selling 500 chickens a month. On the first day, Bahadur Ali released a tiny ad in the newspaper. This advertisement mentioned the rate as well.

"I calculated the rate as production cost multiplied by 2... I was afraid it might be too high!"

When the shop opened its shutter, there were 300 chickens in stock. By 12 noon, on the very first day, the entire stock sold out.

"*Mujhe ek energy mili...ek market ka scope dikha. Bas, meri apni soch ka poora tareeka badal gaya.*" (I got energised. I could see the scope of the market. My whole way of thinking changed overnight.)

There was, in fact, more demand for broiler chicken than there was supply. This was a big opportunity, but how to take advantage of it? Bahadur Ali returned to Rajnandgaon and discussed the situation with Sultan Ali.

"We decided to expand our poultry farm with full speed and urgency."

In fact, Bahadur Ali already had an order from a hotel in Nagpur to supply 2000 chickens a month. And the farm did not have the capacity. So they decided to order the chicken through a trader in Hyderabad and supplied it to the hotel.

"*Deficiency market se fulfil karke idhar hamney production badhaana shuru kiya.*" (We bought from outside to fulfil demand and meanwhile increased our own production.)

To do this, he needed money, so he went to the Bank of India. From Day 1, the bank lent its support. Initially, the loan amounts were small – ₹10-15,000, with a family friend standing as guarantor. Gradually, the loan amounts increased. In 1987, Bahadur Ali received a loan of ₹10 lakh – a very big amount back then.

> ***"Sabon mein kaam karne ki badi tammana thi…"* (All of us brothers had a strong desire to do some good work.)**

"*Hamari performance and turnover se adhikari prabhavit the…* (Bank officials were impressed by our growth.) Whenever I went to them with a project to finance, they gave me full support."

In 1990, the bank extended a loan of ₹40 lakh, for further expansion.

A broiler farm essentially needs 3 things – land, chickens and chicken feed. In the late '80s, land was available cheaply – as low as ₹500-1000 per acre. Hence the money basically went into construction, as well as buying chicks and feed, to raise them. Another big cost is transportation. But this was one area which Bahadur Ali outsourced.

"We did not invest in vehicles of our own, we used the trucks which run on the Raipur-Nagpur route on a daily basis."

All the money from the bank, as well as internal accruals, was invested in the core business – poultry farm and retail shops. By 1996, the Indian Broiler group was producing 40,000 chickens a month and the turnover had increased to ₹5 crore. But, Bahadur Ali's mind was not at ease.

"1984-1996 *ek aisa period tha jismey hum aagey zaroor badh rahe the par main khud satisfied nahi tha. Mujhe aisa lag raha tha ki mai ismey kuch mistake kar raha hoon…*" (During '84-'96 we were growing as a company but I was not satisfied. I was not sure whether this is the correct way to run a poultry business.)

There were several doubts in Bahadur Ali's mind and he had no one to turn to. Then, in November 1996, the World Poultry Congress was held at Pragati Maidan in New Delhi. For Bahadur Ali, it was a revelation. The answers he was searching for were found.

Along with his 2 sons and brother-in-law, Bahadur Ali went from stall to stall, seeking out experts.

"*Kyunki mujhe angrezi nahi aati thi toh mere bachche aur mere jeejaji meri madad karte the.*" (Since I could not speak English, my children and brother-in-law helped me communicate.)

Bahadur Ali's biggest question was – how should I plan the expansion of my farm? What is the best, most scientific way to run the poultry business?

At the breakfast table, he happened to share his dilemma with an American consultant. The man said, "Come see me at 3 o'clock – I will explain everything."

The consultant spent 2 hours with Bahadur Ali, drawing out an entire roadmap. The growth of any company happens in stages and, at every stage, there are certain challenges.

"*Unhone takneekon ke bare mein bataya, aur yeh bhi ki kitne bade level par kya takneek viable hoti hai.*" (He advised us on technology including at what level of operation you need to make that technology viable.)

The basic recommendation was simple: even as you grow, make sure you keep the production cost low. Invest in technology, adopt best practices and think like the best in the business.

"He gave us the example of the Australian company called Tasman and how we can reach that scale."

The consultant was an American, simply sharing friendly advice. In Bahadur Ali, he found a man with curiosity, a man eager to learn.

"*Mera naam bhi nahi poochha. Bas yeh tha ki koi itne achhe question kar raha hai, toh yeh jo knowledge hai meri aap mujhse le lijiye.*" (He did not even ask for my name. It's just that I asked question after question and he willingly shared his knowledge.)

Neither does Bahadur Ali recall the consultant's name. What he took to heart was the roadmap laid out by the gentleman.

"*Main 100% convince ho gaya, humne woh roadmap pakad liya aur uske aagey peechey kuch bhi nahi socha.*" (I was 100% convinced, we adopted that roadmap and did not look back.)

Bahadur Ali thus embarked on a 10-year project, to create a 'world-class' poultry business. With a bank financing of ₹1 crore,

***"Hum ne hamesha doosron ke anubhav ka laabhu thaya."* (We always took advantage of other people's experience.)**

the company began investing in the best-available technology. As well as manpower.

The first veterinary expert to join Bahadur Ali was Dr R K Jaiswal. He was earlier working with a company called Phoenix Farms in Jabalpur, which supplied chicks to Indian Broiler.

"Since 1992, I used to visit Rajnandgaon regularly as an 'after sales' service. At that time I noticed, Indian Broiler has the best productivity among all the farms I visited."

In fact, by 1997, Indian Broiler's required 80,000 chicks a month, which exceeded the production of Phoenix Farm itself. By this time, IB was operating 24 broiler chicken shops. The next logical step was to start a hatchery to incubate fertilised eggs and produce chicks.

However, even fertilised eggs were not available in such large numbers, hence Indian Broiler set up a 'breeder' farm. At this farm, roosters and hens mate and produce the egg itself.

"*Bahadurbhai ki soch aur vision ko dekh kar maine unki company 1997 mein join ki*," says Dr Jaiswal. (Impressed by Bahadurbhai's thinking and vision, I joined the company in 1997.)

Working at Indian Broiler was a completely different experience. The good doctor recalls his very first day in the new job, when there was a disease outbreak at one of the farms. After treating the birds, he went back to Bahadurbhai and proudly said, "*Ab sab theek hai*." (It's all fine now.)

Bahadurbhai was silent. Later that evening, he called the new recruit and said, "*Doctor saab dawaiyon ke naam aap jitna jaldi bhool jaayein utna achha hai*." (The faster you forget names of medicines, the better.)

The doctor was stunned. How would he do his job, if not with medicine?

Bahadurbhai added, "*Aap yeh jaanne ki koshish karo ki bimaari aayi kyun.*" (Instead you find out why the disease occurred in the first place.)

On investigating this angle, the doctor reached the conclusion that it was a respiratory infection caused due to stale air. To solve this problem, Indian Broiler invested in environmentally controlled houses with heat sensors and cooling pads.

"People thought he has gone mad to spend so much money…but he stuck to his guns."

The philosophy of 'prevention is better than cure' became a driving force at the Indian Broiler group. *Achhi hawa*, *achha paani* and *achha feed* (good air, water and feed) were the areas of focus. The air and water could be taken care of by technology, but feed remained an issue.

Most companies, engaged in production of soyabean oil or nuggets, provided the husk which is a byproduct, as animal feed. But the quality of this feed was not good enough.

"*2003 tak humne yeh problem face ki. Humko quality soya nahin milti hai, milawati hai, phir humne decide kiya ki apna banana chahiye.*" (We faced this problem till 2003. We did not get good quality or genuine soya, so we started producing our own.)

The rising price of soya was another concern. Bahadur Ali could see that input cost was slowly but surely affecting his bottomline. Thus, complete 'backward integration' made good economic sense. On the one hand, Indian Broiler set up a 500-ton soya solvent plant with a focus on high-quality DOC (De-Oiled Cake). The first of its kind in the country.

On the other hand, the company worked with local farmers to increase soyabean production in the area.

"We gave free seeds and interest-free loans to farmers, and promised to buy directly from the growers at a fair price."

The elimination of the middleman was a major attraction to the farmer. Within 5 years, the supply of soyabean increased manifold. A similar story was repeated with *makka* (corn).

> ***"Unhoney humsey do ghanta jo meeting ki, woh hamari strength ban gayi."*** **(That 2-hour meeting with the expert became our strength.)**

Indian Broiler's entry into the feed business was a turning point. A byproduct of this operation was soyabean oil – that became a new line of business. The company set up a 250-ton refinery and began selling under the brand name ABIS Gold*.

The roadmap Bahadur Ali had drawn out for the company was completed 2 years ahead of schedule – in 2005. During that period, the overall industry was growing at 5-7% while Indian Broiler grew by 25-30% year on year, taking its revenues to ₹200 crore. However, the year 2006 brought the biggest crisis Bahadur Ali had ever faced – the bird flu scare.

The H5N1 virus was discovered in Navapur, Maharashtra, and Ucchal, Gujarat. 4,00,000 birds in these areas were slaughtered as a precautionary measure but media hype created a 'fear factor'. The sale of chicken dropped by 80-90% affecting every company in the poultry business.

"*Teen mahina humne bahut tension se guzaare…mere IB group ki life mein yeh sabse bada challenge tha.*" (I spent 3 months in a very tense state, it was the biggest challenge of my life.)

Bahadur Ali and his team spent those months studying medical and scientific evidence. And became convinced that there was no permanent danger to human life.

Hamne mehsoos kiya ki disease utni khatarnak nahi hai jitni media ne use khatarnak declare kiya tha." (We realised the disease is not as deadly as the media is making it out to be.)

Like any other disease, bird flu can be contained and eliminated. If there is no new case 3 months after the original outbreak, as per international protocol, a country is declared to be free of bird flu. This is exactly what happened, restoring public confidence. And that of the industry as a whole.

---

* ABIS is an acronym for the 4 Ali brothers – Amir, Bahadur, Iqbal, Sultan.

Indian Broiler continued to forge ahead, looking for new opportunities and new markets. The company diversified into dairy and egg production, which was logical. But also, into a completely different and little-known sector. And it happened like this.

A company called CP (Charoean Pokphand) used to buy soya from ABIS in large quantities. One day Bahadurbhai wondered – Why? He discovered that CP was in the business of shrimp feed.

"Why don't we also enter this business?"

At that time, fishermen in India were still using rice bran tied to a bamboo stick. While this is the traditional method, it is highly inefficient. To catch 1 kg of fish, at least 4 kg of feed is required. In fact, 75% of the rice bran is not eaten by fish – it simply settles on the riverbed creating silt.

After consulting the American Soyabean Association and surveying the industry globally, Bahadur Ali set up a fish-feed plant. The concept he introduced was extruded fish feed, which floats on water.

"Our feed floats for 40 minutes, fish come to the surface to eat it. To catch 1 kg of fish you need only 1.2 kg of this feed."

Launched in 2008, ABIS fish feed quickly became the No 1 fish feed in India, generating revenues of ₹200 crore. The overall turnover of the IB group crossed ₹2200 crore in March 2013, with 50 lakh birds produced in farms spread over 30 sq km.

"*Hamara saara production chaar states mein bik jaata hai, ded sau retail outlet hain, khud ke karmachari dwaara rate kholke har market mein dete hain.*" (Our entire production is sold in 4 states through 150 retail outlets where our employees set the rate for each market.)

The IB group stronghold include Chhattisgarh, Orissa, MP and parts of Maharashtra. These are not the most prosperous states of India, yet the rise in sale of chicken points to the fact that here too incomes are rising. In fact, the company pegs its growth with the GDP growth, based on one simple principle.

"*Jab ghar mein paisa aata hai to sabse pehle khaane pe aur peene pe kharch hota hai.*" (When incomes rise, the household expenditure on food and liquor go up first.)

"Hum criticise hue ki jo investment karne jaa rahe ho galat hai, risky hai. Magar humne kisi ki baat nahi suni."
(I was criticised for investing so heavily but I followed my gut.)

Based on this assumption, Bahadur Ali believes his company can even grow by 50% year on year, in the coming decade. And it's entirely possible as per capita consumption of chicken is still very low in the country. And there are many new markets beckoning.

Raipur being in the centre of India, live chicken can be transported up to 600 km away. Over the next 2 years, IB chicken will be available in 8-9 states. However, there is a bigger gameplan. In 2015, the company will start processing and make frozen chicken available all over the country with a depot in every state of India. By 2020, IB group will also get into ready-to-eat products.

Despite its name, Indian Broiler is not a company centred solely on chicken.

"*Hamara business hai protein pahuchaane ka business, chahe woh chicken ho ya egg, milk ya soya.*" (We are in the business of protein – whether it is in chicken or egg, milk or soya.)

While chicken constitutes 50% of IB's business, the other 50% is equally important and growing fast. Soya protein in particular is very exciting, as a substitute to *dal.*

"In 5 years' time dal will be too expensive for the common man...*uske liye hum taiyyari kar rahe hain* (we are preparing for that day)."

IB group will soon start producing value-added soya products – dal, nuggets, milk and biscuits.

Thinking and planning ahead is not an accident – it is a choice. Take a simple decision like how to transport poultry feed. While the standard method is packing in polypropylene (PP) bags, IB group employs bulk feed tankers.

"At the time we took this decision PP bags were very cheap but now tanker is far more economical."

Profit margin in the poultry business varies widely – when there is surplus production, chicken prices fall. Hence, every paisa saved is a paisa earned. However, being cost conscious does not mean being stingy. Where it matters, Bahadur Ali never holds back.

Dr Jaiswal recalls, "Even 15 years ago we had a good office in Rajnandgaon. *Bahadurbhai ki soch thi ki agar kursi chubhti ho aur paseena aata ho toh worker achha kaam nahin kar payega*." (Bahadurbhai's thinking was that if the chair is uncomfortable and it is hot, my workers will not perform.)

In the year 2012, IB group moved into new and completely state-of-the-art corporate headquarters. The next generation – Fahim Sultan and Zeeshan Bahadur had joined the company after completing their education from Christ College, Bangalore. While Fahim's focus is more on poultry production, Zeeshan manages the soya and fish-feed business.

More importantly, the next generation also brings in fresh ideas and ways of doing business.

"*Adhunik office ka sapna yeh bachchon ka aur hamara mila-jula sapna hai. Samay ke hisaab se badalna aur upgrade hona zaroori hai*." (This modern office was our joint project. We must change and upgrade ourselves with the times.)

Today, that change can be seen with the ERP system, connecting head office to every farm. Vaccination, production, sale & dispatch information is available on a daily basis. Even as an IB truck is loaded, its weight can be seen in real time.

As consumers change, the company must change with it. So far, IB outlets sell 'live chicken' but pre-washed and dressed

"*Dawai dene ke bajaye bimari ka kaaran dhundhna chahiye.*" (Rather than treat a disease, find its root cause.)

> ***"Kaam mein jo aaram milta hai woh aaram karke aaram nahi milta."***
> **(The pleasure I get in work, I do not get in pleasure.)**

chicken may soon be the norm. What will not change, however, are the founding principles of the business – honesty, integrity, customer first.

Every IB retail shop has a signboard which declares: "If any customer has a complaint, please call our MD." And right there, alongside, is Bahadur Ali's direct number.

The bank must be paid on time, suppliers must be paid on time, salaries must be paid on time. More than 8000 people are directly employed by the IB group while another 50,000 farmers and traders are indirectly connected with the company. From labour to supervisory staff, the employees are all from the neighbouring villages.

And that's a matter of great pride.

"Agar aapki soch achhi hai aur kuch achha kaam kar sakte hai toh iska faayda aap apney alaawa aur kitne logon ko de sakte hai… yeh cheez dekhni hai." (If you think positive and put in sincere efforts, many people can benefit from your work.)

While several investors have shown interest, the Alis don't feel a need to divest their stake at present. Nor does the idea of 'cashing out' hold any interest.

"*Maine kabhi yeh nahi socha ki paise se mujhey aaraam ki zindagi paana hai...aaraam ki zindagi main usko samajhtha hoon jo kaam karne se milti hai.*" (I have never thought of money as a means of leading a comfortable life. I am most comfortable when I am working.)

While Bahadur Ali is the public face of the IB group, elder brother, Sultan Ali, remains the silent backbone. He has managed all the small day-to-day issues, maintaining harmony and empathy with the staff. Even as he encouraged Bahadur Ali to keep forging ahead, thinking ahead.

"*Woh hamesha kehte hain – tu kaam kar, peechey jo hoga usko mai dekh raha hoon. Chhoti-chhoti problems jissey mujhey stress aati thi unhoney sab apne upar le liya.*" (He always says – keep working, I am behind you to handle all the small issues which cause you stress.)

Equally unconditional has been the support from Mrs Bahadur Ali (Azmina Bano) and Mrs Sultan Ali (Afroz Bano).

"*Thakey haarey aatey the toh badi achhi chai milti thi, kaam jyaada karne ki shikayatein nahi milti thi...khush thi ki hamarey husband, hamarey devar aagey badh rahe hai.*" (When we came home tired and frustrated, we got a hot cup of tea and no complaints. They were happy to see our progress.)

The fruits of progress must fall from the tree and nurture the community. The Alis are staunch believers in education – years ago, when Muslim girls were rarely given a chance to study, their younger sister, Noor Bano, completed her MBBS. Now, Bahadur and Sultan Ali want many more to get such opportunities.

"*Humne apne pitaji ke naam se ek bina shulk ka angrezi maadhyam school khola hai, apne kisan aur labour bhaiyon-behnon ke liye.*" (We have started a free-of-cost, English-medium school in memory of our father for the children of farmers and labour working with IB group.)

More power to India, more *poshan* for each Indian. The world is now a global village and every village of India must reach out to that world.

ADVICE TO YOUNG ENTREPRENEURS

Youngsters ke liye toh kaam karne ka future hi future hai. (The future is bright for any youngster starting a business today.)

Jab humney kaam karna shuru kiya toh na phone hotey the na sadak hoti thi, na parivahan ka sadhan. Aaj mail hai, phone hai, iPhone hai, car, flight sab hai. (When I started, there was no phone, no road, no vehicle. Today you have phone, iPhone, flight – everything)

India mein paison ki koi kami nahi hai, market ki koi kami nai hai…sirf kami hai toh karne walon ki. Aapko bas ek line dhoondhni hai jahan apko jaake apni energy use karni hai. (In India, there is no dearth of money, or of market, only of people who want to work. You have to find some line of business and put your energy into that.)

Imandari ko apne business ka usool banaiye. Doosra, apko sab ke liye positive sochna hai. Kisi ka bura karke apna achha nahi kar sakte. (Make honesty the basic principle of your business. And adopt positive thinking. By thinking ill for someone else you cannot prosper.)

Meri soch bahut simple hai – jo aap khud chahte hai woh apko doosron ke liye karna hai. Main achha chicken khaana chahta hoon, main sabko khilaoonga, main achha doodh peena chahta hoon, main sabko pilaoonga. (My thinking is simple – treat others as you would like to be treated yourself. I would like to eat good chicken and good milk, so that's what I will provide to others.)

Main jhooth pasand nahin karta, iss liye main khud sach bolunga… (I dislike falsehood, hence I will speak the truth myself.)

Iss tarah ki soch ke saath aap har manzil ko paa sakte hai. (With such an attitude you can reach any and every goal.)

RETURN OF THE NATIVE

They spread their wings and flew to fine institutions and foreign lands. But one day, they returned, with a dream of making a difference.

MISSION IMPOSSIBLE

Deepak Dadhoti – Servocontrols India Belgaum (Karnataka)

A young engineer gave up his green card to return to Belgaum and start a high-precision, high-technology company. 10 years later, Servocontrols is a key supplier to Indian aerospace and defence, with revenues of ₹100 crore p.a. and a dream to soar much higher.

As a little boy, Deepak Dadhoti was fond of playing *galli* cricket. In the middle of an exhausting match, he would run across to the house of the venerable 'Raosaheb', which stood at the corner.

"*Ma, mala paani payaje*," he would say and the kindly lady would give the little lad in knickers a glass of water from her kitchen *matka*.

Years later, knickers gave way to business suits. Deepak was now working with a famous international company, flying to client sites in private jets. At Belgaum's tiny, infrequently used airport he met the same Raosaheb.

"You are from Belgaum, no?" the feisty old man enquired.

"Yes, Raosaheb," said Deepak.

"*Mala Konkanacha California karayecha* (I want to make Konkan another California)*!"* thundered back the older gentleman.

But who is to make it happen? While the states of Maharashtra and Karnataka continue to fight over the city of Belgaum, 'development' in the official sense remains on hold.

Yet, this town in north Karnataka, blessed with pleasant weather and enterprising people, is finding its own way forward.

In 2003, Deepak Dadhoti gave up his lucrative job in the US to return to Belgaum. He started Servocontrols India in a garage, along with his brother, Dinesh.

10 years later, Servocontrols India is a critical cog in the giant wheel of Indian aerospace and defence. Whether it's pylons for light combat aircrafts, or the intercept launchers we will use if ever attacked by Pakistan.

"We give the perfect pitch and roll capability for launchers with servocontrols...built right here in Belgaum."

Deepak never made it to an IIT, but few IITians have made what he has. His story is an inspiration to every small-town technical graduate in India.

Fall in love with engineering! Master your subject!!

Become the backbone of this proud nation.

MISSION IMPOSSIBLE

Deepak Dadhoti - Servocontrols India
Belgaum (Karnataka)

Deepak Dhadoti is a Belgaum boy.

"Ours is a very ordinary middle class family. I studied in a government school in Kannada-medium, where we literally used to sit on the floor."

Deepak's father was in 'service' (he worked as a cashier in Sangli Bank), but his uncles ran a *kirana* shop and sold coconuts in the bazaar.

"We lived in a joint family and owned a lot of cows and buffaloes – around 25-30 in number."

Deepak would help with milking the cows every morning as well as selling the milk door to door. He loved to go to the shop after school and hang around there. Doing odd jobs, just watching the hustle and bustle.

"Uncles liked me because I was very responsible with money. They would always give me things to do."

It was his mother who made sure Deepak did not neglect his studies in the bargain.

"She used to lock me in the bedroom and teach me maths and

science. Or I might have got into the kirana and milk business – not higher education!"

Deepak excelled in academics. But he was also very naughty – a rough and tough '*galli*-type' boy.

"Teachers used to constantly complain about me but I used to do very well in exams. So the complaints got nullified!"

By the time he completed SSLC (Class 10), Deepak was clear about one thing. He wanted to become an engineer. One of his uncles, Mr Vasu P Hanji, was a big industrialist in Belgaum at that time and became a 'role model'.

"I used to visit his foundry and machine shop (Ashok Iron Works). And I found it very fascinating."

In Class 10, Deepak joined B K Model High School – the school which produced the topper for the entire Belgaum region year after year. The school offered Sanskrit, which was known to be a very scoring subject.

Meanwhile, family and friends advised Deepak, "You must try for IIT."

Deepak went to Kolhapur, as well as Bangalore and Bombay – to find out about IIT entrance exam coaching. But somehow, he was unable to figure out where to join, what to do.

In 1987, Karnataka introduced an objective-type entrance exam for the state engineering colleges. Deepak decided to focus on this exam, instead of IIT JEE. He attended coaching classes at National College, Basavangudi, in Bangalore. The result was very good.

"I got admission to 3 colleges – in Davangere, Bangalore and in Belgaum. My father insisted that I stay at home so I joined K L E Institute of Technology in the mechanical branch."

The first year was a bit tough. It took 6 months to adjust to classes in English medium. But it had to be done and somehow, you cope.

Engineering was a subject Deepak took to naturally – like a fish to water. Only he wanted to swim not just in ponds, but bigger oceans.

"I used to read a lot, out of syllabus. Then I used to go to my uncle's factory and sit there whole nights…you know…to understand the various machines."

During his third year of engineering, India built its first indigenous supercomputer (Param). This inspired Deepak to teach himself Pascal as well as AutoCAD.

"That also prompted me to take up a real challenging project in my final year of engineering…and that project was a turning point in my life."

The project was titled 'Computer Design and Drafting of Hydraulic Cylinders'. The idea was simple but elegant – Belgaum was the 'hydraulic city' of India. The cylinder is the core product in any kind of motion control system. Could these cylinders be designed and drafted using a software program?

To test this theory, Deepak learnt AutoLISP – an Artificial Intelligence language which is the building block of design and drafting software. It was an ambitious project, by any standards. What's more, while other students were working in groups, Deepak chose to go solo.

"We had only one computer with Math Coprocessor in the entire K L E Engineering College at that time. That was mainly used by the PG students."

Deepak took special permission from the principal as well as his guide to work on this computer. The only slot available was 3 am to 6 am, which he happily accepted.

"I think it was just passion, I didn't care about anything else at that time!"

The project was presented at the Karnataka State Council for Science and Technology in Dharwad and stood first in the entire state. It also landed Deepak a job with Oligear Towler Polyhydron Ltd (now called as Polyhydron Systems Pvt Ltd), a local hydraulics company which had sponsored his project. The young engineer's salary was ₹1100 pm.

The year was 1991.

Deepak joined the company but was also preparing for GMAT and GRE.

"My final year engineering project gave the foundation of my life."

"I scored 680 in GMAT and 1350 in GRE, so I got admission to several top universities in the US. But I did not get financial aid."

So he dropped the idea of further studies and focused on the job. The idea was to work for 2-3 years and then apply again. But along came another exciting opportunity.

A chance to work for Moog Inc – a US-based company and world leader in the field of precision control.

"I was interviewed by the UK facility for a position of 'application engineer' in Bangalore."

Deepak was familiar with the technology – Oligear Towler equipment used 'precision control' products (commonly known as servocontrols). In fact, every industrial machine, medical equipment, military and commercial aircraft relies on servocontrols.

It's the 'brain' within the body which regulates precisely what you do.

Let's say you are driving a car. When you go uphill, the car slows down, when you go downhill it speeds up. This is an 'open loop'.

Servocontrols create a 'closed loop'. The system senses the RPM (rotations per minute) and automatically throttles the accelerator. Irrespective of gradient, your car will maintain a constant velocity.

If that's too much for the non-technical types and *kachcha* engineers to handle – just understand that servocontrols are hidden everywhere, all around us. In planes, in cars, in steel factories, in power plants, in satellites.

We humans use servocontrol in our day-to-day lives. As we cross the street – we see a car coming head on, we dash across the road.

"You got it – that's a classic example of 'servocontrol'," laughs Deepak.

Without this 'system', you would not be here.

And neither would modern life, as we know it.

In the industrial world, servocontrols must make corrections in milliseconds, for movement that occurs in microns.

"Human hair is about 40 microns. The human eye can see only 25 microns. In servocontrols, we are talking of 1 micron and 2 microns."

So we are talking about very high technology, very hard for laymen to fathom. But for an engineering enthusiast like Deepak, joining Moog was a 'Charlie and the Chocolate Factory' kind of moment. A once-in-a-lifetime opportunity he grabbed with both hands.

The company deputed the young engineer abroad for training to its centre in Tewkesbury, UK.

"I never felt intimidated although it was my first time outside India and it was very hi-tech stuff."

When you enjoy an area of work, you welcome a chance to dive deep into it. You master new things quickly.

Deepak returned to India to provide the technical and implementation support to Moog's India office. It was a small set-up, headed by a 40-something Indian CEO. And a young engineer from Belgaum, all of 26 years of age, heading the technical team.

"The important thing was that I could grasp the client's requirement and deliver the results."

Organisations like Vikram Sarabhai Space Centre (VSSC) and HAL (Hindustan Aeronautics Ltd) were already Moog customers. So were many of the steel mills. However, demand from the aerospace activity had slowed down due to restrictions imposed by the US. New markets had to be found.

"I was given the task of developing the plastics industry – a very large industry but using rudimentary technology."

Using servocontrol systems, plastic could be manufactured in a better, more cost-effective manner. But to make it happen in India, you have to keep in mind economic viability.

"When I came to Belgaum in 2002, people said, 'He will go back to US in 6 months.' I proved them wrong."

"I encouraged companies to indigenise wherever possible, to cut down the hardware cost."

While aerospace, steel and power industries came to Moog, the company had to do hardcore marketing to convince plasticwallahs. This was another skill Deepak picked up, as a consequence.

From time to time, Deepak was also sent for training to Moog subsidiaries in different countries. In Germany, he saw firsthand how servocontrols are used in large industries. In Japan, he trained in 'higher electronics.' And in Italy, he learnt how technology is commercialised in a price-sensitive market.

"It was a very exciting and challenging time for me!"

While Deepak was having the time of his life, his father was worried. After all, he is travelling to so many countries – what if he is smitten by some foreign *memsaab*?

"The day I returned from Japan, my parents showed me a marriage proposal. I liked the girl and said 'yes.'"

Deepak took 20 days' leave for the wedding celebrations in May 1996. At that time, Moog was implementing a big project at a plant in south India. The company insisted on keeping the installation on hold, until Deepak returned to work.

The vice president of the company joked, "You are getting married and I am losing sleep!"

Deepak hurried back from his honeymoon to make the project functional.

Fuelled by such passion and dedication, Moog India grew by leaps and bounds (from $150,000 to $5 million in just 3 years). In 1998, the company posted Deepak to its head office in East Aurora, New York. He moved to the US, with family.

Working with the Moog R&D centre, Deepak was exposed to technology at its very core.

"I worked in a big laboratory with a lot of genius IQ people – all PhDs. It reminded me of my student days, it was such a thrill."

In 2001, son Ankur was born and Deepak and Jyoti wondered, "Should we settle in the US and raise a family – or go back to India?"

The company had applied for a green card on Deepak's behalf. Everything was going well but, on introspection, Deepak realised two things.

Firstly, the lab was fun but he was not really a lab person. He missed *doing* things.

Secondly, the US economy was on the decline while India was booming. There were so many opportunities which never existed before.

"I was also very much inspired by Abdul Kalam Sir, whom I had met in DRDO."

What's more, Deepak's father was keen that he return. He often quoted the phrase, '*Janani janmabhoomishacha swargadapi gariyasi*'.

In the Ramayan, after conquering Lanka, Lord Ram says to Lakshman, "Even this golden Lanka does not appeal to me. Mother and motherland are greater than heaven."

It was on this emotional level that the decision was taken, bags were packed. Before the final move, Deepak made a visit to India and looked at where to settle. Bangalore or Hyderabad were the logical choices. But Deepak chose Belgaum.

"My father had retired and wanted us to stay with them. I too thought that children would grow up with grandparents and get the correct *sanskaras*."

Locating in Belgaum was not wise from a professional point of view – but somehow it felt right.

Deepak purchased a plot of land in the industrial area of Belgaum. In April 2002, he shifted back to India. That same month, along with brother Dinesh, he started a company called 'Servocontrols India'.

"Dr Kalam has said, 'What is the fun of basking in the glory of another's country…' Those words kept ringing in my mind."

"I had a clear idea of what I wanted to do. But had no money to do it."

Manufacturing servocontrol devices is a very capital-intensive business. You need to import high-end equipment and set up a world-class facility. Which would cost a minimum of $10 million.

"I knew that nobody would lend me that much money – I had no collateral or security to give. Nor a past track record."

So, then what? Deepak used his 'galli' instincts to start a more practical business. He decided to get into servicing of servocontrol devices. A project which required an initial investment of ₹10 lakh. An amount he could invest on his own.

Valves are the most widely used mechanism in servocontrol. A malfunctioning valve can bring to a halt an entire assembly line, or even a plant.

"I knew how crucial valves are hence we started servicing servo valves and proportional valves of any make."

There was huge demand for this kind of work.

"Repair is always cheaper than replacement. So this is an evergreen industry!"

Of course, approaching the same clients then – as a Moog employee – and now, as an entrepreneur, meant two different things. Companies wanted not just servicing, but 'total support'.

"It was like – go there, make it work, then only will we pay you the money."

And Deepak accepted that challenge.

One day, at the HAL workshop, the supervising engineer pointed to a gunny bag full of defective valves. The valves were lying idle because they could not be serviced in India.

The man poured the entire lot in front of Deepak and said, "Can *you* make them work?"

"I said – give it to me. We will go back and study them and let you know."

Deepak knew that the valves were worth at least ₹4-5 lakh. It was a challenge worth taking. But, at that time, he did not even have a testing facility. All he had was bare land.

"We were running from pillar to post to get an industrial license to build our facility. But there was so much red tape and officers demanding bribes!"

With the HAL project in hand, there was no time to waste. A problem calls for a solution, it cannot be kept 'on hold'.

"Let us build our lab in the garage of our house," decided Deepak.

The car was parked on the road and the garage converted into a testing facility.

"Not that I had done this before, or knew how to do it. But I had no choice!"

Using the *'jugaad'* method, Deepak and Dinesh created a laboratory which could test valves with high sensitivity – in milliampere rating.

They also used extremely clean hydraulic oil. However, the main USP was the proprietary information, which Deepak had. Not just about valves manufactured by Moog, but rival companies.

"It was my job to know about and study every new servocontrol device in the market."

But Dinesh played an equally important role.

"I call my brother 'Vishwakarma'. You delegate to him – do this job – he will get it done."

Still, it took a great deal of ingenuity. Contacting the right people for the right part, importing a particular raw material and using trial and error method. What hundreds of engineers sitting in HAL could not do, two young entrepreneurs managed in 6 months.

"We repaired 70-80% of the valves!"

The HAL people were elated and sent across more work. The

billing from HAL and other steel mills itself was ₹65 lakh in Year 1. The margin for the company was 50-60%. Thus, with very little investment, in its very first year, Servocontrols India made a profit of around ₹25 lakh.

To grow the business, Deepak realised he needed to build a strong team. Dinesh was a diploma engineer but having spent all his life in Belgaum, he needed more exposure.

"I sent Dinesh to the US, Germany and Russia for training at our partner facilities. Quickly, he started thinking similar to me."

Servocontrols also hired 7-8 diploma engineers and trained them on the job.

"We also paid them almost twice the industry standard."

An unusual policy for a small company, which paid rich dividends.

In 2004, Deepak happened to meet Sajjan Jindal at the 'Fluid Power Exhibition' at the Indian Institute of Science in Bangalore. Jindal mentioned that steel mills were facing a tremendous recession and were keen to cut their costs. This industry too used servovalves to maintain the thickness of steel guage. Malfunctioning valves resulted in expensive downtime.

"We started servicing valves for the steel industry. The savings they got ran into lakhs of rupees."

Power plants were the young company's next big customers. One idle turbine can bring the entire grid to a halt. The plants are in remote locations, not easily accessible. So, companies would actually send a chartered plane to Belgaum – to get the 'service magician' in as quickly as possible.

"It happened with BALCO* at their Korba plant and also with some of the State Electricity Boards."

What's more, such clients were willing to pay a handsome fee.

The servicing business was good, but Deepak soon spotted a second opportunity. Every valve is supported by a sensor – a position sensor, pressure sensor or controller. These sensors were not available in India, and neither was the technical support.

* BALCO is now Vedanta Corporation.

"We tied up with sensor manufacturers both to distribute their products and as their technical partners."

Meanwhile, construction of a proper factory finally started. But what about the clearances and licenses?

(*Deepak smiles*)

"One of the officers told me, 'See the Tamil film *Sivaji* starring Rajnikanth.'"

In the film, the superstar plays an NRI who returns to India and wants to build a free hospital.

"If Rajnikanth has to struggle, imagine ordinary fellows like me," chuckles Deepak.

The one advantage the Dhadotis had was a father who had been a banker. Deepak had been operating an NRI account with State Bank of India (SBI) as well. These 2 factors helped Servocontrols secure its very first loan from SBI for construction purposes, without any collateral security.

The initial plan was to have a very small setup, just for valves. But after servicing clients and understanding their many needs, the duo became more ambitious.

"Expectation of our customers was so high. They said – you must have an electronics lab, a systems lab, different kinds of sensor labs..."

From ₹1 crore the project cost ballooned to ₹5 crore. Luckily, profits from the existing business were healthy enough to meet this requirement.

The state-of-the-art Servocontrols India laboratory at Udyambag Industrial estate in Belgaum was inaugurated on 15 August 2005. It included 'clean room' facility, oil-cleanliness test setup and an anti-static electronics lab.

At the time, the company had 20 employees and a turnover of ₹4 crore.

Soon, Deepak realised that testing would not be enough. Instead of importing all the raw material, it made sense for the company to have its own manufacturing facility. "We were a small company then but we thought – let's think big."

"It is one thing to have the 'know-how' and another to convert your know-how into a commercially viable business."

The second facility was set up at a cost of ₹5 crore, again aided by SBI. The Chief General Manager for the Bangalore branch at that time was Mahapara Ali.

"Madam had noticed we were borrowing a lot of money from the bank. She wanted to know, who are these guys? She wanted to visit our company."

Madam Ali was duly impressed and agreed to support Servocontrols' ambitious expansion plans.

But one problem remained. The plot Deepak had purchased in the Udyambaug industrial estate was not large enough. At that time, the man holding the neighbouring plot, an engineer called Mr Vibhuti, came forward.

He said, "Deepak, you are doing a great work. You take my land. It will be blessed."

Deepak purchased the plot and started construction. The state-of-the-art machine shop for manifold blocks in aluminum/steel/castings and special alloys was completed in 2007. At the time, Chip Emery, former Vice President of Honeywell and CEO of MTS Corporation, was visiting India as part of a business delegation. MTS Minneapolis was a Servocontrols customer and expressed an interest in visiting Belgaum.

Deepak took this opportunity to have his new plant inaugurated by Chip. The American simply could not believe that such a facility could be built in this remote part of India.

"This is the reaction of anyone who visits Servocontrols India," smiles Deepak. "The only problem is bringing the clients here."

Air connectivity is a major issue with very few flights in and out of Belgaum. The road journey from Goa is 5 hours long and not very pleasant. Despite this, many large aerospace customers started visiting Servocontrols.

"I knew the aerospace companies from my Moog days. But what really helped was the government's offset policy, announced as part of the Defence Procurement Procedure (DPP) 2005."

The offset policy is simple: foreign firms who win major defence contracts must pump back at least 30 per cent of the contract value to the Indian manufacturing sector. This was a huge opportunity as servocontrols and sensors are integral to combat aircraft.

Aerospace is a lucrative but uncertain business. You have to first 'qualify' to bid. The testing and certification process itself takes 2-3 years.

What's more, the aerospace and defence industry is highly capital intensive. Where would the money come from? Even as Deepak was pondering this question, he got a chance to visit Moscow as part of the Prime Minister's delegation in December 2005. Subsequently, Servocontrols signed a contract with a tier 1 supplier for the Sukhoi 30 aircraft.

The same year there was a technology-transfer agreement between Russia and India. HAL Lucknow was chosen as the Indian manufacturing partner and Servocontrols India became the supplier for flight-control actuators.

"That gave us an edge and a burning desire to excel!"

In June 2007 came another high-five. At a symposium organised by the Aeronautical Society of India, Dr A P J Abdul Kalam visited the Servocontrols India stall. Amazed at the work the company was doing he exclaimed to Dr Saraswat, Programme Director (Air Defence) with DRDO.

"*This* man...give him a push! I want him to do lot of projects, give him proprietary tenders. Make him work hard, he is young."

That opened many doors.

"We also put up a stall at the Bangalore Air Show in 2007 and the Paris Air Show in 2009. It created a lot of awareness – that there is a company called Servocontrols in Belgaum."

A large American corporation called Spaceage Controls and Firstmark Aerospace wanted Servocontrols to represent all its products in India. At the same time, Servocontrols was approached

"Entrepreneurship means going out and cutting deals. You can't just sit in your office and expect orders."

by the Russian company Voskhod, makers of aircrafts actuation systems. They too were looking for an Indian partner in order to make India a manufacturing hub.

All defence-related deals in Russia are done through a state agency called Rosoboron exports. Dealing with such agencies is a long and tedious process. And more so for a small Indian company competing with multinational giants. But that did not deter Deepak.

"We decided to incorporate a separate company called Servocontrols AeroSpace India Private Limited. After that, we went in for the AS9100 certification which gives you worldwide recognition as a supplier of products to the aerospace and defence industry."

UL India audited Servocontrols systems – a difficult and detailed process. The audit covered all areas from design to manufacturing, servicing, assembling and onsite installation. After a lot of *ragda-patti*, Servocontrols India obtained AS9100; RevB Certification for Aerospace components and systems in the year 2009.

"Then we started venturing in bigger projects. Many large foreign companies were looking for good suppliers in India so there was no dearth of business."

Sensing an opportunity, other established players like L&T and Godrej had jumped into the fray. Multinationals such as Honeywell, Eaton and Boeing* set up manufacturing facilities in India, as well. But the pie is large enough for all players to carve out a niche.

"We specialise in actuation systems for aircrafts – both commercial and fighter jets. Our other area of strength is space applications and UAVs (unmanned aerial vehicles, also known as drones)."

* Boeing set up in India as a joint venture with Tatas.

It's a knowledge intensive business, with a steep learning curve. The client literally works as a 'partner', providing technology training and specifications. Down to the correct way to pack and ship products.

"There are engineers at Honeywell who have devoted 40 years of their life to solenoid valves. When they come and train us, it is a unique experience."

In 2009, Servocontrols India put up another facility for sophisticated technologies like laser welding and embedding. Now the company could create its own special alloy fusion, as per project requirement. 12 acres of land were also bought to set up a fourth plant – a turnkey facility for aerospace projects.

The cost of this critical infrastructure was ₹35 crore. The new facility added 40 employees to the existing 120. As always, these were mostly 'localites'.

"We don't go for highly qualified people or those with too much of experience."

The idea is to identify bright diploma-holders as well as BTechs from the many colleges in and around Belgaum. Take best available raw material and mould them into 'real engineers'. To do this is a painstaking process.

"We have an HR department but I still conduct a personal interview before we make the final offer. I always look for the young people with tremendous potential."

Servocontrols does hire more experienced hands from time to time. These are the folks who left Belgaum to make their careers in companies like HAL, Godrej or Honeywell. Keen to take this opportunity to work in their hometown.

"We have received '*maan dhan*' from numerous public sector companies. The amount could be as small as ₹500 but we always preserve it."

"For every cellphone we buy, a dollar goes to Motorola, because the IP of cellular technology is still with them. I want to make that sort of innovation happen in India."

"We find the experienced useful when there is a lot of statutory documentation. They know the industry inside-out."

Knowing your industry makes you known in the industry. That's how Servocontrols India was called upon to work with the Tatas. Being a nodal agency for defence projects, the Tatas get large orders which they sub-contracts to specialist companies.

"Their people came and evaluated our work and we were chosen as a key partner for actuation systems."

During a bid for a very large project – in thousands of crores – Deepak was asked to come and present to Ratan Tata himself on 14 October 2009.

"It was a great experience, a great feeling!"

Apart from the stay at Taj, the dinner and the actual interaction, Deepak remembers one unusual fact. All visitors have to undergo security check before entering Bombay House. With one exception. "There was a dog coming in and going out and no one paid it any attention. Afterwards I learnt it was Ratan Tata's personal dog!" (*smiles*) In the pedigree of aerospace, Deepak is but a young pup.

"Many people I meet say – 'We did not expect you would be so young! Do you have enough experience to take up our project?'"

That's where they get another pleasant surprise.

"I remember a critical project from the Tatas related to T-72/T-90 tank and simulators. Normally, it takes 8-10 months but we executed in 3 months, working day and night!"

In recognition of the young company's contribution, the Tata Industry Services Ltd (TISL) CEO, Kamesh Gupta, wrote a letter to Deepak on 7 July 2011.

"...What is most credible is that despite critical challenges of volume, cost, quality and most important, credibility of India to deliver aerospace and defence products, you have managed to accomplish the task at hand."

The same year, Servocontrols India's revenues crossed ₹30 crore ($8 million). 60% of the business came from manufacturing, with services bringing in the rest. The combined employee strength of both companies crossed 200.

What next? From a global perspective, Servocontrols was a tiny player – an ant in the company of giants. A large global company in aerospace industry is minimum $10-12 billlion.

"We have a very, very, very long way to go!" laughs Deepak.

Clients and well-wishers exhorted Deepak to 'think big'. To become the 'Infosys' of aerospace and defence industry. Institutions and investors have shown interest, but Deepak is afraid of giving away 'too much'.

"We are control freaks... The foreign companies can easily chew you and spit you out in no time."

One option is to cash out and 'enjoy life'. A couple of years ago he got a call from the Curtis Wright Corporation, a company whose aeronautical heritage goes back to the original Wright brothers.

"They were very interested in buying out my company but I declined."

But why keep slogging it out? Whenever he is in need of motivation, Deepak recalls his visit to Israel in 2012. A friend took him to a place called 'Nobel Laureates Street' built in honour of the 232 Jews who have received the Nobel Prize till date.

"I was amazed by the spirit of entrepreneurship in Israel...despite

"We dream of building an entire Unmanned Aerial Vehicle in our factory. It will happen someday."

"After struggling with all the possible government departments, from electricity board to excise, service tax, customs, sales tax and even CBI, finally the government gives you an award!"

the conflicts and hardships they have produced cutting-edge technologies."

The desert land of Israel is a pioneer in drip irrigation. Water is brought to the major cities all the way from Golan Heights.

"Every plant in Israel is watered. If even one tree falls they feel that a person has died..."

It is that sense of passion – and national pride – which keeps Deepak going. He recalls the misery India went through after Pokhran 2, when the transfer of technology from US and Europe came to a halt. But it led to indigenisation – a blessing in disguise.

"I believe we are doing work which is critical to this country. We want to work with Indian organisations."

This includes the likes of ISRO, Vikram Sarabhai Space Centre (VSSC) and Bhabha Atomic Research Centre (BARC).

After India signed the Nuclear Non-Proliferation Treaty, the CIRUS reactor, which supplied plutonium for India's atomic explosions, was shut down. As a result, BARC could no longer supply isotopes for treatment of cancer patients in hospitals across India.

One fine morning, the head of BARC's Research Reactor Maintenance Division, Mr Kharpate, walked into the Servocontrols office, without an appointment.

He said, "Deepak, *mala he karoon payaje* (You have to do this job for me)."

Over the next year, Servocontrols India worked with BARC to upgrade the Dhruva reactor and restart production of radio isotopes in India.

"In November 2011, we were publicly felicitated for helping BARC achieve self-reliance in nuclear handling technologies."

In 2011, Deepak also received the Kaigarika Ratan Prashasti Award from the Karnataka Small Scale Industries Association.

"After struggling with all the possible government departments, from city corporation to electricity board to excise, service tax, customs, sales tax and even CBI, finally the government gives you an award," he smiles.

The year 2012 brought with it storm clouds. The Parliament was rocked by scams like 2G and Coalgate bringing defence and aerospace tenders to a grinding halt. This affected the 30% of Servocontrols India's business which came from the government sector.

"For 6 months, things were so bad…I was completely frustrated. The situation looked hopeless."

When the pressure got too much, Deepak went to America with family for 2 months. He visited Disneyland and Niagara Falls, as well as customers, friends and relatives.

"I took my son, Ankur, to the Millard Fillmore Suburban Amherst hospital where he was born – it was an emotional moment."

When he returned, nothing much had changed. But, Deepak himself was more optimistic and less weighed down.

"Fortunately, we were able to get some orders from the Israeli aerospace industry and that helped a lot. We even decided to go ahead and put up a 100% EOU (export-oriented unit) in the aerospace SEZ at Hattaragi, Belgaum.

In March 2013, Servocontrols India reported revenues of ₹100 crore and an employee strength of 210.

"After understanding the Jain philosophy of *syadavada* (relativism), my mind has gone into a totally different spin."

"In the next 5 years, I think we can easily cross ₹200 crore ($35-40 million)."

Goals are important, but so is a sense of detachment. This is the spiritual aspect of life which Deepak has imbibed from his mother, a devout Jain.

In December 2010, Deepak spent a month at Mangalayatan, a *teerthadham* near Aligarh set up by NRIs from the Jain community. Apart from a temple complex it also houses a university and research centre which has digitised more than 8000 *agamas*[*].

"I used to be a sceptic, I never believed in the concept of reincarnation...but now I do. And it has reduced my stress considerably."

Jain doctrines such as Anekantavada propagate multiplicity of viewpoints, encouraging you to consider the views and beliefs of rivals and opposing parties – which is so important in life as well as in business.

Similarly, there is the philosophy of Syadavada (relativism) which explains how each truth can be represented in 7 different ways.

"After understanding these philosophies, my mind has gone into a totally different spin."

While he loves to hang out with friends and family and with cows ('my first love'), finding time is not easy.

"One has to juggle between family, wife, kids, clients and employees..."

The principal of the K L E International School put it into perspective one day when she remarked, "Your contribution to your child's growth is zero. You better do something!"

"I am trying to spend more time with my sons, Ankur (12) and Ankit (8). I know there has to be more to life than business."

And there has to be more to business than profit.

---

* Agamas are Buddhist, Jain and Hindu scriptures which encompass temple architecture, philosophy and meditation practices.

"I believe we must share the wealth with employees, pay all our taxes and also give back to Belgaum."

Konkanacha California honaar ya nahi? (Can the Konkan become like California?)

If more young engineers and entrepreneurs believe in such dreams, *anything* is possible.

ADVICE TO YOUNG ENTREPRENEURS

Don't all of a sudden jump into a manufacturing project. You have to have the basic skillset and the financial backing – if you match these two then only you can only become a success.

Selecting the right business is important. Don't be blinded by passion alone.

You have to be very, very humble. I left a very good position and when I was on my own I found I have to be responsible for every smallest thing.

You should be jack of all but master of one technology. That is my principle. Even if all the employees leave, you should be able to do it yourself.

You have to know your technology. But you must also understand the 'hidden red tape' in your business. Do not rely on outside consultants – study these aspects personally.

A lot of companies in India fail because they don't understand the legal aspects of business.

You must also be able to handle finance. You will have a CA and an accounts department but don't expect them to do the thinking for you.

An entrepreneur doesn't get promotions – you have to motivate yourself. I have seen in foreign countries that you can work hard and also have a lot of fun. Learn how to keep up your spirits.

At the end of the day, my mother always says – *do bhakri fakht lagtat* (a man needs only two meals a day).

Don't be greedy, whatever you get enjoy that.

BISI BELE APP

Rohith Bhat – RoboSoft
Udupi (Karnataka)

This young engineer shifted base from Mumbai in 1998, convinced that he could create a world-class IT company from his hometown. Today he heads a ₹35 crore company with 350 employees. Proving, that it *can* be done.

When I think of Udupi, I think of crisp, golden-brown dosas.

Rava dosas, masala dosas, ghee rava masala dosas. Idlis, vadas and bisi bele bhath.

Growing up in Mumbai, the Udupi hotel was our most-loved 'eating out' option. Decades before McDonald's, the enterprising *annas* of Udupi set the standards for cheap, clean, quick-service restaurants.

So when I reached Udupi I had just one objective – to eat at one of the 'original' Udupi restaurants.

To my surprise and horror, I could see mostly Punjabi, Chinese and fast-food joints.

"Udupi is not what I thought it would be," I sighed. And certainly, it was much more than I expected.

To my surprise and delight, I discovered Robosoft. An IT company headquartered in Santhekatte (New Udupi) but thinking and acting like this was Bangalore. Serving global clients, creating innovative apps and games. Hungry and foolish and confident, about achieving much more.

Like the hoteliers of Udupi, Rohith Bhat went to Mumbai to find his fortune. But, in 1998, he decided to return to his roots.

"I didn't need to be in a big city. With Internet and mobile phones, I realised I can be anywhere."

Being 'local' is Rohith Bhat's strength. 80% of his employees are young graduates from the engineering colleges in and around Mangalore. Just like he is.

On the other hand, Robosoft 'acts global'. The company has ambition, it has vision. And it has a fabulous office building. The kind every hard-working IT employee expects and deserves.

From the old Udupi to New Udupi.

What an idea, Sirjee.

India needs lots and lots and lots more.

BISI BELE APP

Rohith Bhat - RoboSoft
Udupi (Karnataka)

Rohith Bhat was born and brought up in Udupi, a small town in south Karnataka.

"My father had a factory, a small-scale unit which made plastic sheets and pipes. I understood how hard it is to run a successful business at an early age."

As the youngest of 4 siblings, Rohith followed a path set by the elders. Like his brother and sister, Rohith went on to study engineering. Computer science had just been introduced and, at his brother's suggestion, he opted for the course. Hardware was expensive and very few institutes had the required equipment. One of them was a newly set up private college called NMAMIT in Nitte, a village in Karkala taluk, 54 km from Mangalore.

"When I joined in 1988, not many people really knew 'what is computers'. We used machines with 8086 processors – so slow and ancient by today's standards."

Despite that, Rohith enjoyed tinkering with the machines. The hardware side interested him much more than the software. Rohith's fourth-year project was on 'speech recognition and synthesis'. It was a team of 4 and here too, his role was more on the hardware side – burning the PCBs, designing the PCBs and so on.

"Our goal was to have the best and most talked-about project. And we succeeded in that."

After graduating from college – like all the young engineers of his time – Rohith set out to Bangalore to look for a job.

"Ours was the third batch to graduate and we had no campus placement option."

The job hunt did not yield any result. Rohith's sister was living in Bombay. She said, "Come here, stay with me and look for a job. There are more jobs here."

Rohith took her advice and eventually joined a small company called Industrial and Business Machines for a salary of ₹1200 per month. The company made devices for banking known as 'adding machines'. But Rohith's job, ironically, was in the software side.

"Computerisation had not yet started because the unions were resisting it. But everyone knew that it was inevitable."

The company realised that its hardware business would soon be extinct. Hence, they wanted to develop software which the same clients could use to get their work done.

"My job was to build 'clearing' software, i.e. when a cheque is presented in the bank it gets cleared."

Coding had never been the young engineer's forte. But now, he had no choice.

"I was quite a novice even by newbie standards. The fact that I knew nothing motivated me to learn everything – as quickly as I could."

Rohith would work in office and carry work home. Using his brother-in-law's computer, he would continue coding, testing and refining his programs.

"I worked with my heart and more than was strictly necessary. This made my boss like me a lot."

After 9 months, Rohith moved to a Japanese company called Recosoft. Again, it was on the software side but with a twist. The company was creating an equivalent of Microsoft Word for the Japanese market, but on the Macintosh platform. At the time, the world was mostly MS DOS and Wordstar. GUI (Graphical User Interface) was hardly known.

"I was thrilled to work on something new, something different from anything I had ever seen before."

But the most exciting part of the job was exposure – to Japan and Japanese culture. The company posted Rohith in Japan for a year and it opened his eyes to a new way of working and thinking.

"I saw this country that was totally destroyed in World War II but which had rebuilt itself and was once again at the pinnacle."

Japan was kicking the US on every front, be it in technology, manufacturing or even automobile design. What's more, you could sense passion and determination in everyday workers – at banks, shops and service stations. A passion born out of national pride.

"I thought, if this country can do something like this, some day I should go back to my country and do something, start something."

Rohith came back to India after a year to work in the company's Bombay office. After two and a half years with Recosoft, he decided to move on.

"At that time I was 26 years old and struggling with myself – should I take up another job or start my own company?"

Rohith's mother advised, "Don't get into business – I have seen enough of your father struggling."

But his father and brother encouraged him. "Enough," they said. "It's time you do something on your own."

Rohith did take up a job with L&T but quit after just two months. Because there comes a time when you take a leap of faith.

Once you jump in, you will figure out a way to stay afloat.

So where does one start? The very first thing Rohith did was to get a telephone line in the company's name (Robosoft). The next was to put an ad in the 'Yellow Pages'.

"I thought that if you take out an ad, people will look you up and come to you. I was so young and idealistic!" (*laughs*)

Rohith knew his focus had to be the Macintosh. This was the technology he knew and there was nobody offering services for this niche. To do this, the basic requirement was an expensive Apple Macintosh machine. Using the money he had saved up from his Japanese stint, Rohith acquired an Apple Mac.

"I used to dream of living abroad, living comfortably. After going to Japan, I was determined to do something in my own country."

One man, one machine and a zero-rental office (his sister's house). But how does one get that first contract? It takes some thrashing around, and a bit of luck.

"I had a friend living in Pune near the Osho commune. The Oshos had a lot of Macs so I thought they might give me some work."

When they met, the Oshos said, "Can you create a spellcheck program for us?"

"Yes," replied Rohith. And he did the coding, with the help of a friend.

Apple Computers had just entered India and they heard about this. The company approached Rohith and asked, "Can we bundle your program with our OS?"

That was the young company's first major breakthrough, in mid-1996. Apple bought 3000 copies of the spellcheck software with an upfront payment of ₹5 lakh.

'It was a very large sum for me, at that time."

Apple released a local language kit to support the Macintosh in India. They requested Rohith to provide support with all their software – in Hindi, Gujarati, Marathi and other Indian languages.

"They even took me on the road show. I was giving presentations as part of their delegation and that gave a lot of credibility to my work."

The next project Rohith bagged was with C-DAC (Centre for Developing of Advanced Computing). They heard of his work in local languages and got in touch for a related project. Meanwhile, more projects came in by word of mouth and through referral by Apple.

"People came to know, if you want to get some Mac work done, these are the guys to go to..."

With more projects in hand, Rohith hired 2 programmers. There was still no 'office'. Rohith worked from his sister's place while they worked out of their own homes. Co-ordinating the work was becoming an issue. It was then that Rohith had his 'eureka' moment.

"Let me shift to Udupi."

The year was 1998 and the internet was in its infancy. But Rohith realised one important thing.

"With the internet, it does not make much difference – whether you are in Bombay or Udupi."

Or Timbuktu, for that matter.

Unfortunately, on further investigation, Rohith found that there was no internet available in Udupi. But there was an internet facility in KREC Surathkal (Karnataka Regional Engineering College, now known as NIT-Surathkal). In fact, under a scheme called STEP (Software Technology Entrepreneurs Park), startup companies could make use of both the internet as well as the REC students – for project work.

This sounded attractive enough to Rohith. In January 1998, he closed shop in Bombay and shifted to the KREC campus. Office space in STEP came in June and Robosoft began operating there on 15 July 1998.

"My 2 employees did not want to leave Bombay. So once again, I became a single-person startup!"

That's when Rohith returned to his alma mater – NMAMIT – and decided to hire some fresh graduates. The seventh batch of students was passing out and was happy to get a 'campus placement', that too so close to their hometown.

Rohith's friend, Ram (M Ramachandra Acharya), was teaching at KREC. He helped train the fresh recruits, and also shared the load of programming.

The outsourcing era was upon the world and with it, Robosoft prospered. Foreign clients would call Apple India and say, "We are looking for Indian programmers who are good with Macintosh... can you recommend someone?"

"There were so many Windows programmers, so many companies giving Windows services. So I decided to focus on Apple Macintosh which was just entering India."

That's how Robosoft won its first international client – a company from Israel. Rohith travelled to Jerusalem, met the party and bagged the deal. The task was to create a multimedia encyclopedia and the billing was a whopping $25,000.

"Suddenly I could stop worrying how to pay the next month's salary and focus on the work."

But delivering was a huge challenge. The team was young and inexperienced, the project, a large one. Rohith persuaded Ram to quit his teaching job and join Robosoft*. Together they struggled for more than two and a half months to complete the final leg of the project.

When the money finally came in, Rohith was on top of the world.

"That's when I bought my first fridge, first television set..." (*smiles*).

In its first year of operations at Surathkal, Robosoft earned revenues of ₹8 lakh. At that time, the company did not even have its own website. But the company grew rapidly – from just 2 employees to 19. After two and a half years, Rohith decided to move out of KREC and set up his own office in Udupi.

"We rented the second floor of a commercial building, it had the capacity to seat around 50 people."

The employees were thrilled.

"Oh...my god! This is such a big office..." was the constant refrain. Standing at one end, they would stare at the other end and feel yes, we are making progress!

Of course, working from Udupi brought its own set of issues. There was no dial-up connection in Udupi or Mangalore in the

* Ram Acharya is still with Robosoft, as SVP Engineering.

year 2000. The only way to get on to the net was through the *jugaad* method.

“I would redirect my mobile to the BSNL landline number in Bangalore, then dial into my mobile number and use the net. That way it was a local call for me.”

What helped Rohith in those early days in Udupi was his engineering college experience.

“When I joined the college, we had no building, no classrooms... everything was under construction. We had to find a solution for every small thing.”

Adversity is a boot camp which creates that fighting spirit. So necessary to do *anything*.

The year 2000 also saw the dotcom bust. Although Robosoft continued to enjoy steady business from its many overseas clients, sentiment was affected. There was doom and gloom about the future of IT companies.

“We had hired some 7-8 people...quite a few of them quit the company thinking we too might go bust!”

Nevertheless, Robosoft continued its growth trajectory. By 2003, the company outgrew the office which had seemed ‘so big’.

“We opened another office in the same building and, in 2004, we added a third office.”

In 2004, the employee strength had risen to 150 and Robosoft had 4 separate offices in the city. This was the time when Rohith decided to take a quantum leap.

“All our friends work in big, fancy buildings in Bangalore. Why can’t we create such a building right here in Udupi?”

Employees would love it. Customers would be easier to convince.

“Getting a project was a big thing...so we said yes to whatever was offered. Only then we would worry about how to do it!”

"Over the years we outgrew every office we had. So I thought, this time let me think big and make this our permanent address."

When they visit Udupi they would see the same infrastructure, same facilities, same work environment as any big city. And certainly, that would bring in more business.

It was a big vision for a small company. At the time, Robosoft had 160 employees and a topline of just ₹4 crore. The cost of construction was over ₹10 crore.

"I decided to go in for a bank loan."

Over the years, Rohith had learnt to deal with banks. It was always a struggle to convince them but seeing the steady and timely inflows from foreign clients they had extended loans both for capital equipment and overdraft.

"The goodwill of my father and brothers in the plastics business also helped."

But why build a a five-storey building with basement, gym, cafeteria, sports facilities and an auditorium. A one lakh square foot facility which can accommodate 800 people?

Because of a vision.

"I knew we will grow. I knew we will need the space!"

Looking at the company's past record, the almost 100% year on year growth, the bank agreed to provide funds. Robosoft provided 33% margin money and kept the property as collateral. The final cost of the land and building was close to ₹13 crore, including interiors and workstations.

"We did not furnish the building completely, that part we keep adding as more people join and need the space."

Space is not just a physical reality. There is a space in the mind from where you create your own reality.

As you expand, so does your world.

Rohith realised that Robosoft's growth would not come in numbers. It would never be an Infosys which would put 300-400 people on a single project.

"I had chosen a niche for my business and my goal was to be the best in that niche."

Robosoft had a who's who list of clients – Canon, Epson, Umax Logitech and HP (majority of HP's printer drivers for Macintosh are coded by Robosoft).

"We were something like the Taiwanese who used to be vendors for all the global PC giants."

The Taiwanese eventually decided to step out of the shadows and build their own brands like HTC and Acer. A strategy Robosoft has adopted in the software space.

"We were doing great work, but it was outsourced work, for clients. In 2007, we thought, let us start creating our own products."

Thus began a new journey, a journey of discovery and learning. And unlearning. The mindset of a product company is different from that of a services company. Hence a separate team was created for product development.

"Within products itself we have 2 brands – Global Delight, which creates utility apps, and 99Games, which is focused on creating games"

As always, the platform chosen was Macintosh. While solving engineering problems was the company's strength, product development required some new skills. Such as how to conceptualise a product from scratch. With that came the issues of market size, user interface and creating kickass art and design.

"Then we had to switch from the sales mode to the 'marketing' mode – you understand the difference don't you?"

"Do not start a business thinking I will try this...if it doesn't work...I will go back. It will definitely fail."

"Margins in the IT services used to be quite high but are falling. Hence it makes sense to diversify into products. "

Global Delight and 99Games started attending trade shows such as Macworld. The idea being to give demos, meet the press and try to get reviews for your products.

Of course, you have to try ten things and find one 'success story'. And you never quite know *what* might take off.

"We did not create a blockbuster right away...it's all trial and error and some luck also!"

In 2007, Apple launched the iPhone and this was a major inflection point. Suddenly there was a whole new app economy* and Robosoft was in the thick of it all. The company was already developing iPhone games and apps for clients.

"Quickly we also started making our own."

On 1 October 2009, Global Design released an app called 'Camera Plus'. This free app allows iPhone and iPad users to shoot better photos, with several features not available in the camera provided with the device. The free version of Camera Plus has attracted over 20 million downloads.

"When we saw how popular the app was, we created a paid version."

More than one million people have paid between $.99 to $2.99 to download this version of Camera Plus. The company has 5 other apps, though none quite as successful in terms of numbers as its first release, but just as successful in terms of revenues.

On the gaming side, 99Games has released 12 games so far and seen one big hit – 'Wordsworth'. Among the first word games released on the iTunes App store, it scored both positive reviews and a large user base. Over 400,000 downloads in the last 5 years.

---

* When iPhone launched with 200 apps, 5 of them were created by Robosoft (for clients).

"The latest versions of Wordsworth are available for iPhone and iPad as well as Android phones, Kindle Fire and NOOK."

Although built on the cult of Macintosh, Robosoft cannot afford to ignore other, larger markets. The company now works on the Windows and the Android platform for clients, as well as for its own products.

In March 2013, Robosoft posted revenues of ₹35 crore, the bulk of which still came from services. But its own apps and games now contribute 16% and Rohith expects the balance to shift further.

"Earlier we were not breaking even on products – now we are. The revenue per person in the product team will soon be more than it is in services!"

The story has another happy side to it. In 2008, the entire IT industry was affected by recession. One of Robosoft's clients – HP – tightened its purse strings. But that same year, the iPhone took off, followed by the iPad.

"What we lost from our traditional clients, we made up by developing apps and games for the new platform."

From an export-only focus, Robosoft is now looking to serve the Indian market as well. The company has developed the iPhone and iPad apps for several media houses such as NDTV, *Dainik Bhaskar* and *The Economic Times*.

The latest feather in Robosoft's cap is the Dhoom 3 game, through a licensing agreement with Yashraj Films (YRF). Developed in a record 6 months, the D3 racing game achieved 1 million downloads in just 20 days, making it a runaway success.

"We have a multi-year, multi-game deal with YRF and are open to collaborating with more film studios."

So all izz well and all but one question remains. The IT business is built on the nimble brains of its coders, animators

"The Mac industry is a very small and tightly knit community. Everybody knows everybody else – your relationships and your past track record matter a lot."

and testers. How does a company situated in a small town attract that talent?

Rohith has a simple solution – he focuses on hiring young people just like himself.

"80% of our 350 employees are from in and around Mangalore. They are from the local engineering colleges of south Karnataka."

Local boys and girls attracted by the quality of the work and comfort of living close to home. A job at Robosoft pays as much or more than Infosys or Wipro. And it's actually more prestigious.

"We don't recruit in bulk – just 2-3 students from each college. Because we want the best, the ones who are looking for a challenge."

Robosoft also offers internship projects to BTechs and conducts coding competitions.

"Everybody likes the kind of work that gets done here – that helps us attract the right talent!"

The company is also robust at the management level. Some of the early joinees such as Shylaja Rao, Srinidhi Rao and Pradeep Kumar (all NMAMT graduates like Rohith) and Ram Acharya have been with Robosoft since its KREC days. When the company shifted to Udupi in the year 2000, Rohith's brothers sold off their plastics business and joined the venture. While Purushotham Bhat is responsible for the overall operations, Sudheer Bhat takes care of accounts and finance.

"I remember the early days – when we were giving our first salary, I wrote the cheque without deducting any tax. We realised our mistake only after a year!"

Such slip-ups don't happen anymore but at every stage in life you realise – "I can do better."

"Small things we have not paid a lot of attention to in the past... suddenly those things start becoming more important as you start looking into the future!"

Robosoft continues to be a privately held company, grown through internal accruals and debt finance.

The family and early founders own the entire equity, but going forward Rohith thinks a stake sale or public issue may be necessary.

"I want to take the 99Games and Global Delight business to a totally different scale."

Lower costs and higher loyalty of employees are the plus points of the Robosoft model. Will we see more such success stories? Yes and no.

"For large companies it will always be a challenge. For people like me – who have grown up here, studied here, it's an opportunity."

And a big one at that....

All work and no family life makes Jack a dull boy. After many years spent building the company, in 2005, Rohith tied the knot. Wife, Shilpa Prabhu, is also from Udupi, and a computer engineer who was working at Robosoft since 2002. Shilpa is now spearheading 99Games.

"We have a 7-year-old daughter and, I must say, I work far less now but travel a lot more."

When in Udupi, Rohith is in the office at 9:30 am and leaves at 8 pm. Weekends are off though the calls and emails continue. Travelling on work more than 150 days in a year, he travels for pleasure as well.

"I own a Mahindra Scorpio (bought in 2004) and recently bought Mahindra XUV500." *(Note the preference for an Indian built, world-class car.)*

Driving down to Mangalore, Goa or Agumbe on weekends is a favourite pastime.

"I owe a lot of my success to family and friends...even the friends who discouraged me when I started this company."

They said, "You are a fool Rohith...you have such a good job. Why are you leaving it – for what?"

"Once I started the company they were the guys who helped me, who gave me support through all the tough times."

May thousands of enterprises bloom, may they find support. When bold young minds decide – this is our time. To make a difference, to make a mark in this world.

ADVICE TO YOUNG ENTREPRENEURS

The key to success is perseverance. I have seen a lot of people who look at this building and say, "Hey, we are also going to do something like this!" They try it and within one year, one and half year, they find it's difficult. And they head back to a job at an MNC. I don't think they tried hard enough.

If you are serious, you must persevere and keep hammering. I never for one moment thought I am going to go back. That thought was never there, even though there were difficulties and even today, there are difficulties. I always thought we are going to fight it out!

Certainly, this is a great time for somebody to be an entrepreneur because of this whole app ecosystem. You can create an app, put it in the iTunes store or Android store and if you have thought enough, if you have been passionate enough, if you have done your homework, you might create the next big sensation. You don't need a lot of investment to do this either!

Geography is really irrelevant right now. You should just be tuned in, know what is happening in the technology space. Attend conferences, talk to people, stay in the self-learning mode.

In the first 2 years of my life, I learnt how not to run a company, then how to run a company. I say the same thing about product development. We have figured out what not to do, we are still figuring out what we need to do. It's an ongoing process!

And lastly, I never felt the need for any business management degree. Doing business, I learn business – so can you.

WORDS WORTH

Sriram Subramanya – Integra
Pondicherry

Starting with one computer, from their home in Pondicherry, Sriram Subramanya and Anu Sriram started an outsourced e-publishing company. 19 years later, Integra is among the Top 10 publishing BPOs worldwide, with revenues of ₹72 crore and 1200 employees.

People come to Pondicherry in search of enlightenment. To drink in divinity. They wear loose clothing, buy *agarbattis* and discuss the meaning of life in bistros around Aurobindo Ashram.

Sriram Subramanya came to Pondicherry for a different and materialistic reason.

"I always wanted to start my own company. My wife, Anu, is from Pondicherry, so it made sense for us to be here."

In 1994, Sriram and Anu ventured into the brave new world of outsourced publishing. Operating from a small town back then was not easy.

"To get an Internet leased line, I had to get a form from Chennai!"

Yet the young couple never regretted their decision. With dedication and determination, they managed to do what few thought possible. A world-class business, regardless of location. Creating from scratch, whatever was needed.

Manpower, office building, professional practices.

"Ministers used to recommend candidates for jobs, I said, we can only take those who qualify."

With the idea of excellence in every action, Integra grew from strength to strength. Along the way, Sriram discovered that enlightenment comes in many forms.

"I have chosen the path of action or Karma Yoga."

The meaning of life can be found in an ashram. Or whatever you pour your soul into, the work you choose to do.

WORDS WORTH

Sriram Subramanya - Integra Pondicherry

Sriram Subramanya was born in Madurantakam, a small town in Tamil Nadu.

"My entire family is in agriculture. My father is the first educated person, he was a postgraduate and also principal-cum-correspondent of a school."

Sriram did his early schooling in Madurantakam, in Tamil medium. In Class 7, he moved to the Ramakrishna Thapovanam – a gurukulam-type, residential school near Trichy.

"The school helped in my all-round development and shaped my entire life."

Independence and confidence were two important lessons Sriram learnt early. From age 11, he travelled alone from home to hostel by bus, including changing a bus midway.

Subsequently, he joined Anna Malai University in Chidambaram to do his BE in Mechanical Engineering. After graduating in 1986, Sriram appeared for the GRE, scoring 97 percentile in the Quantitative section. But his Verbal and TOEFL scores were not up to the mark.

"Being from Tamil medium, my English was weak."

This was the time he decided, "I want to start something of my own." After graduating in 1986, Sriram spent 2 years exploring 'what to do', which business to start. To keep himself occupied, he also took up a computer course and also practiced transcendental meditation.

"I was doing whatever is required for life – both professionally and personally."

Since his family owned land, initially, Sriram thought of setting up an agro-based industry, right after graduation. But well-wishers advised him to first get some experience.

"Work for 4-5 years – then start."

Thus, in 1988, Sriram joined an auto-ancillary unit in Chennai as a graduate engineer trainee. After working in various departments from maintenance to process engineering, he was selected to head a greenfield project in Bangalore.

"That gave me big exposure – how to do everything, from getting a license to erecting the radiator assembly plant."

With its big-bad-city vibe, Bangalore was also a culture shock. But again he classifies it as a 'learning experience'. During this period, Sriram also got married to Anu – an arranged marriage, through family connections.

"My wife is a BE in Electronics from the same university, but 2 years junior to me. She also completed her MBA."

Bangalore was a challenging assignment. Sriram was not working in a specific department – he was responsible for the entire unit. He had to go deep into every aspect of production, in order to get the best out of his people. As a pilot project, Sriram's brief was to implement various new ideas. One such innovation was hiring only female workers.

"The women worked harder and with more cooperation. With proper training, we were able to improve productivity by more than 100%."

The company took notice of the young manager's efforts. In 1993, Sriram was once again selected to set up a greenfield project in Pondicherry.

"Anu wasn't very happy to hear this. She is born and brought up in Pondicherry and was keen to live in a big city at that time."

Nevertheless, the opportunity was too attractive to pass up. The company sent Sriram to Mühlacker, near Stuttgart, for training, as it was a German collaboration.

"I got a second end-to-end exposure, how to set up a new venture. Then I realised – it was more than 5 years since I started working. When am I going to start my own company?"

Once again, Sriram began exploring – what business to get into. Agro-industry remained an option, as did auto ancillary. He also began looking into IT, which was a sunrise industry at that time. But IT is an ocean, you must choose *one* entrepreneur-friendly island and survive on it. Sriram chose Desktop Publishing (DTP).

"We started in a small way with one computer, working from our house."

The year was 1994. Initially, Anu fronted the enterprise while Sriram stayed put in his job, supporting her in the evenings and on weekends. The work was mainly designing brochures, flyers and project documents for local merchants.

"Side by side we took some courses in DTP so we can learn to do the job better."

The first big client was Pondicherry University, which was starting distance education. Hence, they required a lot of course material to be typeset. In 1995, through a friend's contact, Integra landed its first overseas client – a British company with an office in Singapore.

"This was the first time we worked on a journal for a foreign publisher."

With more work coming in, the team expanded to 5 members and shifted to a rented office. In 1996, Sriram decided to quit his job and plunge into the venture full-time.

"I was grateful to my company, but I felt ready to be on my own."

Liquidating 8 years of his savings and with the help of a small loan, Sriram had invested ₹2.5 lakh into running the company. However, the company was still in the red.

"My first job, I used to commute around 2 hours everyday. During this time I was always dreaming, when will I start my own company."

"When I resigned, I told my parents, 'I want your help and support until the business starts making profit.' "

They said, "Go ahead…we will support you."

It wasn't easy. Computers were slow, technology primitive. Postscript files had to be physically loaded onto an iOmega Zipdrive and couriered to the client.

"After transferring the files they would send the drive back."

Then there were crisis situations. Like a toothache, they come without notice.

In the midst of an important project, 2 employees suddenly resigned. Anu had to jump in and work on the fly, learning how to use PageMaker and CorelDraw on the job. To complicate matters, she had just delivered a baby. Yet, she was able to get back to work with the support of her parents and an ayah.

"That's when she understood the advantage of being in Pondicherry – she started liking it."

There were also infrastructure issues. It was impossible to get a phone line on *tatkal* basis without recommendation. Luckily, one of Anu's cousins had several lines and he transferred one of his numbers to them.

Email was another 'must have', but available mostly through *jugaad*. Since the local dial-up line was always busy, Sriram used a roundabout method.

"I started travelling abroad in 1995-96 so I took an Ipass account from VSNL. When I was in UK or Singapore, I could make local calls at local rates."

Taking advantage of its roaming facility, you could dial a Singapore number and go online from Pondicherry. It was expensive, but useful in an emergency.

"We would download mails and then immediately disconnect!"

It made sense to have a leased line, but in 1996-97, the Pondicherry Department of Telecommunications (DoT) was clueless.

"I knew that IT companies in Chennai had leased lines so I went there, got the application form and gave it to the general manager in Pondicherry DoT."

He said, "I will get back to you."

After a long wait, the leased line was granted. At such times, did it not seem like a good idea to shift back to Bangalore?

"Never. Actually, the most important thing was that we had my in-laws support in Pondicherry, to take care of my son."

Even the extended family was very helpful. When Sriram tried to rent his first office, the landlord said, "You are new in business – we can't trust you will pay on time."

It was the recommendation from a relative which sealed the deal. Similarly, when the company applied for a loan, Karnataka Bank asked for collateral. That condition was waived when Anu's cousin signed as the guarantor.

Integra's struggling startup phase lasted 3 years. Despite pumping back all that they earned into the company, there were no profits. At one point, Anu's jewellery had to be sold, in order to pay the salaries. An initial partner decided to quit and pursue further studies, while Sriram and Anu plodded on.

In 1997, finally, Integra broke even, then came the growth phase.

"Initially, you are hands-on, now we must learn to delegate. Otherwise it will be a bottleneck…the company will not grow."

Sriram's focus shifted to acquiring customers. Sensing potential in outsourced publishing, Integra began participating in the prestigious Frankfurt and London Book Fairs.

"I used to try for appointments, but often I did cold-calls."

At the very least, such gatherings yielded a goldmine of company brochures, to follow up on email. It helped that publishers were warming up to the idea of outsourcing their grunt work.

India scored on cost as well as quality. What's more, Indian companies were ready to take on large volumes of work.

"In business, there will be a lot of new opportunities but you must stay focused on the one you want to grow. "

"DTP outfits in foreign countries are mostly mom and pop shops, with 10-20 employees. We were ready to keep expanding."

The company also got into some new areas such as advertising and software development. But too many pies only make for sticky fingers. Sriram quickly realised that it was not possible to manage so many diverse activities.

"We decided to focus only on our core business of outsourced publishing."

With this resolve, Integra grew by 70-100% year on year between 1997 and 2002. There were some hiccups, like the sudden departure of one of the company's 2 biggest clients. But captain and crew held steady through the storm.

"We fought hard and acquired new customers."

By 2003, the company had over 400 employees working across 14 different buildings in the Jawahar Nagar area of Pondicherry. The locals started calling one of the crossroads, the 'Integra Street'.

The premises were not fancy, just existing houses converted into offices.

"We did not even have air-conditioning facility at that time. Just basic tables, chairs and computers."

The work was also quite basic, in the beginning. The client would provide design specifications – typesetting and layout was handled by Integra. But, like Oliver Twist, hungry companies started asking for 'more'. It started with one client outsourcing 'core' activities such as copy editing, indexing and proofreading. Critical areas, with no room for error.

"We had no experience but we did have one employee called Daisy who was an excellent proofreader."

Daisy volunteered for the project and, working with the client, understood the ins and outs of the job. She subsequently set up the entire unit. Sriram realised that he would need many more Daisys, to take the company to the next level. With this in mind, Integra had set up a training facility in 2001.

"Initially, we took 'freshers' on board as employees and trained them free of cost. But anything free is not taken seriously."

The company then started a certificate course where candidates paid a fee to join. Employment is offered to deserving candidates, on completion of training. The duration of training ranges from 6 weeks to 12 months, depending on the complexity of the task. Copyediting is the most technical role requiring higher English-language proficiency.

90% of the staff is from Pondicherry while 10% are from surrounding areas.

"We preferred locals at that time because people from big cities expect a higher salary. Also, they may not fit in with the culture and values of the company."

As the company was growing rapidly, Sriram took the help of a consultant to help put in place an HR policy.

"My goal was to hire good people, people smarter than me. Especially in areas like finance where I am not an expert."

A quality-control consultant was also hired, to make homegrown methods more robust. A central quality team was set up to conduct regular process audits, as well as check random samples of completed work.

Along with intellectual capacity, a company must build its physical capacity. The search for a 'good office' began way back in the year 2000. But unlike Chennai, Bangalore or Mumbai, there was no readymade building you could just walk into.

"We did not want to block our money in construction activity but we had no choice!"

A one-acre plot of land was purchased and loan sanctioned. The *bhoomi puja* took place in 2003, but the 60,000 sq ft facility took 3 long years to complete.

"We had some objections from neighbours, we had to get numerous approvals... One has to be patient!"

"If you can provide a good ambience in office, staff is motivated and ready to extend more time on the job."

Working with an architect, Sriram was personally involved in designing each and every floor, nook and corner. Picking the right contractors and consultants for electrical and civil work was one of the major challenges. To hire one, you need to meet and study detailed estimates from at least 3. Sriram's modus operandi was to finish all the regular office work and then put on the 'construction worker' hat.

"I used to work with my team on all these issues from 8 pm till midnight. Those days were really crazy but exciting."

In January 2006, Integra's stylish new corporate headquarters on Pondicherry's 100 Feet Road was finally inaugurated. The staff was thrilled to move to modern workstations and a pleasant environment.

"We specifically chose colours which help concentration and are good for the eyes."

The building also has an atrium or *Brahmasthaanam* as per Vaastu Shastra, which is said to create positive energy.

"We had 800 staff back then, but planned such that we can expand up to 2000."

An entrepreneur 'sees' that which is not visible. He sees through the mind's eye. While many make business plans, few make a vision plan.

"It is my habit to scribble down 'what I want in life'. Even when I was a young engineer, just joined the company, I had written how and when I will either become the CEO, or start my own venture."

Those handwritten notes still exist. Plan A, Plan B, how many years, what you need to get there.

"Frequently dreaming...that's what the plan shows."

It's the same story with his own company. Imagining the future, creating in the present, building on the past. The entrepreneur must juggle all 3 balls – in every day and every moment.

"By 2006-7, we were a US $6.5 million (₹30 crore) company. Investment bankers began calling."

As a 100% export-oriented ITES unit, Integra enjoyed tax exemption. Working with reputable foreign publishers, there were no bad debts and few delays in payment. Working capital and term loans had already been secured from Canara Bank and State Bank of India.

"When any investor called, I would say, 'Not interested'. I thought why waste their time and my time in having a meeting!"

This attitude caused some to label Sriram as 'arrogant'.

"I thought, okay, let me have a face to face meeting and then say 'no'," he chuckles.

However, the market was changing. The publishing industry was seeing numerous mergers and acquisitions and customers started expressing concerns.

"We are giving you a large volume of work but there is so much competition...will you be able to stay in business?" they asked.

Sriram decided it was time to 'think big'.

"I decided to take some money and go for aggressive growth."

Many publishing companies are niche players providing high-end value-added services. But such companies cannot grow very fast. This makes them a target for acquisition.

"We decided to go for scale. Instead of somebody trying to buy us, we will go out and acquire other companies."

Sriram's vision of becoming the 'No 1' player in the world attracted investment from Baring Private Equity. The fund acquired a majority stake in Integra in early 2007 and the business went into hyper-growth mode.

In such a mode, there is bound to be learning and unlearning.

"Sometimes we'll miss on timely delivery or quality takes a hit. That is when we started spending more time and attention to process stabilisation."

"You can either be a niche player or a scale player. We decided to go for scale."

Continuous innovation became the need of the hour. An R&D department was set up by Sagayaraj, a key manager. Its task is to develop software for work-flow management, production tracking and order delivery. Such that customers can see, in real time, how the job is getting done.

The second focus area was automation.

"Wherever people are doing mundane work, I decided we should automate."

Take citations in scientific journals. You can write a software program which automatically checks for references at the end of each article. The program also verifies that first name, last name and year of publication appear in the format specified by the publisher.

However, machines cannot take over when it comes to the 'language' portion.

"Copy editing is bound by rules yet it needs human judgement."

Judging where to take your business is also an art. Sriram realised that although Integra was working with almost all the major publishers, the company was handling barely 2-5% of their outsourced workload. Whereas in his judgement, a client could outsource 20-25% of such activities to any one vendor.

"You have to engage the customer and align with their requirements."

The beauty of this approach is that you don't need to constantly search for new customers. You can grow by serving your existing client-base better.

"The same companies who once treated us as a supplier, began seeing us as partners."

With higher levels of trust and collaboration, customers began to outsource more and more of their core activities. At the same time, Integra decided to expand its customer base beyond Europe and beyond STM (Scientific, Technical, Medical) publishing.

"We decided to enter school and college market, as well as trade publishing."

To make this happen faster, Integra acquired 2 US-based publishing companies. One of these is the Chicago-based Elm Street Publishing, which caters to the college textbook market.

"When our US customers wants to know whether we are 'onshore' or 'offshore', we can say 'both'."

These acquisitions also enabled Integra's entry into content creation and editorial development, which require higher skillsets. Even in Europe, Integra decided to expand its portfolio by adding more languages.

"For 14 years, we worked mainly with English language publishers, maybe a little French. Then we started hiring people to handle Italian, German, etc."

The advantage of Pondicherry is that it attracts numerous foreigners. Hence hiring 'native' speakers was not very difficult. Integra now handles work in 7 languages, with a core team of 14-15 multi-linguals.

In 2007, Integra also started recruiting senior professionals – such as a CFO and Head of Global sales & marketing. Getting such employees was a big challenge.

"First of all I had to sell our growth story. Then I talk about the future – that we will acquire companies, we will go for IPO. We also have an Employee Stock Option Plan (ESOP)."

The idea of working for a young and dynamic company is attractive. But location is a stumbling block for many.

"They live in gated communities, their children study in IB or ICSE schools. When they visit Pondicherry, they feel it will be difficult to adjust."

Ultimately, some do take that leap of faith. Their cultural background, work ethic and experience enrich the boardroom.

"I learn from my managers, we grow together as a company."

Cultural differences also come into play with acquired companies. Integra has retained the original teams, with mostly American employees. Their style of working is more independent.

"Each time you have to learn something, you will make mistakes... How you are able to fix that is the key point. "

"In the US, initial agreement will take time, but then we need not supervise. In India, they will quickly agree to 'everything' but require constant supervision."

However, Indian workers are capable of multi-skilling, i e, handling 4-5 tasks at a time. In the US, you rarely get that. Understanding such differences makes integration much smoother.

However, the path to progress can never be completely smooth. In 2008, like all outsourcing companies, Integra was impacted by world events. There was a dip in the bottom-line as well as increased pressure on pricing.

"When we started the company, we had high-profit margins – 30-40%. Now, because of cutthroat competition, margins are slim."

Even so, clients demand further reductions.

"We have to work hard to convince them otherwise because if we reduce further, the business is not sustainable."

Another area of concern is attrition. With Chennai becoming a hub for outsourced publishing, Integra is an ideal poaching ground.

"Few of the other companies want to invest in training."

Yet, Integra continues to build on its reputation and expand its business. By March 2011, the company had clocked revenues of ₹68 crore and a 1000-strong workforce.

Along with growth, employee welfare has been a priority. More than 60% of Integra's employees are women, and this is no accident. Special attention is paid to the problems which prevent women from performing at their best. This starts with something as basic as a health check-up.

"Many women were complaining of fatigue. On conducting blood tests, we found that many are anaemic."

Juggling family and work commitments is the other big challenge.

The company offers flexible working hours and a daycare facility on campus to enable young mothers to return to work. A 15-member team headed by Anu mentors female employees on a regular basis.

"Women are very sincere, very competent, but they don't want to take promotions."

To encourage them, the company has training programs as well as personal counseling. These efforts were recognised when Integra won the award for 'Excellence in Gender Inclusivity' from NASSCOM in 2009.

"My goal is to have 50:50 at all levels. I want a mix of people – male, female, rural, urban, local and from all parts of India. That will bring in new ways of thinking."

In its own small way, Integra has brought in new thinking into small-town life. Ministers and babus often put in *sifarish* (requests). "Please give so and so a job."

There is a clear policy to deal with such requests.

"You can recommend 100 people and I am willing to take them for training. But unless they clear the test and interview, I cannot give them a job."

One time, a candidate recommended by a sales tax commissioner did not pass. When he was refused a job, the commissioner made his displeasure known by conducting a raid on the company.

"Yes, it was a harassment but we are extremely transparent, we have nothing to hide. The case was withdrawn.

On paper, anyone can have principles. What matters is sticking to them, when the going gets tough.

Over the last 2 years, the company has moved from books, journals and data conversion into e-learning and multimedia

"I want to be number one in my business, but my ultimate aim in life is to get enlightenment. "

"My ancestors did a lot of social work, I too am giving back to society through the Sriramchartiabletrust.org."

services. Ranked in the Top 10 globally, there is still some way to go to reach the No 1 spot.

After 19 years in business, Sriram still keeps a punishing schedule. 30% of the time he is travelling, meeting clients. While in Pondicherry, he is in office from 9 am to 9 pm. The goal is to cut down these hours, with more delegation, more handover.

"In the first few years, I gave 24 hours to my work, including holidays and weekends... Now at least I spend weekends with family."

Anu leads a more balanced life. She handles the important portfolios of Finance and HR but makes it a point to go home at 3 pm every day when her younger son, Advaith, comes home from school.

"She couldn't do that with our elder son, Dhanvin, and feels bad about it. So those 2 hours in the evenings she may still work, but from home."

On the one hand, there is business development, on the other, spiritual development. Every morning, Sriram spends half an hour doing yoga and pranayama, followed by transcendental meditation. Only then does he read newspapers or check email.

"That's how I am able to manage all my stress."

Sriram also has a spiritual mentor, who he met right after college. He speaks to his guru almost every evening, seeking guidance in all matters.

"It has nothing to do with astrology, Guruji believes each one must take his own decisions. But he is my inspiration and support."

There are different paths to enlightenment – Bhakti Yoga (the path of devotion), Jnana Yoga (the path of knowledge) and Karma Yoga (the path of action). Sriram believes he is on the path of Karma Yoga.

An employee once remarked, "Sir...we are all working for you."

Sriram replied, "No... *I* am working for you."

Working to ensure a salary is paid, to every employee. And working for the greater good as well. Once he achieves his business goals, Sriram says he will shift his focus more and more towards philanthropy.

"I have already set up a charitable trust which is working in areas of healthcare, women empowerment and education, in the rural areas."

In the last 2 years, Sriram has also become a weekend farmer, converting a barren piece of land into a lush green haven. Using organic methods of cultivation and percolation ponds to recharge the rainwater.

"This is a sustainable, model organic farm – anyone is welcome to visit us and learn how to replicate these methods."

An enterprise is but the planting of ideas. Sow your seeds and tend them wisely – to reap a bountiful harvest.

ADVICE TO YOUNG ENTREPRENEURS

You must first start dreaming. Have dreams both in your professional life and personal life. First you must dream, then you must do. Put your vision on paper and then focus on execution.

Keep looking at your plan, your vision – see whether you are on the right track. Is there anything you need to do for course correction?

Thirdly, you must unlearn and learn…this is a critical phase. For example, you will be a doer when you are in the startup phase and must be hands-on with everything. Then you will move to continuous growth phase or high growth phase.

You have to let go of the work you once did and learn what is required for the growth phase. Or you will become a bottleneck and the company will get stuck.

Patience is required. Sometimes you have to make mistakes, learn from the failures.

Success will be the next phase. It will happen.

GENIE IN A BOTTLE

Sandeep Kapoor – Perfume Station
Jodhpur (Rajasthan)

From a dream job with ITC, Sandeep Kapoor spread his wings to Russia and then China. In 2010, he returned to his hometown, Jodhpur, to set up retail outlets for perfume, aimed at the Indian middle class.

In ancient times, young men in search of adventure set sail on merchant ships. To one day make a truimphant return, laden with spices, silk and gold.

Young men continue to seek adventure, far from the land of their birth. Sandeep Kapoor is one such 'mariner'.

He set sail from his native Jodhpur, a city of majesty and royalty. But with no 'future' for a man of ambition.

"I joined my grandfather's photography business in Kanpur, and then stayed on because of other opportunities."

The big break came when Sandeep landed his 'dream job' at ITC. The tides of destiny led him to a company in Moscow, where he got into the business of perfume. The winds of commerce then took him to China.

Ultimately, he returned to Jodhpur, with a fragrant new idea. A retail outlet for high quality, affordable perfumes, aimed at the Indian middle class.

The first 'Perfume Station' was launched in Jodhpur in 2010 and was a runaway hit. The brand is slowly expanding into other similar-sized towns.

"I see a lot of potential in 'B' and 'C class' cities, that's where my market is."

Because young people everywhere have hopes and dreams. Some will set sail in search of adventure, but many will seek fortune beneath their feet.

Because opportunities are now there, just waiting to be found.

GENIE IN A BOTTLE

Sandeep Kapoor – Perfume Station
Jodhpur (Rajasthan)

Sandeep Kapoor was born in Allahabad but grew up in Jodhpur.

"My father was a chemistry professor in the university and my mother was also teaching in the home science college."

Sandeep completed his schooling in Kendriya Vidyalaya (Central School) and then attended Jodhpur University, where he completed his Master's in Economics. After graduating, he joined his grandfather's photo studio, a well-established business in Kanpur.

"It was quite famous in Kanpur. There was a saying – 'If a girl is having difficulty getting married, she should go to Chitra Studio and get her photograph taken'!"

Apart from the studio itself, Chitra had exclusive distribution rights for Kodak and Konica films in UP.

When Sandeep decided to join the business, he imagined a cushy life as the owner's grandson – sitting at the cash counter, ordering people around. What *dadaji* did was put him on 'cleaning duty' for the first 3 months.

"I later understood that he wanted me to grow from the ground up…which was indeed very good for me. I still follow and respect that way of working."

At Chitra Studio, Sandeep learnt the basics of business. How to run a small organisation, deal with people, how to keep a team together like his grandfather had – for 50 years.

"I also learnt a lot about photography itself. Since that was my hobby, I enjoyed my work even more."

But after about a year, Sandeep grew restless. The young man and his grandfather had different ways of thinking, about the future, about how to run the business.

"I decided it was time to go out and explore the world."

Kanpur was a city of industry and opportunity, a city where he could find a job. Instead of waiting for advertisements to appear, Sandeep would simply go from office to office, carrying his CV.

"I would try to meet the branch manager, talk to him and keep following up."

That's how Sandeep landed his first job selling paints for Goodlass Nerolac, in 1985. The salary was ₹1200 per month, the lessons invaluable.

"Tough selling and tough living is what I learnt in that job."

Travelling across rural UP to sell paint is not easy. The market is extremely competitive, the distributor literally makes you wait for hours, especially when you go to collect payment.

"I used to stack paint cans, help out in the shop while I waited for hours. This is how I learnt the art of patience!"

Sandeep also learnt that the best way to sell a product is to know everything about it. So he studied everything he could about paints and painting.

"To convince someone else, first you have to convince yourself."

Every tour mean a trip to the railway station. On the way to the station, Sandeep would notice the ITC office and think to himself, "Now that's a company I should be working for!" So one morning, he walked into the ITC office and handed over his CV. As luck would have it, there were some vacancies.

"I was called for an interview and offered a job, the very next week!'

ITC was a much bigger organisation with a very different working atmosphere. Seniors took juniors under their wing and taught them the ropes. Ozair Ahmed, branch manager, Kanpur, was a mentor to Sandeep.

"His ability to handle people, take quick decisions and get out of any problem impressed me. I learnt a lot, working with people like him."

Above all, ITC was a 'school of marketing'. A new product launch included everything from hoardings, in-shop POP, free sampling and consumer interaction. Sandeep enjoyed all this action thoroughly. In 6 short years, he got a record 4 promotions. Everything was going very well but, along came a new opportunity.

"I spotted an advertisement in *Business India* magazine – a company in Russia was looking for a general manager for its tobbaco business."

It was a large sales and distribution company by the name of Agio Counter Trade PTE, owned by an Indian in partnership with a Russian. The company did not manufacture anything – it imported everything from tobacco to garments and electronics.

Russia was an exciting market in 1993 – it was just opening up. In fact, there were certain peculiar opportunities which it offered. India and the USSR used to have a rupee-rouble agreement. This allowed India to buy defence equipment in rupees. The rupees were used by Russian importers to buy goods from India.

When the Soviet Union broke up, India owed the USSR a lot of money. The debts were distributed to the various newly formed republics and to individual factories.

"It was my job to talk to the plant management and say that you need to recover 'x' amount of money. The government has allowed this payment to be made in the form of goods. So, we would give them goods, they would sell that and recover the money."

Thus, Sandeep's job was to bring in container loads of saleable goods from India. The tobacco division somehow never came up but the experience was exciting enough. In fact, the very day that he landed in Moscow in September 1993, there were tanks on the road.

"I thought – oh my God! Where have I come!"

"Working with ITC was my most important phase in life – it taught me sales, marketing, people relations. More than a job, it was a 'learning school' for me."

Mikhail Gorbachev had been ousted, rival factions were battling for power. However, the real difficulty for an Indian in Moscow was not the politics – it was the weather. Impossibly cold!

"Language was another issue – hardly anyone spoke English so I was forced to learn Russian."

By 1995, Sandeep was no longer enjoying his job. He missed the professionalism of ITC and decided to pack his bags and return to India.

"My old bosses said they'd be happy to have me rejoin the company."

Sandeep was now in exit mode, spending his last few days in Moscow. One evening he was having dinner at an Indian restauarant. There was another Indian seated at the next table.

"We greeted each other and started talking."

Dinesh Singh was representing a company called Starion International, a British-Indian-owned company in the UK. The company manufactured perfumes which it exported to Russia and was, in fact, looking for a general manager.

An informal 'interview' took place over dinner and by dessert, Sandeep had a job offer.

"I joined Starion as head of the CIS operations. I worked with them for about 8 years and that taught me everything about perfumes."

Making perfume is no 'rocket science' – it's basically a mixture of alcohol, water, fragrance oil and certain stabilisers. Most companies use French fragrance oil as it adds value in the customer's eyes. But the kind of perfumes which Starion manufactured and sold were essentially mass-market.

There is no 'brand' here, the perfume should smell nice and bottle should look nice. But pricing is *the* most important thing.

"Essentially, people buy one expensive brand and use it on a special occasion, but on a daily basis, they would use our perfumes."

Eventually, Starion decided to export the perfume in bulk-packaging to Russia and get it filled locally. For this task, Sandeep found Tamene, a Russian of Ethiopian origin, who was willing to set up a factory.

In 2003, the Russian offered Sandeep an equity stake in the factory, which he accepted. The time had come to quit the job and go into business.

"I was looking after the whole factory in terms of manufacturing, sales. I was contacting the clients and getting orders to make sure we were running at full capacity."

The clients were all large wholesalers and some of them also required design services. They would come and say, "I want a new perfume in musk."

Sandeep would put together a turnkey solution – concept, bottle, cap and formulation. While he handled the front-end, the Russian partner managed the back-end. In particular, complying with the laws of the land. Running a perfume factory in Russia requires a license, as the product contains 75% alcohol.

"Actually, the alcohol is 'denatured' so that it's not drinkable."

Yet, in rural areas, people were actually consuming it like alcohol. Because a litre of eau de cologne was cheaper than a litre of vodka. To curb this, the Russian government came up with strict new laws in the year 2005.

"This affected our business very badly. Ultimately, we decided to shut down the factory."

At that time, the busines (York Transnational) was worth about $10 million (30 million bottles) a year. But shutting the factory didn't mean shutting the *business*.

"We went to the guy who was our alcohol supplier and struck a deal with him – take our equipment, make our perfume."

"The engine of the economy today is B and C class towns. Our franchise business is picking up from the smaller towns – Jaipur, Jodhpur, Udaipur, Ajmer.

Freed from the hassles of production, York could now focus on sales and marketing. Finding new clients, bigger orders and new concepts for perfume. In order to remain cost-effective, the company also started importing bottles, caps, spray nozzles and other components from China.

"We were dealing with an agent but there were a lot of quality issues. So, in 2006, I decided to visit China myself."

Sandeep landed up in Yiwu, a vibrant trading hub 300 km south of Shanghai. The city is a vast 'global supermarket' which draws traders from all over the world. It made sense for York to set up its own sourcing office with local staff looking into quality control. In fact, it made even more sense to start manufacturing perfume in China itself.

Once again, the company chose the contract-manufacturing route.

"We supplied the design, the formula as well as the components – their job was to assemble and fill the bottles."

The plan was to now start exporting to more countries. York began taking part in various exhibitions such as the Canton World Fair 2008. At the fair, Sandeep secured his first client from the United States. Packaging and formulations had to be tweaked a little to suit this market.

"Russians like very gaudy designs and fruity, lemony fragrances, while Americans like simple designs and mild perfumes."

On the other hand, in countries like India, people prefer deodorants to perfumes, because they are available for as little as ₹150. In fact, whenever Sandeep visited, he was struck by how expensively perfumes were priced – out of reach of the average consumer. What's more, the buying experience was not very pleasant.

"I was standing in a store in Jodhpur and I just wanted to test a fragrance. The shop boy came running and said, 'No no, do not open it'!"

Sandeep realised there was a gap in the market. There should be a store where people can walk in, smell various perfumes and buy them at an affordable price. And where better to test out this concept than in his own hometown.

"In 2010, I set up the first 'Perfume Station' retail outlet in Jodhpur, as an experiment."

To manage the finance and logistics of the project, Sandeep roped in his elder brother, Piyush. A chartered accountant by profession, Piyush used to run his own paint factory which he had recently sold, in order to lead a peaceful, retired life.

"I managed to get him out of retirement and into the thick of this new venture!"

The very first 'Perfume Station' outlet was launched with FM radio advertising and TV actress, Kavita Kaushik, cutting the ribbon. The shop stocks perfume and only perfume – rows and rows of it. Prices start at ₹250 and go up to ₹1000.

"Nobody is going to disturb you, you can try as many fragrances as you want. We also have trained consultants who provide assistance."

People liked the concept and the store broke even in its second month of operations, with sales of ₹3 lakh per month. The perfumes are shipped from China to Mumbai, and further to Jodhpur by road transport. These are the same products which York sells in the US, Australia, Hong Kong, Russia and Singapore.

"For the Indian market, we have an exclusive 'Archie' range of perfumes which we have licensed from Archies comics."

Sandeep believes that the perfume market will grow exponentially over the next 5-10 years so it makes sense to start creating a national retail chain. While most brands prefer the 'trickle down' effect and first launch in metro cities, 'Perfume Station' has gone the opposite way.

"We have started franchise outlets in Udaipur, Jaipur, Ajmer, Aurangabad and Vijayawada."

With 6 stores now operating, 'Perfume Station' is clocking revenues of ₹8-10 lakh per month. And the plan is to continue expanding – the target is 50 outlets in 3 years.

The model is profitable because the outlets are not located in malls, where rentals are high.

"However, we are experimenting with the idea of small kiosks inside malls."

Interestingly, it is the big cities which are posing a bigger challenge. A franchise store which was set up in north Delhi, near Delhi University, did not click with customers.

"We faced 2 problems – people are more brand conscious and fake branded products are easily and cheaply available!"

However, 'Perfume Station' has not given up on the city. Another outlet has been set up in west Delhi's Rani Bagh, a haven for budget-conscious shoppers. In fact, even the failure of its first store in Delhi has been an important lesson for the company.

"We realised that in big cities, people will pay 4-5 times more for a brand-name perfume. So we have decided to make these products available in our store as well."

And there are bigger changes afoot as well. York Transnational is shifting its manufacturing operations as well as its export office to India. There are 2 sound reasons for this: costs have increased in China and, with the fall of the rupee, exporting from India is more lucrative.

However, Sandeep has no plans to set up his own factory – he will continue to rely on contract manufacturers.

"I realised one thing, it is best to concentrate in the area you know best. Ours is a sales and distribution company, running a factory will dilute that focus."

This approach allows you to remain a very lean company. With an employee strength of just 10 people spread across India, Russia and China, York is doing a business of $15 million – with 50% coming from Russian sales and 50% from exports to other countries.

"With our Yiwu office moving to Ahmedabad, I will be in India more often. So more attention on growing our business here as well!"

Life had become a little too hectic for Sandeep in recent years. Travelling between Russia, China and India meant little time for anything apart from business. He now wants to get back to photography and make more time to enjoy '80s and '90s music and jazz.

A man can travel the world but his heart still wonders – where is 'home'.

"Sometimes it all gets too much and when I fill up the form at the immigration, they ask me, 'Which country do you belong to?' "

Beyond narrow definitions of nationhood and manmade barriers on maps. The citizen of the future is a citizen of the world.

ADVICE TO YOUNG ENTREPRENEURS

Keep your ears and eyes open, look for opportunities and go for it! And, yes, it is hard but the best part is, if you enjoy what you do, it will feel easy.

PLAY STATION

Virat Khutal - Twist Mobile
Indore (Madhya Pradesh)

In 2009, Virat Khutal started a company to make mobile games and, in a short time, achieved remarkable success on Nokia's Ovi platform. The enterprise is now focused on the android market and dreams of creating the next 'Angry Birds'.

Indore is a city of 'bijness'. Everyone is buying or selling *something* – from cement to pharmaceuticals to the famous *namkeen sev*.

The typical white kurta-pyjama and *bahikhaatha* (accounts book) has been replaced by pant-shirt and computer terminal. But, at its heart, Indore retains the 'trader' mindset.

That's what makes Virat Khutal's story so different and interesting. His 4-year-old gaming company is like an ant riding up an elephant. But the audacity and velocity of his journey makes me go, 'Wow'!

When I first met Virat in 2011, he was flush with his first early success. Indore-based Twist Mobile had been invited to speak at the Nokia world conference. To share a stage with EA and the creators of Angry Birds!

Yet, the young entrepreneur could not help commenting on the exorbitant price of coffee at the Trident Hotel.

"I hate this corporate bullshit," he said. "I always prefer to travel by bus from Indore to Mumbai."

Two years later, I meet Virat to get a 'status update'.

Everything has changed.

Twist Mobile has got venture funding, it is more structured and scientific and catering to a completely different market. But what about its soul? And the young entrepreneur himself?

Virat 2.0 orders red wine with authority. He speaks like a man who has experienced more in 2 years than many of us do over a lifetime. This personal expansion and growth is reflected in the trajectory of the company.

"In the mobile space everything changes in 6 months. 2 years is a lifetime!"

To stay in 'bijness', you have to be agile and mobile. Discard old ideas and practices yet retain your values.

"I still travel by sleeper bus from Indore to Mumbai, whenever I can!"

For even as you create a better version of yourself, never lose sight of the original. Version 1.0 where you started your journey – as a 'common man'.

PLAY STATION

Virat Khutal - Twist Mobile
Indore (Madhya Pradesh)

Virat Khutal was born in Rau, a village 14 km from Indore.

"My father was a farmer but later shifted to the construction business."

Virat studied at St John Higher Secondary School, near his home. At the age of 12, he joined the prestigious Indore Public School but he wasn't too serious about studies. At home, it was pretty clear that marks did not matter – ultimately he would be joining the family business.

"I took this as an excuse to often bunk classes and hang out at my dad's office."

The only subject he enjoyed in school was mathematics. And extra classes for learning computers after school. Not surprisingly, Virat scored a very ordinary 57% in the Class 10 board exam.

"It was only after that I became a bit serious."

Although Virat's heart lay in Computer Science, his dad pushed him into Architecture – a useful degree to have in the construction business. So Virat spent the next 5 years at IPS Academy, Indore, studying for BArch.

Virat's biggest success in this period was winning the Annual

National Design Competition, held across 120 colleges. But it was not enough.

"In third year, I realised that I am not going to continue as an architect... I don't enjoy this field, I won't be any good at it."

By this time, the family construction business was also in shambles. The mindset had changed – taking up a job seemed to be a better option. But not in architecture.

In 2001, Virat completed the BArch course but never registered himself with the Council of Architecture. Instead, he went to Pune to do Master's in Computer Management.

"I wanted a college where attendance was not compulsory."

PICT (Pune Institute of Computer Technology) was one such place. Virat attended just a few days in the entire semester and sat for the exams. The rest of the time he was busy doing his own R&D.

"At that time my family was supporting me... Even after MCM, I continued my own work. I did not take a job."

Virat's routine was a little weird. He would be tinkering around, working on programs, until 4 am. Then sleep till 12 noon. Eat, read newspapers till 4 pm. Again sleep and wake up for dinner. These experiments continued for a year and a half, when he and his buddy Kapil finally decided to shift from Pune to Delhi, to take up a job with a company called System Life Cycle.

"Actually, I had made a game based on an ant colony and proposed to the company, 'Let's get together and help sell it'."

Instead, they offered him a job at ₹17,000 per month. Which was pretty good for a fresher, back in 2004-05.

"By this time I was single because my girlfriend left me...she thought I was aimless and crazy and would never change."

The irony was that the girl fell for Virat because he was 'different' and 'exciting'. But then, priorities change and you have to adapt yourself. To new people, new situations, new ways of work.

From PCs, games were moving to the mobile platform. Virat realised it was time to join the mobile bandwagon. An advertisement on naukri.com caught his attention. Gameloft, one of the world's leading mobile game developers, was setting up an office in Hyderabad.

Virat applied for the job.

"I cleared the test, which is normally meant for Computer Science guys."

The salary was a little better – ₹22,500 – but Virat had a blast. Yet, he left after just 6 months.

"I had made a lot of friends and contacts and decided to work from home again…on my own ideas."

Within a year he had run out of money, so Virat once again joined Gameloft. This time as a 'Game Designer'. As a developer, Virat was coding to specification. As a designer, he was *giving* those specifications. Imagining how the game would be played.

"I grew up playing Prince of Persia so to work at Gameloft – a sister company of Ubisoft (which created Prince of Persia) was a dream come true."

A rival company tried to lure Virat with a better pay package – he refused. The work at Gameloft was that good. But then, problems started. An important project got delayed and Virat refused to pass the buck.

"I am protective of my team…I took responsibility. I was fired."

Virat asked to be relieved immediately.

"I didn't want to do 15 days' notice, I said, let this be my last day."

In November 2007, Virat went back to Delhi, where his good friend Kapil Raj was still working. At age 27, he was back to square one – sitting in his bedroom, tinkering with programs. Doing what he loved best – dreaming up new games.

And what did Virat's family think of this career path? Weren't they worried about his future….

"Of course…but let's be clear. If you want to do something, you have to 'kill' your parents."

Not literally of course, but kill the expectations they have for you. Otherwise, your own dreams will die, before they *ever* see light of day.

> **"I have been programming from fifth standard... I wrote a software when there was no Photoshop, no CorelDraw!"**

Kapil (working part-time) and Virat (working full-time) started 'Twist Future'. The company started licensing content from abroad and publishing to Indian operators. But this was a very low-margin business. A second revenue stream was making mobile apps. This involved 'client servicing' – which Virat hated – and work which was neither challenging nor creative enough.

But, they had no choice.

In any case, before the company could really take off, Virat's father passed away suddenly. He returned to Indore, to be with the family.

"I also agreed to get married, for my mother's sake."

It was an arranged match but, like everything else in his life, came with a twist. At the first meeting with Pallavi, Virat learnt that she was just 19 and still studying in college. His mother rejected the girl saying that she was 'too young'.

But Virat and Pallavi had hit it off so well, he insisted he could marry no other girl.

"I was earning barely ₹10,000 a month from Twist Future...but she liked my ideas and had faith in me."

On his part, Virat insisted she not give up her studies, even after marriage. Right after their honeymoon, she got busy with her second year BTech exams while Virat went right back to being a 'struggling entrepreneur'.

The struggle was a choice, not a compulsion. Virat's family owned a whole lot of property. Why not simply use that, make the path easier?

Because, a company which lasts is built on blood and sweat.

"The best part is that my parents didn't give me money to do business. If they had, I would have become spoiled and very easily satisfied."

Virat continued with Twist Future, working from Indore. But he was feeling restless – for something more. A business idea came from Achal Choudhary, owner of the well-known IPS Academy in Indore and a family friend.

"I want to start a new college which teaches game development. Will you join this project?"

Virat agreed but the idea did not take off. The fees were too steep, the concept too radical. But Virat had a Plan B – mobile games. The low-hanging fruit for any entrepreneur is to be a service provider.

"Isn't it better to make your own products and try to rule the world?"

Friend and business partner, Kapil, had no objection to Virat starting a new company whose mission was to develop and publish its own games. Thus, in January 2009, Twist Mobile was born with Achal as partner and investor.

It wasn't a very formal, structured investment.

Mr Choudhary simply said, "Every month, whatever money you require, take it from me."

Virat hired one developer and one person to keep accounts. Office space and computers were provided by Choudhary. The question was – where do you start? At Gameloft, Virat could simply focus on building a game. Here, it was much more complex – dealing with everything from selecting the right idea to finding a platform to publish on.

"I met a lot of people, pitched ideas. I hired someone to help with marketing."

Initially, Twist Mobile tried to sell mobile content to cybercafés – that did not click. To stay afloat, Virat agreed to work with Webdunia, a portal run by the local newspaper *Nai Dunia*. Twist Mobile would create BREW games, for use on CDMA phones. Webdunia acted as a 'middleman' and published these games to operators.

Since no money was given to Twist Mobile up front, there was no 'risk'. When there is no risk, there is little hunger for return.

"We worked on revenue-share basis and hardly earned anything."

In the first 6 months of operations – from March to November 2009 – Twist Mobile lost close to ₹7 lakh. All of it, put up by Choudhary.

"I used to share clothes with my brother, then we became rich. Then once again we lost it all. Money comes and goes, it is not everything."

The company had 5 employees, including developers with 2-3 years experience. The total salary bill was ₹60-70,000 per month.

Virat himself took no salary at all.

In desperation, Twist Mobile started making mobile apps for clients such as Zee Studio and Chevrolet. But Virat was beginning to lose hope.

"We launched a car race gaming – it made just ₹3000. I began to doubt whether any money could be made from games."

In December 2009, came a turning point. Virat attended a Nokia conference in Bangalore. Meeting developers from across India and listening to their experiences Virat realised that making games *had* a future.

You just have to find an idea which clicks.

For Twist Mobile that idea came in the form of an idea from a client.

An agency called and asked, "Can you make an app which shows how a person will look after 30 years?"

"Sure," said Virat.

As the project required heavy image processing, he quoted a price of ₹9 lakh. The client did not give a go-ahead. But by this time, Virat was sold on the idea.

"This sounds interesting to me also...how will I look 30 years from now?"

Virat decided to go with his gut-feel and develop the app independently. A task which took 2 months.

In May 2010, Twist Mobile released 'Age Effect', an app which allows the user to upload a photograph and see it morph into what you will look like – after 30 years. The app was first published in Israel and got an astounding response, with 1000 downloads in a single day. Customers paid $3 each, with Twist Mobile making a cool ₹50,000.

"We got the app published in Israel through a middleman but he was a very good, very fair guy. He shared the online reports, he did not cheat us."

The 'Age Effect' app brought in a total of ₹7 lakh for Twist Mobile from Israel. It was subsequently published in India, but it didn't achieve the same kind of popularity.

"I realised that India is a market where paid downloads don't really work."

So, how does the developer get compensated? *That* was the million-dollar question.

"Companies like Gameloft spend ₹1-2 crore to create a single game while we had a very small budget."

The rule of thumb at Twist Mobile at that time was – no app should cost more than ₹80,000 to produce. An experienced developer, working with an artist, tooks around 45-60 days to create such a game. The trouble is, you never know *which* game would work.

"We got excited by the success of 'Age Effect' and produced many more apps. But they just did not click."

Around this time, Virat bumped into Dippak Khurana, a common friend and founder of the ad engine company, VServ.

"Why don't you try and monetise using in-app advertisements?" suggested Dippak.

It was a good idea but there was a problem. Virat didn't have the bandwidth to do the additional coding. However, VServ had already built a technology called the AppWrapper. A software which allowed developers to easily integrate ads into any application.

"Give me one app – we'll put it online and see the numbers," said Dippak.

The very first 'Wrapped App' was uploaded on the popular app-sharing site, GetJar. The app was downloaded 300 times, free of

"Even when I was not employed, I worked 14-15 hours a day. Working was fun, it was never a chore."

cost. Yet, because of the ad inserted into the game, Twist Mobile earned $3 in the form of 'micropayments' via user clicks.

"It was so exciting watching the live report… I will never forget those 3 dollars!"

Virat had a 'eureka' moment that day.

"The word 'free' is very powerful. Free content attracts eyeballs… you can reach not thousands but millions of people."

Even a penny or two per user adds up to a large sum.

On MobileNine, a website offering free apps, Twist Mobile games quickly got 1.6 million downloads. That's when Nokia took notice and approached the company. On 21 March 2011, the first free 'wrapped app' from Twist Mobile was published on the Nokia Ovi store.

"Adopting the ad-wrapper technology was a turning point for us... it changed everything."

From July 2011, Twist Mobile started making $1000 a day in revenues. Virat stopped taking on client projects, to exclusively focus on original games. One of the most successful such games was 'Psycho Hunter'. The actual game involves hunting a deer. But *how* you play the game throws up a fun analysis on what kind of person you are.

"This was an idea I had 5 years ago…when I used to eat, sleep and play a lot of games!"

Launched on 15 August 2011, Psycho Hunter achieved 1 million downloads in just 15 days, the fastest in Ovi history. Other popular Twist Mobile apps in this period included 'Sketch Effect' (converting a photo into a sketch) and 'Shade Effect'. Both were created from the same gaming engine as 'Age Effect' – a smart use of resources.

While most developers were focused on smartphones, Twist Mobile took a different approach. Like Nokia, Virat believed that even users of the cheapest and simplest phones could be consumers of games.

"I always used to think of my tea stall guy – whatever app I make, it should be on his phone."

By October 2011, Twist Mobile apps had over 14 million downloads, of which 4.5 million were from India alone. In India, the company had the added benefit of special promotions and visibility on the Ovi store.

"In less than 6 months, we became the first company in Asia to achieve 10 million downloads!"

At that time, out of 4,00,000 developers, only 160 had crossed even a million downloads – across all games. So this was really a very big thing to happen. Virat was invited to speak at the Nokia World developer conference in October 2011 in London. Twist Mobile was one of 3 companies worldwide chosen to make a presentation.

"It was a proud moment when Stephen Elop (Nokia CEO) mentioned Twist Mobile in the same speech where he talked about partnering EA (Electronic Arts) and Angry Birds."

At that time, 97% of the downloads on Nokia's Ovi store were free, the question was how would developers get paid for their efforts? Virat freely shared his experience of selling games with 'ad wrappers', a possibility few developers knew about back then.

"I am very open about sharing what I know. I believe more competition is better for industry, better for our future as a whole."

Virat returned from London, pumped up to expand his 15-strong team to 35. Unlike other small developers, he was clear about one thing – no virtual employees, everyone must be on-site. Daily interaction builds trust, builds skills.

"I constantly provoked my team to think for themselves and I could see the results."

Ideas for games initially came only from Virat. But over time, team members started coming up with ideas as well. When one such game got a million downloads on Ovi it was a 'big achievement'.

More so because Twist Mobile's used to hire purely local talent.

"Ideologically I am very different, so it becomes very complex to communicate with others at times."

"My policy was to hire freshers who are from Indore or MP. Many are engineering graduates, but anyone is welcome to apply."

The same hurdle for everyone – an extremely tough recruitment test, followed by a personal interview to gauge energy and enthusiasm. Hiring the right people is extremely important for any business, more so in a product company.

"I realised that our strength lies in less number of people but more efficient people."

To keep employees happy, Virat had his own set of fundas. People leave for two reasons – for want of salary, or want of respect. The first part Virat addressed through a policy of sharing 10% of the company's profits with all its employees. The second part just came naturally.

"I never sat in a cabin…I never looked or acted like the 'boss', I am just one of the team."

As the boss, Virat kept the longest hour, starting at 12 noon and leaving only at 3 am. The first few hours in office were always spent with the team, solving their problems. Even sitting on the PCs, along with programmers. From 9 pm to 2 am was the time Virat used to work on his new ideas.

"I was always here, even on Saturday and Sunday… But I never forced anyone else."

A leader must lead by example, he must *earn* respect. Because of the quality of work and quality of the workplace, Twist Mobile experienced very little friction and attrition.

The relationship with the angel investor remained equally cordial.

"Every week we had one or two meetings where we discussed everything. And more than just money, Mr Choudhary gave me lots of good advice."

One principle of business Virat learnt from him was: "Never work on verbal assurance. Get it in writing."

On the other hand, a relationship is also about trust.

The arrangement between the young entrepreneur and his investor was simple – each had a 50% stake. But as far as day-to-day operations went, Virat was fully in control.

“I never had to ask before issuing a cheque or hiring an employee. Nor did I have to justify.”

By the end of 2011, Twist Mobile had revenues of ₹1 crore with a 60% profit margin. Yet, Virat remained extremely grounded and cost-conscious.

“It’s very easy to fall in the trap of hiring expensive people, people who join you only for money – destroying the culture of the company you built from scratch.”

Virat’s gameplan was to use the cash to build a second office – either in Vietnam or Philippines. Two major markets for Twist Mobile games outside India. The vision was to build a 100-member team in India and a 50-strong abroad. With such a team, Twist Mobile could move beyond Nokia, to other platforms.

“I realised that we had to start working on Android, BlackBerry and eventually, iPhone.”

The obvious route would have been to take the existing games and adapt them for all platforms. But Virat knew that wouldn’t work.

“iPhone users play games like Angry Birds. The quality and complexity you need to sell in these markets is very different from what we were doing.”

Virat realised he would have to ramp up the team and its capabilities. Get better artists, better programmers, be more professional and more methodical. The company had cash reserves and could fund its own expansion. But to do this well and to do it quickly, he would need more money.

Luckily, Twist Mobile had created some buzz and started getting noticed in investor circles. In January 2012, Matrix Capital Partners initiated talks with the company. Even as negotiations were taking place, Virat accelerated hiring.

“I went to all my friends working with Gameloft and Digital Chocolate and got them on board.”

> **"When I say 'Kill your parents' I mean all the mindsets and the orthodox things put into your head. You have to put them aside if you want to create something new."**

Fortunately, things fell into place quickly. In May 2012, the deal was executed. By the end of June, capital transfer actually took place. In July, there was a public announcement. The original angel investor received a 20X return on his investment and made a graceful exit. The sum invested by Matrix as Series 'A' funding remained undisclosed.

So what actually happens when a small startup gets a whole lot of cash? Well, just about everything.

"Instead of fighting five fires at once, we identified *one* problem and focused on solving that."

To make good games, you need good people. To get these people to work with you, you need a good office. So, that's where it all began – working backwards. Twist Mobile rented and refurbished an office with a capacity of 125. Next, they introduced ESOP (Employee Stock Option Plan).

"I believe in ESOP but I find that, in India, people don't join a company for this reason. A better way to attract them is to give freedom."

Freedom to be creative, freedom to choose the timings you work. But with this freedom comes responsibility. To be excellent and to keep raising the bar of excellence. *Nothing* remains still in the universe of mobility. Today's killer app is tomorrow's 'delete'.

"I meet each and every new hire for a few minutes. Just to see their face, to assess if they can adjust to the culture of 'high speed'."

To drive a company in the fast lane, the one behind the steering wheel must focus on the finish line. Every cog, every wheel must spin together – there can be no faulty parts. Exactly one year post-funding, Twist Mobile has scaled up to 77 employees, but only 4 members of the original team remain.

Virat shrugs.

"Business does not run on emotions. If people cannot deliver, you have to let them go..."

Some who quit even started their own little companies, with one artist and a couple of programmers. But Virat is not worried. In mobile technology, everything changes in 6 months. The only way to survive is to think ahead, to anticipate what's next.

From simple games with a maximum of 10 levels in 2012, Twist Mobile graduated to complex games with 90-120 levels in 2013. Such a game took 3-4 months to produce at a budget of ₹6 lakh. With 10-15 such titles a year, Twist Mobile had become one of the Top 5 developers in the world on the Nokia Ovi store. In July 2013, this segment accounted for over 75% of the company's revenues.

Yet, in August 2013, the company decided to stop producing new products for Ovi and focus exclusively on smartphones. It was simply the smart thing to do. Feature phone users are not fanatic and repeat-users of apps or games. And these entry-level phones are simply irrelevant in major markets like the US.

"Heavy Internet usage is on smartphones. That's what will drive high-quality content – that's where we need to be."

The advice from Matrix was crucial in making this tough, strategic decision.

"I still remember Rishi Navani, MD of Matrix Partners, telling me, 'There is a tectonic shift in the mobile technology space. It will be very hard to catch up for feature phone players.'"

But Twist Mobile is willing to put up a fight. The Android market is far more competitive, more demanding. You have to *earn* visibility completely on the merits of your app.

"We are in a learning phase, understanding what we need to do to push our apps in the Android marketplace."

Virat also believes that in the future, more than advertising, it is in-app purchase which will drive revenues. In-app could be premium content, virtual goods, or subscriptions. Creating such games requires a different kind of thinking.

"See, in India, from childhood we have been taught – don't go

> **"We are not France-driven or America-driven. Creative people join us because they get to do great work."**

for momentary pleasure. But in Europe, everything is about momentary pleasure."

The difference in cultures is reflected in every aspect of gaming. If an Indian creates a shooting game, he will say, let my customer pay for the gun, give the bullets free. In Russia, the game designer will say, give the gun free but let the customer pay for bullets.

Virat's original plan was to start a studio in Vietnam, or at least hire some Vietnamese. However, he found them unwilling to shift to India. Then, he travelled to Russia and things were very different.

"In Russia, people know about India, they have no problem working in India."

In fact, it's relatively tough to get a Bangalorean to shift to Indore but Virat had no such trouble in Moscow. He has hired a talented game designer on a 12-month contract and is in the process of recruiting 6 more. It's also very cost-effective, with high-quality Russians artists willing to work for far less than Indians.

The cultural cross-pollination went a step further when Twist Mobile hired a Greek for the market research function. She came to the company through AIESEC*.

In the past, the company developed games completely on the basis of gut-feeling. Now, it's more structured and scientific.

"We call consumers to our office and ask them to test out games. We take their feedback and incorporate it right from concept stage."

In fact, every aspect of the company's functioning is now more organised. In the first 2 years, employees did not get 'offer letters'. Because such a document did not exist! Now there is an HR manager and employer-employee contract.

Twist Mobile is also investing in technology in order to increase

---

* An international non-profit organisation that provides students with leadership training and internship opportunities (www.aiesec.org).

speed of production. Since there was no one platform supporting ioS, Android and Symbian, the company decided to develop its own tools, using Coco2Dx. No easy task but well worth the effort.

The weakest area of all was accounts.

"Our balance sheet was delayed for one year...we had to pay a lot of interest on our profit!"

With a VC on board, there is a quarterly board meeting and performance review. How are things going, *where* should we be going – problems are debated, opportunities explored.

"I can now understand the difference between professional investors as compared to taking money from your father."

The VC investor is pushy, he is answerable to *his* investors. But he is also aware of the limitations, the obstacles likely to be encountered. The company earned revenues of ₹1.6 crore in the year ending March 2013 and this is likely to stay flat.

"The last one year, we focused on building technology and talent. We will use that to produce kickass games and scale aggressively."

Twist Mobile is in the process of raising series B funding of $6-10 million. The company plans to set up a studio in East Europe as well as increase its marketing and PR spend.

Working with a great 'publisher' – the way authors do – is one way to get credibility and visibility. A little-known fact about the success of Angry Birds is that it was initially promoted by Chillingo*, a publisher with several successful titles and a strong relationship with Apple.

The game, which has been downloaded more than 1.5 billion times, is every developer's wet dream. They know it took Rovio Entertainment 6 years and 51 titles to achieve 'overnight' success. A simple game, using a basic physics engine...somehow it just clicked.

That gives you something to believe in, something to hope for. If a worldwide hit can come out of Espoo, Finland**, just maybe it can happen from Indore too.

---

* Following the success of Angry Birds, Chillingo was acquired by Electronic Arts (EA) for $20 million.

** Espoo is the headquarters of Rovio Entertainment, creators of Angry Birds.

ADVICE TO YOUNG ENTREPRENEURS

My advice would be that first decide – you want to do a job or you want to do business...if you want to do business, be prepared to walk a hundred kilometres without shoes, like I did.

Whether you belong to a rich or poor family, don't take money from family. It will spoil you. Whether it's money from parents or from a job, it's easy money.

If the money is made from business, then you will understand its real value. When you make your own money, use it wisely.

It's hard to find an investor in India but if you do, make your investors happy, make them feel that they are important in the ecosystem. Don't treat them like an investor, in the initial years treat them like mentors. Observe how they made money at their time. Use their strategy, not their technique.

If you are located in a small town, make it your advantage. Apart from salary, in small towns, respect and honour are very important. People work for you because they are treated well.

You can never force someone to work more for you. It has to come from within. If they have a sense of ownership they will stay late, they will work all night to meet a deadline. That's when you will see the magic.

Enjoy the days of struggle. When the times were hard, I had more ideas, better ideas. I was travelling by train, wandering in front of toilets, talking to and observing customers.

Don't get infected by other people's thoughts. Look for inspiration from people, places, from life happening all around you. That will give your product a 'human touch'.

AIR SUPPLY

Abhijit Barooah – Premier Cryogenics
Guwahati (Assam)

A young man returns to India in the mid-'80s with an MS in Chemical Engineering and starts a business in one of the most volatile parts of the country – Assam. Today, his company is helping Oil India save natural gas worth ₹50 crore annually.

In any other part of India, Premier Cryogenics would be just another mid-sized industrial establishment.

In Assam, it is a symbol of hope.

Amidst *bandhs* and curfews, ethnic and political turmoil, it is a miracle to find a company of *some* size and scale. Run by an IIT and US-educated professional who is here because he chooses to be here.

And despite what people say and what they believe, it is possible to do business in Assam.

"Yes, there are bandhs and protests but my factories have not shut for a single day due to these reasons."

In fact, Abhijit took advantage of the locational disadvantage the Northeast is known for, by getting into the right business. When Abhijit began producing liquid nitrogen, companies like ONGC and Oil India – with oilfields in Assam – quickly became his customers.

No doubt it hasn't been easy. The most basic issue was an erratic power supply which affected production on a daily basis. Yet, Abhijit remains optimistic about his home state.

"We have problems here, but if I were to go elsewhere, there would be other problems!"

Positive thinking and positive action have made it possible to come so far. Now, Premier Cryogenics wants to spread its wings and soar above its geography – beyond the cocoon of the Northeast.

But the mission in his mind is much bigger.

"Entrepreneurship is not just my profession but my passion… I want to see many more entrepreneurs come out of this region."

May this land be flooded with ideas. And young men and women, who swim against the tide.

Bandh karo yeh jhagda, shuru karo kuch kaam. (Stop this fighting, let's create some enterprises.)

Peace of mind, peace of business, the people want it and deserve it all.

AIR SUPPLY

Abhijit Barooah - Premier Cryogenics Guwahati (Assam)

Abhijit Barooah was born and brought up in Assam.

"My father was an engineer with the state irrigation department and my forefathers were in the police service."

Yet, from an early age, Abhijit had an inclination towards business. It was a secret ambition, to do 'something of his own'. The young boy was fascinated by his father's cousin, Hemendra Prasad Barooah.

"He was the first person to go to Harvard Business School from Northeast India. My parents always encouraged me – 'You should do something like Hemen *bordeuta.**'"

Abhijit was a good student – in fact, it was the 'only thing' he was good at. He topped the Cotton Collegiate Higher Secondary School in the Class 10 board exam, standing second in the state. With equally spectacular results in Class 12, Abhijit got admission in IIT Delhi to study chemical engineering. The year was 1978.

At one of the first few classes in IIT, the professor asked each student, "Why did you choose chemical engineering?"

Abhijit answered, "I have heard this is a good qualification to have, if you want to start a business."

"Ah," said the professor, "So you want to be an entrepreneur!"

That was the very first time Abhijit heard of this word, which was to define his very life.

---

* In Assamese *bordeuta* means 'uncle'.

"One thing I have learned that to be a successful businessman, you need to know little bit of everything."

But first, like most IIT graduates of his day, the young man headed to the US on a full scholarship. After completing a Master's degree at the University of Rochester, he was keen to do an MBA.

"I got into Wharton Business School, Berkeley and Cornell, but I was fascinated by Harvard Business School and did not want to study anywhere else."

HBS did not offer Abhijit admission because he had no work experience.

"Go and work for some time, come back after 2-3 years, maybe we will take you," they said.

Abhijit took the advice to heart and did a surprising thing – he returned to Guwahati. What's more, he was clear that he would not take up a job.

"I thought I will start a small business and after 2-3 years, I will go to Harvard."

Family and friends were shocked but Abhijit remained unaffected. He started looking around for some 'business idea' – something new, or something for which there is a good market. In this quest, he travelled across Assam, visiting factories and talking to people. One such location was the ONGC operation in upper Assam.

There, Abhijit discovered that a product called 'liquid nitrogen' was being tried out in ageing oilfields, in order to boost production. This product was not available in Assam; it had to be brought all the way from Sindri in Bihar. Liquid nitrogen is not easy to transport and the supply was erratic.

"So then I thought, this seems like a good idea – it's not available here and there is a market for it. That is how I decided on the product."

The project was capita intensive and Abhijit didn't have much money to invest. But he was in the right place at the right time. After long years of agitation and unrest, Assam got a new government in 1985 headed by former members of the AASU (All Assam Students' Union).

"There was lot of talk of how to be self-sufficient and how to encourage local people to get into business. So the government was very supportive."

The idea of an Assamese returning from the US to his home state to start a business was very novel. Wherever he went, people went out of their way to help. In those days, IDBI had a scheme for technical entrepreneurs.

"I got a low-interest loan for ₹10.5 lakh and the government of Assam also gave some equity contribution."

Thus, Abhijit himself had to invest only ₹5-6 lakh out of a total project cost of ₹1 crore.

The very first task was to get land for the factory. Abhijit purchased a small plot in a place called Sivasagar, because it was located near ONGC's eastern headquarters. And ONGC was the biggest potential customer.

"Sivasagar was a very remote area, it still is. But, in those days, we had to travel one hour to Jorhat, to even make an STD call."

The factory took 2 years to be set up. In the first year, it was a single-man venture. Abhijit did everything himself – from typing letters to overseeing the engineers installing the machines.

One of the suppliers remarked, "When I go to install our machine, there are many people – someone handling finance, someone marketing. But here you are the director, you are the producer, you are the clerk – you are everything!"

In 1987, Abhijit's sister, Anamika, was studying for her MBA from Gauhati University. To form a company, you need two directors. Abhijit asked his sister to be the second director and, with some hesitation, she agreed.

In early 1988, the Assam Air Products factory began production. The implementation of the project was relatively easy – machines were available or they could be imported. The real challenge was running the factory on a daily basis.

"I never did a job, so my first designation was Managing Director."

"We had no experience of production, handling machines, breakdowns and what-not."

All the workers were local hands, living 1 km from the factory. Except for one diploma engineer, the rest were just matric or even school dropouts. Many had been working on-site during the civil construction, as daily-wage labourers.

"Those who seemed more hardworking and motivated, we offered them jobs. Probably they had no option but to work with me and I had no option but to work with them!"

Abhijit did try to hire an experienced person to look after production – a gentleman from Kolkata who had taken voluntary retirement from an MNC. However, he kept dithering and ultimately decided against joining. The same was the case in sales. This time, the man did join but quit within a month when he got an offer from an older establishment.

Assam Air Products produced liquid nitrogen and oxygen gas. For liquid nitrogen, there was a bulk customer who was as interested in buying the goods as the company was eager to sell them.

"ONGC people used to keep asking – when will your factory start production? They were facing a lot of difficulty in getting the product from 1500 km away."

Locational disadvantage became an advantage. Abhijit was able to sign a contract worth ₹15 lakh and get a captive buyer, from the very first day. However, oxygen gas was a different story. Industrial oxygen gas is required by small workshops as well as large factories. Then there is medical oxygen, which is widely used in hospitals.

"To reach these diverse customers we needed to do a lot of sales and marketing. Both Anamika and I did that in the initial period."

At that time, a company called Indian Oxygen Ltd was already quite well known. Assam Air Product's strategy was to offer a free trial.

"Take 5 cylinders, use them and if you are satisfied, we will give you more."

In its first year of operations, Assam Air Products did not meet the initial projections but did manage to break even. Slowly, the business grew, with Oil India also becoming a customer for liquid nitrogen. By 1995, Assam Air Products had modest but steady revenues of ₹6 crore. However, the business faced one intractable problem – power.

"When I ventured into Sivasagar, I did not know much we would struggle with this. A factory like ours simply cannot function without good-quality, 24-hour electricity!"

With power failure 8-10 times a day, running the factory at any kind of optimal level was impossible. Abhijit decided to make a thorough study of the situation across the state. Not only did he talk to people, he actually visited sub-stations and asked to see their records. That was the only way to accurately pinpoint how many failures occurred in the last month or last year.

"I probably know more about the electricity situation in different parts of Assam than most people in the electricity board!"

Abhijit came to the conclusion that the best possible power is available only in the capital city. Hence, Assam Air Products would have to shift its production to Guwahati. To do this, a new factory would have to be set up. This expansion was to be financed through an IPO.

"We incorporated a new entity by the name 'Premier Cryogenics' and floated a very small public issue to raise ₹2 crore."

The issue was mostly subscribed by institutional investors such as IDBI (Industrial Development Bank of India), IIBI (Industrial Investment Bank of India), AIDC (Assam Industrial Development Corporation) and NEDFI (Northeast Development Finance Corporation). An investment of ₹51 lakh was also made by the venture capital wing of IFCI (Industrial Finance Corporation of India).

Thus, Premier Cryogenics got listed on the Calcutta and Guwahati Stock Exchange. The expansion also helped Abhijit attract qualified professionals such as Company Secretary Anjan Talukdar, and General Manager Tridib Borah who had worked with Oil India Ltd.

"We hired people who were only Class 5 or Class 8 pass but they had the right attitude and today some of them are my key persons."

"Mr Borah has been instrumental in the growth we have achieved over the years!"

Among many daily struggles, a major challenge which the company faced was supplying high-purity liquid nitrogen to the Numaligarh Refinery (a joint venture of Bharat Petroleum, Oil India and the government of Assam).

"It was a big opportunity but we had never supplied such high-quality products before. When we sent the first consignment we did not even have the equipment to test the purity – and did not know whether it would be acceptable or not!"

The consignment was rejected. The team went back and tried again, and again, until finally, they were able to produce the correct specification and consistent production. With the crucial liquid nitrogen, the Numaligarh Refinery was commissioned in October 2000.

"Due to this, within a month, our plant achieved a 100%-capacity utilisation for the very first time!"

When Tridib Borah later paid a visit to Numaligarh, people came up to him and shook his hand, "Had it not been for you people we would never have been able to commission this refinery on schedule!"

The feeling that you have contributed in a small way to a big project is certainly a good one!

Thus, the enterprise was built project by project, product by product. The Premier Cryogenics unit began functioning in 1996, with liquid nitrogen and liquid oxygen production. In 2003, a 'dissolved acetylene plant' was added, followed by nitrous oxide production in 2011. Now the plant also converts liquid carbon dioxide into CO2 gas and dry ice.

"We have shifted most of our production from Sivasagar to Guwahati. Even within Guwahati we have chosen our location carefully."

The factory is situated at Lokhra, which is just 1.3 km away from the biggest electricity sub-station of the Northeast. Power is no longer a bottleneck. However, the old factory is also being put to use – as a compressing station. The Lokhra factory makes liquid oxygen and it is transported by tanker to Sivasagar. Here, it is filled into cylinders and distributed across eastern Assam.

"The cost of transporting cylinders is very high. Hence, in the last 5 years we have established 4 such oxygen bottling plants."

The plants are located in the 4 corners of Assam – Lakhimpur (north), Silchar (south), Bongaigaon (west) and Sivasagar (east). These plants are not power-hungry and can even function on generator.

The business has some unique aspects, the most peculiar being the fact that 'raw material' is free. Air is everywhere, you simply need the equipment and know-how to extract individual elements. However, industrial gas is classified as 'hazardous' and hence, factories must follow stringent safety procedures.

The other strange fact is that a 7 cubic metre cylinder of oxygen costs only ₹140. However, the cylinder itself costs ₹7000. These cylinders are continuously recycled and must be kept track of.

"Initially, we lost a lot of cylinders as we were unable to monitor our customers!"

The company now classifies clients as 'high risk' and 'low risk' and visits their premises at least twice a year to take stock of its cylinders.

"Only in the last 2 years we have been seriously thinking where we are today and where we want to be... Now we want to go beyond Northeast."

"Assamese people have traditionally been mild-mannered and peace-loving... what has happened in last 20 years is unfortunate."

95% of Assam Air Product's sale is within the Northeast region, where it has a 70% market share. The remaining 5% goes to Bengal, Bhutan and, through a contract with the Indian Air Force, to other parts of India. By 2007, the two companies had achieved combined revenues of ₹20 crore with steady year on year growth of 15-20%. But the company is now taking a whole new direction.

"Recently, we have ventured into a new area of oilfield services."

These services started in a small way when Assam Air Products gave a mobile air-compressor on hire to ONGC in 1997. Subsequently, 2 more such units were hired out. In 2010, the company made further inroads and bagged a contract from Oil India to set up natural-gas compression stations.

"We were given the task of setting up these stations in the marginal oilfields where they were not finding it feasible to do it themselves."

It is common for natural gas of low pressure to be compressed so that it flows smoothly through a pipeline. However, in marginal oilfields where the quantity of gas is small, the gas is simply 'flared' or burnt.

"Our job was to put up compressing stations such that we draw the gas from them at low pressure and pump it into a high-pressure pipeline."

The main bottleneck to do this job is procurement of land. More so, when the contract requires putting up 6 stations in a period of 7 months! At the time of signing the agreement, the team had not identified this crucial resource.

"We thought let's start and somehow or the other we will manage it!"

And that's exactly what they did. You go to a village one day, second day, third day. By the fifteenth or twentieth day, you find someone willing to sell their property. There were some complications – like a court case at one place – but Abhijit and his team completed the project on the deadline, as promised.

Oil India officials were amazed and said, "This is unthinkable – we cannot put up 1 compressing station in 7 months!"

The 6 units have been in operation since May 2011 and 3 more have been added since. These compressors have helped Oil India to stop flaring of natural gas worth ₹50 crore annually. This is not just business but, in a way, national service!

The success of this first-ever, build-own-operate model for compressing operations is paving the way for more such contracts. Another project with ONGC will include not only supplying liquid nitrogen but also providing the equipment and managing the pumping operation. This is also an opportunity for the company to venture beyond the Northeast – into Bengal and Bihar.

"Oxygen/ nitrogen is still 80% of our business but we gradually foresee the oilfield and project services being more and more important!"

In March 2013, Assam Air Products and Premier Cryogenics reported combined revenues of ₹44 crore with a ₹6 crore profit. Which is good but, of late, Abhijit has been asking himself – is it good enough?

"For the last 2 years we are thinking – how can we grow to ₹100 crore, even 1000 crore? We never had that kind of ambition before..."

The future is still being written, but the road travelled so far has its own lessons and learning. Abhijit employs over 400 people, of which 220 are on permanent basis. The work culture of Assam Air Products remains unaffected by Assam itself.

"I am not always thinking about how to take my business forward. I make time and effort to play a role in the community and development of the state."

"Writers, singers and actors get awards – so why not small entrepreneurs! We must recognise and encourage them."

"Even if there is a bandh, we have 99% attendance at our factory... not a single day in our history have we shut down due to any agitation or protest."

However, business does get affected. Due to a bandh, vehicle movement is restricted, customers are unable to function.

"I certainly wish we had peace and stability...our economy would be bigger and better!"

The development of the Northeast is as much on Abhijit's mind as the development of his business. He has consciously taken on a larger role and responsibility, to benefit the community and the state. These include chairmanship of the State Financial Corporation as well as heading the committee which is formulating Assam's industrial policy. Abhijit is also active as a 'voice of industry', working with bodies like FICCI and CII.

However, his pet passion is encouraging entrepreneurship. One such project is a joint venture between the Assam government, CII and Bhartiya Yuva Shakti Trust (BYST).

"I am also one of the promoters in a 'Bamboo Technology Park'. It is a public-private partnership 70 km from Guwahati where we are setting up common facilities for different bamboo-based industries."

All these activities leave little 'free' time. But that's how he likes it. Abhijit's wife is herself an entrepreneur, also extremely involved in her work – 'Kalpana Barooah 91 Degrees' is well known in the region for high-quality exclusive wooden furniture.

Their 3 children are all living abroad. Jahnabi joined Princeton to do her BS in Computer Science, though she shifted to Financial Engineering and finally graduated in Economics.

"But her real interest is in Comparative Religion. She is currently doing her post graduation at the Harvard Divinity School."

Jahnabi's sister, Urvashi, majored in International Politics and Economics from Middlebury College, Vermont, and is a China-specialist. She is now working with E&Y in New York.

"Urvashi has aptitude for business but has not shown much interest to join me yet!"

That leaves Neil, the youngest in the family, who is studying at the United World College in Hong Kong. Abhijit is hopeful that someday, he may return to Assam and take over the mantle.

Which way the river will take – winding or straight – we do not know. We must let it flow, with majesty and intensity towards the ocean, where all becomes one.

ADVICE TO YOUNG ENTREPRENEURS

The world is full of opportunities; today it has much more opportunity than 30 years back. India had never been in a better position than where it is today and young people must definitely take advantage of this. Now we can think in terms of starting a global business, not just a local business. So I would advise everyone, whoever has the inclination, to grab the opportunities.

From my experience, I have seen that if you have the will and if your mind is very clear, intentions are good, everybody will come forward and help. Do not be discouraged by negative news that you hear like corruption or a 101 other problems. In spite of all that, the opportunities are more than the problems.

Those who want to start a business in a region like Northeast, remember that every place has its plus and minus. In other states, the competition is more, here there are many virgin areas where you can enter and do a good business. Since the Northeast is a priority for the government, you also get a lot of concessions and relaxations. So for someone to start, this is a great place. After gathering some experience, you can always venture out in the rest of India or globally as well.

Focus on recruiting the right people and building the right culture from the very start. I look for 3 things in a person – how capable is he, how sincere is he and how much does he need the job. The right 'fit' between a person and a job is the most important. Even today, I conduct the final interview for any candidate myself.

THE HEAT IS ON

Vibhor Agrawal – Multimax Engineering
Meerut (Uttar Pradesh)

IIT-IIM graduate Vibhor Agrawal left a lucrative consulting job to return to Meerut and take over his father's tiny engineering services firm. In 7 short years, he has professionalised the business and grown it 25 X.

Meerut is a town stuck in time. *Chhoti dukaan, puraane makaan*, *aur ek ajeeb sa*, *ruka hua sa ehsaas.*

The English word for it is 'inertia'.

It's as if the Sepoy Mutiny, which almost ended British rule in 1857, was that one, brief shining moment in history when Meerut became the epicentre of India. And then, it went back to sleep, while the rest of the country surged ahead.

It is this lethargic environment that a young man chose to return to. Leaving the buzz of Bangalore city, the fizz of 5-star lunch-meetings and a fat paycheque.

"People could not understand what an IIT-IIM guy will do in Meerut… Surely he has gone mad!"

Yes, the young man was mad enough to take over his family's tiny engineering business. A company whose annual turnover was less than an IIM graduate's salary at Goldman Sachs.

Far from the rarefied world of power-point presentations and XL sheets, Vibhor Agrawal found himself on the shop floor. Re-engineering himself, his company and its outlook towards work.

"People talk about ethics and corporate principles. But standing for something you believe in is never easy."

In the world of contracts and tenders, to keep your quality and hold your price is a difficult proposition. But it is a principle Multimax Engineering lives by.

"People in the industry know that once this company gives its word, it keeps that word."

A solid business is built on solid foundations. In 7 short years, Vibhor has demonstrated that a business can come alive – even in Meerut.

If you put energy and passion into work. Refuse to accept '*sab chalta hai*' (anything goes). That is modern-day mutiny. Freedom from ignorance, from inertia, from sloth.

THE HEAT IS ON

Vibhor Agrawal - Multimax Engineering Meerut (Uttar Pradesh)

Vibhor was born into a business family of Meerut, UP.

"Nobody is much into academics except for my father who studied at IIT Roorkee and IIT Bombay."

As a student of St Mary's Academy, ICSE, Meerut's only convent school for boys, Vibhor was always a topper. He was also the school head boy and won the 'best student' of the school award.

"From a young age, I knew I wanted to be an engineer and nothing else."

This dream was realised when Vibhor completed his BTech and MTech from IIT Bombay in the year 2003. He then joined IIM Bangalore and, after a summer stint at Deutsche Bank in London, opted for a consulting role at A T Kearney. The job was stimulating – as well as cushy – but after a year and a half, Vibhor was restless.

"Every day when I used to read in *ET* about some entrepreneur making it big, I felt I was wasting time doing consulting."

Why build financial models for somebody else's business when you have your own business to run back home? That business was 'Multimax Engineering', a firm started by his father in Meerut in 1979.

"People would say *nahi yaar, sorry aapki company ka naam nahi suna* (we haven't heard of your company so), we would not be able to join."

"Actually, Dad started this business after graduating from IIT but it never took off. So he went into the family business of jewellery retail and Multimax was continuing on a very small scale, on auto pilot."

The idea of going into business had always been on Vibhor's mind, it was only a matter of *when* to take the plunge."

"I consulted my thesis guide at IITB, Prof Uday Shenoy*, who is not only a teacher but an entrepreneur himself. He pushed me to take the step sooner than I had thought."

The immediate family was happy with Vibhor's decision. But the rest of the world was not convinced.

"*Arre*, why did you leave such a good job? Why do you want to get into the headache of a business??"

At that time, Multimax Engineering had a tiny turnover of ₹1 crore, not even one-tenth the size of the jewellery business. But, that was the challenge!

"I decided that I am going to take this business from ₹1 crore to ₹100 crore in 5 years' time."

The journey towards this audacious goal started at the smallest and humblest level. From working on a laptop 24 hours a day, Vibhor had to go to the shop floor and get his hands dirty.

"I relearnt all my engineering fundas in the first 3 months. Incidentally, I am a chemical engineer while our business is hardcore mechanical engineering."

The good news was, there was a basic set-up – an office, a factory, few small clients. The bad news was there was no vision, no goal,

---

* Dr Shenoy co-founded the online education company syvum.com.

no professional outlook, no 'team'. The challenge was to change the typical *'chalta hai'* attitude to a *'chalta nahi hai'* attitude.

With the owner leading by example.

"I started by making small changes, like documenting things in a proper format, teaching people to use the computer for designing and costing."

The second and most urgent concern was attracting high-quality, experienced employees. But how? Gujarat, Mumbai and Noida are the main centres for this kind of industry – few people would like to shift from there to Meerut.

"Plus, I had my own limitations, in terms of budget."

But then any goal is achievable, if you want it badly enough. Vibhor started with posting ads on job portals, scanning applications and calling up promising candidates himself.

"I could not tell them that I am the director calling, because I felt that, you know, they will say *yaar kaisi company hai, director khud call kar raha hai..."(*what kind of company is this where the director himself calls.)

95% of the people he called had never heard of Multimax. And this itself was reason enough to immediately reject the company. But Vibhor wouldn't take 'no' for an answer. He actually went to candidates' homes, convinced them, even promised to take care of admissions for their children in Meerut schools.

"*Main principals se mila, bachchon ke exams dilvaye. Aur prarthna kari ki, bhaiyya, yeh pass ho jaaye nahi to isska father mere ko join nahi karega* (laughs)." (I met school principals, got the kids to take entrance exams and then prayed, that please, you must pass the exams or your dad won't join me.)

Above all, Vibhor explained the difference between working in a settled business and working in a startup.

"I told them what I wanted to achieve and how working with Multimax would be different from any other set-up."

The business of manufacturing heat exchangers and pressure vessels is highly competitive. This equipment is integral to chemical plants, power plants, fertiliser plants, sugar plants and

> **"You have to draw a line, that, okay, this is my *lakshman-rekha*. I will not drop my quality below this level, no matter what the pricing pressure."**

even refineries. Yet companies are shortsighted when it comes to the purchase decision.

"The supplier who quotes the lowest price is the one who usually gets the contract."

To give this price, he will cut corners. Or, go back to the customer after a few months and say, "Sorry this can't be done – unless you pay me more." Neither method was acceptable to Vibhor.

"Our business model is to deliver on quality and on time, while matching the competitor's price."

A tall mountain to climb but first one must reach the base camp – by getting orders. The strategy was simple: visit as many potential customers as possible. Wherever they might be.

Purey desh me jitni refineries hain, jitne plants hain, main khud ek ek mein gaya (All over India, I visited each and every plant and refinery). I made it a point to go everywhere."

Wherever Vibhor went, his IIT-IIM background impressed prospective customers. Initially, he was shy to print it on his visiting card but then realised, it was a way to get a foot in the door.

"I added the words 'MTech IIT Bombay, PGDM IIM Bangalore' under my name and the card itself became a big ice-breaker."

But then, once you are in the hot seat, it's your credentials and your company which ultimately matter. And clients can be extremely ruthless.

After hearing his entire presentation, the purchase head of a large MNC bluntly said, "*Dekho aisa hai, tumhare jaisi pachaas fabrication companies hain. Main kis kis ko inquiries doon, kis kis ko kaam doon*?" (There are 50 fabrication companies just like yours, how many can I work with?)

But Vibhor did not take it to heart. Even as he moved around to get orders, the work of setting his own house in order continued. One important task was converting Multimax from a proprietorship concern to a private limited company. A second one was cleaning, painting and formalising all processes in the factory according to the ISO 9000 framework.

Every small step creating a sense of movement, a sense of purpose within the company. Waiting for a chance to prove its worth.

That chance came from Tata Chemicals. The company had a fertiliser plant in Babrala, a remote area of UP, around 140 km from Meerut. Like dozens of other potential customers, Vibhor paid them a visit. This time, the timing was right.

There was a small expansion project and the head of the project was Mr P K Jain. The elderly gentleman took a liking to the young entrepreneur and allowed him to bid for the project.

"In our business, participation *hi aasani se nahi milta*." (It's very difficult to get a chance to even participate.)

Vibhor put in a lot of hard work to give a technically and commercially sound bid. After the technical consultant scrutinised it and gave his approval, Multimax was given the 'first chance'.

"I was told that our price was 20% higher than the target price set by the company. 'If you can bring it down, we will give you the order,' they said."

Working with his team, Vibhor managed to fulfil that requirement and bagged the order. The real feather in his cap was the fact that officials from Tata came to see the Multimax factory a month *after* signing the contract.

"I could have easily hired sales agents, but unless you first do it yourself, you will not be a depth manager, you will be a shallow manager."

"Every little achievement brings immense satisfaction. Every little challenge pushes me to think for new ideas."

"Normally, in this business, you don't get an order unless the client has visited your premises, conducted a quality audit, met your team, so on and so forth."

It was a measure of the trust that was placed on the young man's shoulders. In fact, when the audit was conducted, Mr Jain was fully satisfied.

"We didn't have a big infrastructure but we had a good team in place. And he said, '*agar team achhi hai, to kaam ho jayega*' (if the team is good, our work will get done)."

Multimax delivered the order on time, along with quality and proper documentation. Tata Chemicals was so pleased that the company sent Vibhor a letter of appreciation.

"I still have it on my laptop," he beams.

In the process, Multimax turnover jumped from ₹1 crore to ₹4 crore in March 2009. And the company also made some profit. Until this point, the focus had been the replacement market. Now, Vibhor decided to enter the 'project' side of the market.

"Meaning, if someone is setting up a new plant and requires 100 heat exchangers – that level of business which we had never done before."

It so happened that Indian Oil Corporation (IOC) had a large greenfield project coming up in Paradip, Orissa, and Multimax secured pre-approval to bid for it. While the total project cost was around ₹30,000 crore, the supply work was split into multiple tenders. Multimax put in bids worth ₹100 crore in these tenders.

Having worked in the replacement market only, Vibhor used those yardsticks to calculate his pricing. Not knowing that project pricing is always much higher, due to more stringent requirements.

"Our bids were the lowest and, like a true PSU, Indian Oil followed the letter of the law. The law states that the contract must go to the lowest qualified bidder."

It was a windfall for Multimax. In a single month, the ₹4 crore company received orders worth ₹40 crore!

And Vibhor was quick to grab the window of opportunity fate had provided.

"Since IOCL has so many departments, nobody realised what had happened. But I knew one day they will wake up and before that we should be fully prepared."

Along with his father, Vibhor quickly met with the bank. On the strength of confirmed government work orders, they secured a line of credit. Machines were bought, shop floor expanded and people hired.

After 3 months, there was a hue and cry at IOCL – at the topmost level. Nobody could explain how such a small company could get such a big order. A committee was formed, to investigate the matter. This committee arrived in Meerut in August 2010 fully prepared to find a small-scale unit with a hundred lacunae.

"*Unhone mann bana liya tha ki hum 50% orders toh raddh kar hi denge, kisi badi sau-do sau crore wali company ko denge.*" (They had pre-decided that they would cancel 50% of the order and award it to a ₹100-200 crore size company.)

But, Multimax Engineering was fully prepared. When the committee surveyed the premises, asked questions, raised doubts – each and every point was satisfactorily addressed. Ultimately, they could find no reason to withdraw the orders.

"Next 2 years, all we did was fulfil those orders! That really propelled us in the market."

"The work culture of our *navratna* PSUs is remarkable. I got such a large contract from IOCL without paying a single rupee to anyone."

"At the end of that project, I had two court cases, a couple of police incidents, and a lot of losses. But *ab mujhe dar nahi lagta.*" (I am no longer afraid of anything.)

The turnover zoomed to ₹9 crore in 2010 and the following year, crossed ₹20 crore. However, the company made no profit. Vibhor had quoted too low a price, because of which he got the contract. But to deliver the required quality parameters within that price was impossible.

"I made a huge mistake…but then you learn only by mistakes."

Luckily Vibhor's father was supportive.

He said, "*Dekho, life mein aisa hota hai… galtiya karogey, seekhogey… tabhi aagey badhogey*." (It happens in life… you have to make mistakes, learn from them, that's how you make progress.)

In tough times like this, it helped that the family had another business to fall back upon.

"Whenever we have been short on money, it is the jewellery shop which has partly financed us, kept us going forward!"

Executing the project brought another set of challenges. Since the workshop wasn't big enough, Vibhor rented another space. Once the jobs were on the shop floor, the landlord became greedy and wanted more payment.

"We refused but he wouldn't allow us to remove our machines from his premises. So we had to go to the police and to the district magistrate."

Ultimately, the case went to court, giving Vibhor many a sleepless night. *Itna bada project leh to liya, ab karunga kaise!"* (I have taken up such a big project, now how the hell am I going to complete it!)

But despite all these tensions, the client was never affected. Multimax earned the reputation of being the most responsive among the fabricators IOCL was working with. Any email received from the 4-5 technical consultants appointed by the client was answered within 24-48 hours.

"In fact, they monitored us very closely and we always welcomed any person who came to see *ki bhai Multimax mein kya ho raha hai* (what is the progress at Multimax)."

When the entire project was completed, there was a sense of achievement. Not only for the top management but down to the last worker.

"*Jin logon ne usko execute kiya* (The people who worked to execute the project), in their own circles, their colleagues in other companies, they still talk about it."

The reputation Multimax built with the IOCL opened up new opportunities in the private sector. Many new clients came on board, but the icing on the cake was the MNC which had once told Vibhor, "*Tumhare jaisi pachaas fabrication companies hain.*" (There are 50 fabricators out there, just like you.)

"A couple of months ago, this company placed a huge order with Multimax. Only because of our credibility."

Kyunki agar Vibhor walon ne kuch kaha hai, to woh deliver kiya hai. (If Vibhor's company has made a commitment, they will honour it). Whether on the employee front or on the client front, even if it results in a short-term financial loss for the company.

"That is the difference between a *lala*-type business and a corporate business!"

In March 2013, Multimax Engineering's revenues were ₹25 crore and the company is no longer in the red. 50% of its business still comes from PSUs, while the remaining comes from the corporate sector. The staff strength has grown from 25 to 224, and Multimax is now a company of choice for prospective employees.

"*Mere ek staff ke bandey ne kaha ki Vibhorji ko dekh kar woh Ghalib ka sher yaad aata hai ki... 'Mein akela hi chala tha jaanib-e-manzil magar, log aate gaye aur karwan banta gaya.*'" (One of my staff members said that I remind him of the poet Ghalib's words – 'I started walking alone towards my destination, people started walking along with me.')

"I sometimes miss socialising with my IIT/IIM friends but otherwise, I am so involved in my work that it really doesn't matter whether my office is in Meerut or Mumbai."

Aur karwan ko aur aage badhna hai. (And the caravan still has a way to go).

Times are tough for the industry right now. There is a slowdown in all sectors, very few new plants being set up. This has affected companies like Multimax. But Vibhor is looking at the bigger picture and planning ahead.

"I have realised that we are a product company. And like any product, there is a growth phase, there is a commoditisation phase, and then there is a decay phase."

At present, the Multimax portfolio is in the 'commodity' phase with many companies in the fray offering the same product. Hence, there is a price war. The way out of this jungle is to continuously think ahead, see what are the requirements of the market and develop more products.

The same plants which need heat exchangers also need many small equipment for piping. These can be manufactured at Multimax's existing factory without any additional investment.

"The only thing that is required is chemical engineering and process designing. Both of which we understand."

Another sector which Vibhor is betting on is natural gas. He believes that, over the next 10 years, it will be the 'next big thing'. Replacing petrol and diesel in cars and LPG in homes. As gas production increases, there will be demand for gas-related plant equipment.

"Those are the products I am now focusing on."

Lastly, the young entrepreneur is turning his attention to exports. The company bagged a small order for a European client which came through a third-party inspection agency. But Vibhor knows that to really 'crack' the market, there is no substitute for legwork.

"I am travelling again, this time to meet companies in the Middle East, looking for orders!"

Business development, project management and HR – these are the domains where Vibhor has excelled beyond doubt. But behind him, like a rock, is his father. Taking care of all excise, labour and all other government and statutory requirements.

"Generation gap was one of the concerns floated by my A T Kearney bosses. However, my father and I have divided work between ourselves nicely."

While there are debates and differences of opinion, there is a healthy mutual respect.

And understanding.

The same goes for wife Garima, a qualified CA who worked with KPMG. She now handles the accounts for the company and often has to point out – "*Yeh number ban nahi rahe hain.*" (These numbers are not adding up.)

And Vibhor will counter – "*Ho jayega.*" (It will happen.)

Just like he convinced her to move to Meerut, in the first place. Born and brought up in south Delhi, Garima was initially sceptical about the idea of shifting to a small town.

"But after a few meetings, she changed her mind."

Just like Vibhor has changed his mind on where he wants to go – in life and business. Ambition, yes, but not at the cost of health or happiness.

"I still want to take my company to ₹100 crore but I know everyone cannot be an Ambani. I don't see success only in terms of 'numbers' now."

And somewhere deep down, this IIT-IIM graduate believes he owes a debt to his country. And that in his small way, he is now 'giving back'.

"If I can run a company which creates 200 jobs, if I can earn foreign exchange through exports… it's making good use of my education!"

Every small town in India needs such young men and women. To lead a small revolution, in their own backyard.

ADVICE TO YOUNG ENTREPRENEURS

I seriously think one should work for few years before taking the plunge. It really makes a huge difference once you've worked under somebody. Plus it makes you more professional, more responsible, gives you a few initial networks to leverage, etc, etc.

If you are doing an MBA, my advice is, select courses that you think will help you become better entrepreneurs. Don't run after grades or CV points which help you get a job.

Entrepreneurship is a seesaw kind of a ride. There are ups and there are downs, BIG downs. When you are in the down phase, don't give up. Persevere.

Many a time I think I've achieved success only to return from near-end point. But with each failure, I am learning and doing it a bit differently next time.

Agar ek baar decide kar liya hai (once you have decided to take the plunge) then don't be in two minds. Don't think about going back to the job ever.

One of my two favourite poems is, *The Road Not Taken* by Robert Frost. "Two roads diverged in a yellow wood. And sorry I could not travel both."

The other poem is, *If* by Rudyard Kipling: "If you can keep your head when all about you are losing theirs…"

Keep these lines in your mind, *chalte jao* (keep going), *kahin na kahin to pahunch hi jaaoge* (you will reach somewhere).

When you do your own business, you may or may not be successful, but it will surely make a man out of you.

THE MILKY WAY

Srikumar Misra – Milk Mantra
Bhubaneshwar (Odisha)

This XIMB graduate had all that an MBA could hope for, but it was not enough. Quitting his job with Tata Tetley in London, Srikumar returned to his roots and to set up a modern milk plant – an 'Amul' for the people of Odisha.

In Odisha, you will find businessmen and you will find mining barons. But you will rarely find an 'entrepreneur'.

Srikumar Misra is one of that rare species.

Like most Oriyas, he aspired to get a good, professional degree and a steady job. But something within him said 'this is not enough'. Ultimately, he moved back to Odisha, to set up his own company.

"People constantly ask me why I left my job with Tata Tetley in London. They can't understand my motivation, my need to do things differently."

In the 4 years since he returned to Odisha, Srikumar has done everything to get his dairy project off the ground, short of milking cows. When venture capital and banks snubbed him, the young entrepreneur decided to crowd-fund his business plan through family, friends and angels.

"The time I spent fund-raising was the most challenging time of my life. But I was single-mindedly focused on Milk Mantra."

In the 18 months since its launch, the young company has shaken up the state-run Omfed. Improved the quality of milk for consumers and standards of living for over 12,000 dairy farmers.

Sitting in the office above the state-of-the-art milk plant on the outskirts of Puri, I see a vast expanse of green. Grass on which cows feast, to give us sweet and nourishing milk.

Ruminate on this miracle. Create one of your own.

THE MILKY WAY

Srikumar Misra - Milk Mantra
Bhubaneshwar (Odisha)

Srikumar Misra was born in the town of Cuttack, Odisha.

"My father was a graduate of IIT Kharagpur and a first-generation entrepreneur. With a lot of struggle, he set up a company called Kalinga Transformers here in Odisha, way back in the '70s."

Srikumar might have grown up without a care in the world, playing *galli* cricket like any other boy in Cuttack. But, in 1985, when he was just 8 years old, there was a bolt from the blue.

"My father died in a car accident and we went into turmoil."

Apart from the loss of a loved one, the family had to face business and legal issues. Srikumar's father had mortgaged the house they lived in to the bank as an additional collateral. This was meant to be a temporary arrangement. However, his unexpected demise complicated the matter.

"The other partners did not get our house released, in fact they ran the company into the ground. So, the bank wanted to attach the property. We constantly had this sword hanging over our heads."

The civil litigation with the bank went on for years together. Even as he was giving his Class 10 board exams, Srikumar recalls running to lawyers and courts. In fact, it was his dream to study at IIT – like his father. But, it was not to be.

"I was spending more time with lawyers than being able to study for JEE."

Srikumar realised that if he stayed in Cuttack, life would continue like this. So he decided to go out, somewhere far from Odisha, to do his engineering. By that time his elder sister was married and settled and his younger sister and mother were supportive. Thus, Srikumar joined D Y Patil College in Pune to study mechanical engineering.

In his final year, Srikumar was preparing for the CAT. But as things would have it, the date of the exam clashed with his final project presentation.

"However I did give XAT and was selected by XIM Bhubaneshwar. So I took that."

An event which Srikumar recalls from his B-school days is the 'India Leadership Summit'. A national-level event held in Mumbai on governance and leadership. Srikumar was shortlisted and travelled to Mumbai to make the final presentation. Competing against students from all across India, he won the top prize.

When he was called on stage to accept the trophy, Srikumar used the platform to make an important point. Addressing CEOs and HR heads of 'Day 1' companies, he said, "I submit humbly, having won this, that recruiters should look beyond the IIMs for talent. Because talent is everywhere."

During campus placement, Srikumar got a job with ICICI Bank. However, he had also applied to the Tata Administrative Service (TAS), which held a national-level selection.

"My CV was shortlisted and then, we went through a rigorous process spread over 2-3 days in Kolkata – GD, in-depth interviews, panel interview."

Srikumar was one of 3 students selected from the East Zone and joined TAS in June 2001.

The TAS induction is a very structured program, where you go to various group companies and interact with their CEOs. Since Tata companies are spread across the length and breadth of India, this becomes a sort of informal 'Bharat Darshan'. You attend classroom sessions at the Tata Management Training Centre (TMTC) in Pune and eat some great food.

But the most important element is the 4 projects you undertake, for 3 months each.

"These projects give you a peek into different industries. At the end of the year, you have a good idea about the sector or the company you want to start your career with."

Srikumar joined Tata Tea, where he had worked on his final project. It was an exciting time, as the company had just acquired Tetley in the UK and was looking to launch the brand in several countries.

"I joined Tetley's global business division in Kolkata and was shuttling around various emerging markets – from Kazakhstan to China!"

In 2002, Srikumar got married to Rashima, a junior from XIMB. A year later, he was posted to South Africa as 'country head'. Which basically meant you had no office, no boss – you were out in the jungle, on your own!

"We were starting from scratch so I worked from home, like a start-up. I set up Tetley's operations from ground up and, in the process, learnt a lot!"

Apart from launching the Tetley brand, another feather in Srikumar's cap was the acquisition of South African tea company, Joekels.

"This was the third largest tea brand in the country, set up by two entrepreneurs. It went on to become one of the fastest growing divisions within Tetley."

In 2006, Srikumar moved to London, to manage a new business that Tetley had acquired in Prague. Two years later, he was asked to head the Mergers and Acquisitions team for emerging markets. The job was an exciting one – identifying innovative, entrepreneur-led companies which Tetley could buy out.

"What happens on a single day in an exam like CAT sometimes affects your whole life. I don't think that's the correct way to decide who is talented."

"As a manager you are travelling business class and staying in 5-star hotels but this is all for something which is not leading to any creation, any other smart guy can easily do the job."

"I got an opportunity to work in several markets across the world. I could see what entrepreneurs have done in terms of creating great food and beverage brands."

This got him thinking about the opportunities back home. Commonsense and experience pointed in one direction: what is happening in other developing markets will eventually happen in India.

"I met two brothers in Turkey – the Karakans – who had set up a $200-million tea business* from scratch. It was quite inspiring!"

Much of the innovation in beverages was happening in the ready-to-drink products. For Tetley, acquisition was not just an engine for growth. It was a way to infuse new ideas into a century-old company. But a smidgen of doubt was creeping into Srikumar's mind.

"Corporates love to talk about entrepreneurial spirit, but, unfortunately, I don't actually see this spirit in any company."

Just 7 years out of B-school, Srikumar was leading the life every MBA dreams of. First, as an expat in South Africa, now in London, on a pound sterling package.

"I was living in Harrow on the Hill in West London, doing very well in my job. Business class travel, 5-star hotels, all of that."

Rashima was also enjoying London, working with a leading education trust. What more could a young couple want?

And yet, Srikumar was not satisfied. Every professional has certain career goals, financial goals but what happens when you've ticked off most of those boxes?

---

* The Karakan brothers' company is called Dogus Cay.

"I realised this would just go on – the next thing and the next thing. In the process, I am not creating anything."

At the same time, Srikumar's gut said that India was a once-in-a-lifetime opportunity. Here was a chance he could not afford to miss.

"From 2007 onwards, I started spending my weekends researching sectors, connecting with people. In fact, I joined TiE London to interact with entrepreneurs."

These interactions made Srikumar sure about one thing – whatever he did, it had to have size and scale. Therefore, it would require a lot of money. But he had no idea how to raise the funds. Around this time, Srikumar heard about a one-week course on Venture Capital and Private Equity at Harvard Business School. He decided to attend it, taking leave from his job.

"I funded it myself but it was worth it. The course gave me tremendous insight into what a VC is all about... That helped me think through how I want to raise money."

Finally, in January 2009, Srikumar put in his papers. By this time he knew that he wanted to create an exciting F & B brand in India. The project must have scale as well as some kind of supply-chain linkage into Odisha. While he explored several ideas, milk was a clear winner.

Dairy is a $40 billion market in India, of which the organised segment is just $5-6 billion. Hence, there is ample scope for a new player.

"Milk is a very old sector, but I felt that a lot of new things can be done with it. In states like Gujarat, Punjab and Andhra already it has happened, but not in Odisha."

"Odisha has no ecosystem to support enterprise. Mostly, we have family business or people making money from mining licenses."

"I selected milk as it was the biggest and most scalable market...there was room for innovation, branding."

What's more, dairy met the criteria of conscious capitalism – of creating an impact within Odisha. Marginal farmers can get a regular income stream from milk, when there is a fair and transparent buyer.

Thus, in May 2009, Srikumar landed in India, with a plan on paper. The project requirement was $5 million (approximately ₹22 crore*). The first and foremost task was to get funding. At that time there had been only one private-equity deal in the dairy industry – Motilal Oswal investing in Pune-based Parag Milk Foods. Overall, there was little interest in the sector.

"I spoke to a few VCs and other investors – most of them wrote it off as a pipe dream. But I had made up my mind, I am certainly going to go ahead and do this!"

Raising $5 million by equity alone was a tall order. Srikumar decided to explore the option of raising some debt. He approached the State Bank of India, Kolkata, where he knew an Oriya gentleman. After studying the project proposal and the promoter's background, he gave a positive response. The bank was ready to extend a loan of up to 50% of the project cost.

With renewed vigour, Srikumar went back to venture capital investors. But the efforts were yielding little result.

"Suddenly, I realised these VCs are claiming to be VCs but all are investing in established businesses doing ₹20 crore turnover, with everything in place. They are not interested in startups!"

An entrepreneur needs someone to *believe* in him. That's why the early investors are known as 'angels'. Who better than your own family and friends to be those angels? Srikumar's first investors were his father-in-law, Suman Kumar Narula, and an ex-colleague from Tata, Sandeep Das.

---

* As per prevailing exchange rate, $1 US = ₹45 in 2009.

The ex-colleague said, "I've always wanted to do something but since I can't leave this cushy life…at least I can invest and live my dream, through you!"

Srikumar decided to first sell his dream to more angel investors. He started talking to his own friends and extended family, to 'crowd-fund' the project. With an investment as low as ₹5 lakh.

But it wasn't just people who knew Srikumar. To raise a large amount, you have to convince complete strangers. After numerous pitches, two individuals from Mumbai Angels agreed to put in their money. Ultimately, a total of 20 angel investors from India and UK came on board.

"This helped me, it made venture capitalists realise – this guy is serious!"

One of the people Srikumar had been talking to was Vineet Rai of Aavishkaar, a social venture fund.

"I knew that my project would be of interest to them since it had a direct linkage with rural development. However, generally they invested in lakhs, not crores."

In this case, decided to raise the bar. Thus, Srikumar finally raised the ₹10 crore he needed in equity funding*. Now, he went back to the bank but there awaited a rude shock. The gentleman who had agreed to disburse the loan developed cold feet.

"I hadn't done any other homework thinking this will work out… suddenly I was back to square zero."

Fortunately, Srikumar managed to convince IDBI Bank. They, too, were reluctant to back a first-time entrepreneur. But looking at his past track record and the equity capital raised, the officer agreed to back the project. The final hurdle was a condition by the bank for significant collateral and 'full personal guarantee' from both Srikumar and his wife.

"I said, 'Look, I have already invested most of my savings into the company so any further collateral will be difficult for me to arrange.' But the bank insisted…"

---

* Stanford has published a case study called 'VC Decision Making Process in India' on the Milk Mantra and Aavishkaar fund-raising.

"VCs told me, 'You have the experience, the background and your business plan is good but it's too early for us to invest.' I was like...that's what a start-up is! What's too early?!"

The last 'buffer' Srikumar had set aside for initial months was also put in. Finally, the loan was sanctioned, completing the first cycle of raising capital. It was January 2011 – a total of 18 months.

During this period, Srikumar made one other important decision – he purchased land for his plant. Initially, he went to the government and to IDCO (Industrial Development Corporation of Odisha), but soon it was clear they would not be of any help.

"I started scouting for a good location which is both close to the milk-supplying villages and to our main market – Bhubaneshwar city."

Finally, he found a parcel of land near Konark in Puri district, which met the criteria. However, the 5 acres consisted of several small holdings – one by one, farmers were convinced to sell.

But this was not the end of the ordeal. Getting farmland converted to commercial use is a long and tedious process. This itself took more than a year.

"Had I waited for the money to come in and then started, the entire project would have been delayed!"

The year 2011 was essentially spent in putting up the processing plant. This involves a complex set of compliances. The much-touted single-window clearance system exists only on paper – in reality you have to run around and deal with 20 different departments.

In fact, when he registered with DIC (District Industries Centre), Srikumar was astounded to receive the registration number '1'.

The officer said, "You are the first medium-scale* enterprise in Puri district."

---

* DIC classifies a company putting up a plant with investment of ₹5-10 crore as 'medium scale'.

Any factory owner will tell you that in India you cannot set up a factory without greasing some palms. The question is how many palms.

"We try and resist such demands. People know it's not easy to ask them for money and get it."

At times, one has to make an appeal to the 'good sense' of the concerned officer. Srikumar recalls the instance where a boiler inspector was delaying approval. Without this approval, a factory cannot start functioning.

"I am going out of station…it will take another 25 days," said the inspector, airily.

"But, sir, we have a loan repayment schedule, I have 20 investors to answer to. This will delay my project by 2-3 months!"

The officer would not relent. After thinking through it for a day, Srikumar decided to approach the seniormost person in the department. After hearing out the young entrepreneur, he agreed to help.

"I will certify your plant myself," he said.

Another time, a senior bureaucrat read about Srikumar's project in a local newspaper. He expressed an interest in seeing the plant. At the end of the visit he commended the young man's efforts and said, "If you face any difficulties, just let me know. I would like to help."

Srikumar promptly took up the offer and the bureaucrat did fulfil that promise.

At that time, XIMB was setting up an incubator. Professor Ramana invited Srikumar to move into the facility. An MOU was signed and Milk Mantra was given office space.

"I did not need incubation as such but having this office took away

"Incubation at XIMB created some buzz which helped us attract talent. We could also involve the rural management students in our extension work with farmers."

"I went to Anand and Banaskantha and saw how much they have developed because of dairy farming. I see no reason why it cannot happen here, in Odisha."

the headache of infrastructure, IT, etc. I could focus on more important things."

Among those things was the challenging task of putting in place the supply chain. Simply put, the sourcing of milk from farmers. Now you may think: I am buying milk from farmers, I am helping in rural development. But what the rural folk themselves want can be something quite else.

"The villages close to the plant actually thought, 'This is some Tata, Birla thing happening. How can we make money out of it?' "

Srikumar and his team went to the village and sat in the *sabha*. The young entrepreneur said, "Look, you might think I am some rich businessman but even my shirt is mortgaged to the bank. I don't have any money to give but yes, I can help you to become dairy farmers."

In Gujarat, the farmers of Kaira district themselves got together and formed the Amul co-operative. Here, there was no such entrepreneurial inclination. The villagers were more interested in getting a job at the plant.

Srikumar realised it would be a slow process to change these attitudes.

"I used to get upset but then I realised they have never seen real development. Someone or the other has hoodwinked them so they only look at the short term, how to make a quick buck."

From the very beginning, Milk Mantra focused on 'ethical' milk sourcing. To head this crucial exercise, Srikumar persuaded his brother-in-law, Ashit, to join the company. A Lt Colonel in the Indian Army, Ashit had taken early retirement and joined the microfinance sector. His understanding of rural Odisha made him an ideal candidate for COO, heading the milk-sourcing operation.

In March 2011, Ashit and Srikumar held a meeting in Subarnapur and Nasikeshwar villages. The farmers were sceptical but agreed to give the newcomers a try.

"Even though our plant was not ready, we decided to start collecting milk. You need to build trust with the farmers, to create supply."

On the very first day, the two young men arrived early in the morning with 2 state-of-the-art bulk milk coolers, with a capacity of 2000 litres each. On that day, they managed to collect just 30 litres. But slowly, collection picked up. Unlike the state co-operative or freelance agents, Milk Mantra was a fair and transparent paymaster.

The company maintains a passbook for each farmer it collects milk from. There is a daily record of how much milk he poured and of what quality.

"The milk is tested in front of him and an entry is made in the passbook, so he knows exactly how much money he should get after 10 days."

This created a lot of positive buzz for Milk Mantra. At the same time, the company began providing extension services such as high-quality cattle feed. This resulted in better yields and better income for the farmer. Tie-ups with MFIs and banks were also undertaken to enable the purchase of more cows*.

"We also started a vet care program and thought of starting artificial insemination, to produce better-quality calves."

The amount of milk collection was steadily increasing but there was still no processing plant to send it to. The only option was to sell this milk to agents. This is when Srikumar realised, first hand, the kind of hardships dairy farmers go through.

Agents operate in a completely arbitrary manner. Suddenly, one day they will tell you, "Your milk is bad, I cannot take it." And they will simply stop paying you.

"I've lost lakhs of rupees dealing with these agents. If they can cheat a company like ours, imagine the plight of farmers…!"

---

* One cow costs ₹20-30,000, it yields 10 litres of milk per day, 8-9 months a year.

"Many dairies add extension services when they have grown to a certain size. We started from Day 1."

At any given time the agent owes the farmer ₹10-30,000. In the hope of recovering his money, the poor fellow continues giving milk. In fact, he has no option. Even the state co-operative is no longer functioning in the interest of farmers. At the village level, the society secretary operates like an agent.

Winning over farmers was one aspect of the milk business but what about consumers?

"I knew that the urban consumer is looking for quality and convenience. So we must put up the best possible, most modern plant."

The equipment was sourced from some of the best companies in the world, through their India offices. In these suppliers, Srikumar found strong technical support. In particular, Anil Burman at Tetrapak provided many valuable inputs. And he continued to do so as an advisor, even after quitting his job.

"I was fortunate to build strong relationships with various people in the industry. They believed in what I was trying to do."

One such believer is Biswajeet Acharya, General Manager, Manufacturing, at Milk Mantra. A post-graduate in dairy technology from IIT Kharagpur with over 20 years of experience at Omfed, Biswajit quit his government job to join the entrepreneurial venture.

"Frankly speaking, I was surprised at the level of knowledge Srikumar had when I was discussing with him," he says. "As well as his commitment."

There was excitement in setting up a 20,000 sq ft integrated Tetrapak milk-processing unit from scratch. The milk comes in tankers, is untouched by hand, and straight away it is pumped into storage tanks, until it is processed and packaged.

"Our homogeniser is an imported one so consistency of milk is much higher. Hygiene is significantly better than elsewhere!"

Before setting up the plant, Srikumar had been to Anand to study how Amul operates, to see and learn from their experience. At the same time, he wanted to create some kind of differentiation. One idea was to launch in bottle format, but that was would add ₹4-5 to the cost per litre, making it unviable. So, then what?

As luck would have it, Srikumar bumped into Satyabrata Mishra of IDMC, a company which specialised in dairy technology and packaging.

"I started working with the company to create an innovation within the pouch format."

Trials went on for 7-8 months. Ultimately, they were able to develop a 3-layer laminate which prevents milk from being exposed to light. This keeps the milk fresh for a longer time. However, the packaging machine Milk Mantra had purchased was not equipped to run this new material. Srikumar and Biswajeet then worked relentlessly with the manufacturer to modify the machine.

"What I am really proud of is that we could introduce an innovation and yet remain cost-effective. Our milk retails at a premium of only ₹2."

The Milk Mantra plant began functioning in October 2011, with the first 2-3 months devoted to pilot production. Now came the ultimate test – cracking the retail market. Srikumar adopted the novel approach of going directly to the consumers, in order to create demand.

"We started the model of direct home delivery, going door to door to explain to customers about our product quality, packaging and so on."

Srikumar's former colleague and investor, Sandeep Das, had returned to India and happened to be in-between jobs. He had readily and enthusiastically agreed to spend a couple of weeks training the sales boys.

Within no time, people were talking about the 'Milky Moo' brand of milk and recommending it to others. Milk Mantra had a base of 2000 households by the time it officially launched! Retailers were now expressing interest in selling this new brand. Milk Mantra quickly appointed distributors for various markets and rolled out in Bhubaneshwar in January 2012. Satyajit Mohanty, joined as GM

(Sales), bringing his experience in the dairy sector in Punjab to the operation.

Initially, Omfed tried to block Milk Mantra's entry into the retail channel. Ultimately, the market prevailed. But sales and marketing remains an ongoing battle.

"Milk requires a cold chain till the last mile, you have to be careful about bad debts. You sell and collect the money on the same day, otherwise it's gone!"

18 months after launching, Milk Mantra is processing 35,000 litres of milk a day, which is approximately 60% of its capacity. The plant is also producing *paneer*, buttermilk, *lassi* and curd. While milk sells only within Odisha, the milk products retail even in Kolkata and Raipur.

The 'taste' is tweaked as per local preference. In eastern India, consumers like their lassi spicy and lassi extra-sweet.

"Our lassi flopped initially because it did not have any essence," laughs Srikumar.

The factory employs 80 workers, of which half are on contract basis. Since there are no other factories in the area, there is no 'working culture'. Late-coming, absenteeism and lack of discipline were some issues which had to be tackled.

"Ultimately, we have to win them over, mould their habits. It's happening slowly, using carrot and stick!"

Milk Mantra closed its first year of operations with revenues of ₹18 crore in March 2013. Srikumar expects to cross ₹50 crore in the second year. The company is still to break even but he is not worried. This is a low-margin, high-volume business which becomes profitable only with scale.

But the impact of Milk Mantra is already evident. The company now has 10,000 farmers in its network. These farmers earn a healthy ₹20 per kg of milk and are no longer at the mercy of agents. On the other hand, Omfed has become more quality conscious. Since Omfed processes and sells 10 times more than Milk Mantra, ultimately it's the consumer who is the winner.

Milk Mantra concluded its second round of funding in February 2013 but to expand substantially, the company will need more funds. Especially for Srikumar's dream project – a milk drink which is marketed nationally.

"VCs & PEs see a big opportunity in the organised food sector, so it is easier for me to raise funds now!"

The flip side of building a large, scalable company in this manner is that the founder ends up as a minority shareholder. Dilution is a painful process but one which Srikumar has accepted. Because he sees value in having a 'small piece of a larger, meaningful cake'.

The pace of work remains hectic, leaving Srikumar with no life 'outside office'.

"Milk is the most intensive sector you can be in! Cows give milk twice a day – we have to collect, process, package, sell and recover our money. That keeps us busy night and day..."

Although Srikumar has given up playing golf, he does make time for his commitments as a fellow of the Aspen Insititute. An international non-profit organisation focused on value-based leadership.

Through all the ups and downs of setting up Milk Mantra, Srikumar had a rock to lean on– his wife, Rashima. In fact, along with professional challenges, the couple decided to take another bold step.

"We had our first baby in June 2009 – a month after we returned – and our second baby in 2011. We discussed it at the time and said, 'Let's take on all the uncertainty we can'!"

Despite this, Rashima took time out to work on all aspects of the Milk Mantra brand communication, centred around the fresh green 'Milky Moo' logo. She also looks after the HR aspects of the organisation.

At the end of the day, a business plan is written on paper but a life-plan is written in the heart.

Srikumar lives in Cuttack, in his childhood home. The home he fought for and finally secured in 2006, through an out-of-court settlement.

Life is not fair. But it is beautiful. Anything you imagine, you can create... If you believe it long and hard enough.

ADVICE TO YOUNG ENTREPRENEURS

Despite all challenges, where we are in India right now is a once-in-a-lifetime opportunity. And if someone strongly believes in the pursuit of creation, this is the right time.

There is nothing more gratifying. I had a pretty successful corporate career but it just didn't seem fulfilling enough. Coming back to a smaller town is a challenge, there isn't a wider canvas to do things. But it's a conscious call.

CHHOTI SI ASHA

Where others see problems, they work on solutions. They are agents of change, harbingers of hope for a new generation.

MAD MEN

Muruganantham - Jayashree Industries
Coimbatore (Kerala)

Educated only up to Class 9, Murugan is a maverick thinker and inventor. Working alone in a modest workshop, he developed a revolutionary machine to make low-cost sanitary napkins. Changing the lives of ordinary women, across India.

Muruganantham is a little mad. Everyone says so, and he accepts it.

"From the childhood I have tried something different. I am away from the normal life. I innovate small-small new things."

Words like innovation entered Murugan's vocabulary very recently. He had no need for English as a workshop helper in the industrial city of Coimbatore. A city of textile mills and auto ancillaries, where a bigger car and a bigger house is the measure of a man's worth. Murugan finds it all very amusing.

"I have many friends who are buying Boleros and Scorpios, wearing big-big chains and they don't put buttons on their shirts. Is that the purpose of the human being life?"

That is mere survival, says Murugan. Educated only up to Class 9, yet he is a thinker, an inventor and a philosopher. A man with a clean heart and a beautiful mind.

It is this mind he applied to solve a problem that affects 90% of women in India. But is never seen, heard or talked about. The problem of women managing their monthly periods. Murugan took up the challenge of making a low-cost sanitary napkin for his wife. Gradually, it became a magnificent obsession. An act of 'madness'.

After years of experimentation and some out-of-the-box thinking, Murugan developed a low-cost machine. His biggest joy is sharing his invention with self-help groups and end-users who benefit directly. In the remotest villages of India and, slowly, across the world.

"I have so many offers by big companies but I don't want money. I don't want Mercedes. I want that 100% of women in India can use sanitary napkin in next 10 years."

In his modest workshop on the outskirts of Coimbatore, he sits at a simple wooden table and chair. Making this grand statement. There is no air-conditioning, but I cannot feel any hot air.

We spend our lives accumulating wealth – material objects which must be left behind.

Maybe Murugan is the sane one, *we* are the ones who are mad.

MAD MEN

Muruganantham - Jayashree Industries
Coimbatore (Kerala)

Muruganantham was born in the village of Pappanaicken Pudur near Coimbatore in Tamil Nadu.

"I was lucky to be born in a poor family. People think it is good to be rich but rich people don't have a real childhood. They don't run behind butterflies or climb the trees like I did!"

As a child, Murugan displayed a keen interest in science subjects. At the Tamil-medium school where he studied, he was lucky to have an encouraging teacher.

"I participated in a school science exhibition and won a prize for a chicken incubator which I had made."

Murugan's classmates were mostly from landed families. He loved visiting their farms, learning about various farm implements and also modifying and repairing them.

"I liked to experiment with mechanical things and moving parts!"

Murugan's father was a handloom weaver but, unfortunately, he was killed in a road accident. His mother Mrs A Vanitha started working on a farm to support the family. Wages were low – just ₹5 a day. Being the eldest, Murugan dropped out of school after Class 9 and started working.

"As a child, I have done many small business like selling fireworks, sugarcane and statues of Ganesha. So I thought I can do something on my own."

Initially, Murugan tried his hand at supplying idlis to factory workers. The venture was successful but the idea was copied. When the competitor threatened his family, the 15-year-old shut the business. He decided to look for a job in Coimbatore – a city of industry and textile mills.

The young man tried various trades but his heart lay in working with his hands.

"I joined a workshop as a helper. Means, not working on a machine, just assisting seniors by buying tea, buying cigarettes…like that."

The adjacent workshop-owner warned Murugan, "Your boss is no good. Don't join."

But Murugan saw it differently.

"My owner is a drunkard…that's lucky for me. I work hard, I learn things and in a short time everybody thinks I am the owner of the workshop."

Like many other small businessmen, the workshop-owner took loans at a very high interest rate. On a loan of ₹10,000, interest payable on a daily basis is ₹100. This workshop owed ₹250 per day towards 'daily collection' as the owner had several loans to his name. But he was usually in a drunken state and hardly bothered.

"Moneylenders saw that I am working, I am repaying the loan. They said, 'Throw out that fellow, you take over the workshop.' "

One day, the drunkard announced he was going back to his village and asked Murugan to take over the workshop.

Thus, one small shed and a welding machine to make grills came into the young man's possession. The enterprise was very small, but it was enough for Murugan. He helped marry off two younger sisters and, finally, got married himself. But his mind was always occupied by small experiments.

"I used to see all grills have same old design, so boring! So I took the *rangoli* pattern and made similar designs in metal."

Murugan's decorative grillwork became popular, yet he never really tried to grow his business in size.

"I never aimed for making more and more money. I don't need a gold bathtub. I want to develop myself."

The one thing Murugan developed early was a personal philosophy of life. As a child, he observed stray dogs in his locality. He wondered where they lived, what they ate? Though he never found specific answers to such questions, a few months later he could see – they had grown, they had survived.

"I understood that survival is automatic, it is natural, it is not in our hands. So every human being should try to do something *beyond* survival."

It was October of 1998, Murugan had come home from the workshop for his lunch and afternoon nap. He noticed his young wife, Shanti, walking across the hall, carrying something behind her back.

"What you are carrying?" he asked.

"It's none of your business!" she snapped back.

This prompted Murugan to get up and run after her. He caught Shanti's hand and saw it was a piece of cloth. So shabby that he would not even use it to clean his moped.

"I understood that she is using unhygienic methods to manage the period days. I asked her, 'Why you are not using sanitary napkins?'"

She replied, "Of course, I know napkin, I watch TV. But if myself and other women in our family start using napkin, then we have to cut our milk budget."

Murugan was intrigued. He went to his neighbourhood medical shop and asked for a packet of sanitary napkins. At the time he didn't even know which brands were in the market, he simply pointed to the most colourful label. The shop girl took the packet, wrapped it in a newspaper and furtively handed it to Murugan.

"I felt like I am carrying a smuggling item."

At home, Murugan opened the packet and discovered that the napkin was simply a 'white bandage'. Holding it in hand, automatically, his brain calculated the weight of the object.

"Immediately I can see it's less than 10 grams and it looks to be cotton."

Murugan knew that 10 grams of cotton cost only 10 paisa. Yet the napkin was selling for ₹4. What a profit margin! He decided to make a low-cost napkin which Shanti could use. There are over 500 textile mills in Coimbatore, so getting the raw material was

> **"I feel sad when I see children in ties going to school in cars and buses. They are living in a golden cage, missing out on the real childhood."**

easy. Murugan bought some high-quality cotton from Laxmi Mills, wrapped it in viscose cloth and, certainly, it looked like a napkin.

"Whenever I made a new thing I would go to my wife and say, 'Close your eyes, Shanti.' Then I give it in her hand. The same way I did for this."

When Shanti opened her eyes, she was surprised.

"See, I made for you. Use immediately and give me the feedback!" said Murugan.

As if the monthly cycle of a woman is timed for experiments in napkin technology.

"You will have to wait for some time," she retorted.

Murugan handed over the napkin and the matter was forgotten. Three weeks later, when he came home for lunch, Shanti opened the door and burst out at him.

"What nonsense napkin you have given to me? It's the worst…I will go back to cloth!"

Murugan remembers this lashing as a 'historical' day. Had Shanti given positive feedback, Murugan would have dropped his research that very moment. Anyone can buy a cotton roll, cut it into a rectangle and wrap it in viscose cloth. But the problem was something bigger, more complex. Now, Murugan was *determined* to get to the bottom of the mystery.

"Like Satyam Raju, I started riding a tiger. My nature is if things become easy, I lose interest. But if it's tough, I cannot drop it until that problem is solved."

Thus Murugan started his research with renewed energy. He made different shapes, sizes and varieties of napkins. But who would test them out? Shanti was available only once a month – at that rate the project would take years! Murugan decided to ask his sisters to volunteer. But they did not take his interest in feminine hygiene kindly.

They called up Shanti and said, "*Anna* (brother) has gone mad. Please tell him not to come to my house until he recovers his senses."

Murugan refused to give up so easily. Where else could he get volunteers? He had a hunch.

"I thought of medical college. Because those girls are studying to be doctors so maybe they will agree to help."

The nearest medical college (Coimbatore Medical College) was 27 km away, near the airport. Murugan hopped onto his scooter and went there. Somehow, he managed to convince a few girls to take part in his research project.

"What do we have to do?" they asked.

"Just give a feedback after using…it's cotton only."

The problem was, even medical students hesitated to have a conversation about their periods. Hence, Murugan designed a feedback sheet. The idea was wonderful, but on the day Murugan returned to the college, he saw 2 girls urgently filling out everyone's sheets. Probably out of courtesy or sympathy but the data was false.

"How can I conduct research on false data?"

Murugan sat in front of the college, sipping a cup of tea. He wondered what could be the way forward. At this point, he was struck by a simple thought.

"I will use the napkin myself."

But how can a man get periods?

"In my family nobody goes for a job…now only I came to know, it is called 'self-employment'."

"Raw material of sanitary napkin is a big secret like Coca Cola formula. That's why few companies have the monopoly on this product."

With a bit of ingenuity and the help of a childhood friend. Murugan asked the local butcher to let him know when he would be cutting the head of a goat. The butcher would ring his cycle bell as he passed by Murugan's house in the morning. That was the 'signal'.

"I go to his shop, fill the hot blood inside an empty football then I wore a napkin. There is a tube connecting my 'uterus' to napkin."

While walking, cycling, going about his work, Murugan would press the bladder and blood would squirt onto the napkin. For 10 days, Murugan experienced what it was like for a woman to go about her daily life during periods.

"My cloth napkin was not doing the job. I became like stinking and my clothes got stained. I understood how much difficulty ladies go through."

The magnificent obsession with sanitary napkins was taking its toll. Neighbours concluded that Murugan was either possessed by a spirit or had some vile disease. Shanti was convinced that Murugan was using the ploy of research to get cozy with college girls. One fine day she stormed out of the house, vowing to never return.

This failed to have any effect on Murugan and his esoteric experiments. With desperation-inspiration, he hit upon a method to get the 'perfect' feedback. Simply collect the used napkin from a lady – it will reveal everything.

"Some are thinking, he is doing black magic, but the medical college girls know me, so they agreed."

The modus operandi was simple: Murugan would supply various napkins along with a black carry bag. The used napkins were to be returned in the carry bag, which he would pick up weekly.

"If I have a French cut or I speak very intelligent, na, they won't help me. But they see me, I am a simple man, not trying to do any *chakkar*, so they say, okay."

There was some method to the madness – napkins were colour-coded, so he could identify who was using which napkin. Along with the homemade napkins, Murugan interspersed branded napkins, to see what is the difference.

"Like that one day I spread all the collected napkins in my house on a table… Same day my mother came to visit me."

All hell broke loose. The old lady was finally convinced that Murugan was indeed mad and declared she would no longer have anything to do with him.

Meanwhile, the experiments were yielding little result. There was *something* different about company-made napkins. What exactly, he could not figure out.

"I sent the Stayfree and Carefree napkins to various labs in IIT, BITS Pilani, SITRA (South India Textile Research Association), etc. For every test I am paying hefty fees – ₹6000, ₹10,000. But all are sending same report."

The report stated that the napkin consisted of a cellulose substance, meaning it was cotton. Yet, no matter what grade of cotton Murugan used, it failed to absorb. Two years went by; finally Murugan reached an important conclusion.

"Those companies are not using cotton…or they are doing some special process on cotton. I have to find out what it is."

After a year and a half of investigation, Murugan realised that the cellulose substance in the napkin was not cotton but wood-fibre. Specifically, pinewood fibre.

"If the problem is tough, you cannot find a single man there…you stand there and you will definitely get an opportunity."

"I was even ready to do the surgery and become a lady to conduct my research! "

"There are no circuits, no coding in sanitary napkin...only the property of raw material. Wood-fibre absorbs liquid quickly and retains shape under pressure. Hence those give better comfort."

So far, so good, but pinewood trees do not grow in India. Murugan realised that he would need to import the material from Australia, Canada or America. This was relatively easy – pinewood fibre is one-fourth the price of cotton and available through the Internet.

Murugan took the help of a professor from the agricultural university to draft a letter and place the order in November 2000. When the Fedex package arrived some weeks later, he could barely contain his excitement. But there seemed to be a mistake.

"I was expecting something like cotton roll, it was just a plain board."

How can one make a soft napkin out of this stiff material?

Every day Murugan would take the board out of the Fedex cover and inspect it, puzzle over it. One day, he accidentally tore off a piece and that's when his heart leaped up. There was fibre inside.

"Immediately I understood the whole secret. But then I found out you need a plant which costs ₹4-5 crore to process the material."

All adding to the ultimate cost of the napkin. So, what was the solution? Murugan spent the next 4 years trying out new and different ways of processing the pinewood board. Through trial and error, *tyaag* and *tapas* he finally cracked the problem.

"I made a small machine in my workshop and with that I am making napkins."

Murugan gave the girls in the medical college these napkins to use. This time, the feedback was very different.

"Anna!" they said. "What happened? This time I tried and I forgot I am using napkin!"

From the 'nonsense' napkin rejected by Shanti to the as-good-as-branded napkin, it was a long journey. Not a few days, or a few weeks, but 4 *years*. The device itself is simple – anyone can learn to operate it within an hour. The first part of the process is 'defiberation'.

"This is a beating apparatus, like a dry mixer. You put the pinewood inside and fibre is separated."

Next, the pulp is compressed into the shape of a pad using an aluminium mould. Thickness can be varied to make either a regular or XL size napkin. This unit is operated by a foot pedal.

The third stage involves sealing the pads in the napkin-finishing machine. In 2005, the cost of the entire machine was a mere ₹65,000. The per napkin cost – less than one rupee.

"I approached IIT Madras and then everywhere in India... The major problem in India is if you don't know English, nobody thinks you are capable."

But someone, somewhere, took notice of Murugan's invention. In 2006, IIT Madras held a competition called 'Innovation for the Betterment of Society'. The low-cost sanitary napkin machine was entered into the contest where it won the first prize.

All of a sudden, everyone wanted to know – who is Murugan?

"Magazines and TV channels were chasing me for interview. Myself I didn't know the difference between ITI and IIT at that time!"

The publicity produced another side effect. Murugan's wife, sisters and mother forgave Murugan for his mad antics. Shanti decided to reunite with her husband and return to his home.

At the same time, Murugan was emboldened to launch his napkins commercially.

"To find a pearl you have to jump in the sea ten times, twenty times, hundred times. You won't find it floating on the surface. "

"I prefer rented house and rented workshop. Ownership is a nuisance and a burden. "

"I tried to come out with my own napkin which is as good as J & J, Procter & Gamble but half the price. "

Murugan's 'Covai' napkins were launched in Coimbatore city in 2006 with a small advertisement in the local paper. But poorly marketed and distributed, the brand flopped miserably.

"I realised the customer thinks if someone is giving 8 napkins for 10 rupees it must be poor quality. I burned my fingers badly and lost ₹50,000."

Murugan suffered this setback in silence. What more could he do? The mighty multinationals were too strong for one man to take on.

"I am having machines and raw material. I gave it to my wife thinking let her at least use it. Maybe 5-10 years she won't need to buy napkins from any shop."

Life once again resumed its routine, Murugan got busy in his workshop. Two months later, Shanti came to him with a strange request.

"We need more raw material."

"But there was enough for 15,000 napkins! What did you do with it?" asked Murugan.

"We are selling napkins," she replied.

"How is this possible?" thought Murugan. "I have already tried and failed!"

Then, he noticed that ladies from the neighbourhood were constantly peeping in from the window. When Murugan was in the hall, they would quietly disappear. But if he was in the other room, they would come inside and take a packet from Shanti. Money was also changing hands.

"5 rupees," he heard Shanti say.

"Why are you selling the packet for 5 rupees?" Murugan asked.

"Oh...you heard 5 rupees? Actually they will pay in installment, weekly 5 rupees. *Seri*?"

Some ladies even stopped by to buy a single napkin. Something no shopkeeper could provide.

This was a eureka moment for Murugan. Finally, he understood *how* he could compete with multinationals. In 60 years, only 10% of India's women had adopted the sanitary napkin. Murugan's target would be the remaining 90% – the bottom of the pyramid.

"My model is one-to-one, here the woman will own the machine. She will manufacture the napkin and sell it to her neighbours."

The whole process of production thus gets decentralised. No transport cost, no hefty profit margin. A high-quality, low-cost product, easily available from somebody I know and trust.

"Actually there are many taboos associated with periods in our country. You cannot change the mindset with a 20-30 second corporate advertisement."

With media and word of mouth publicity, Murugan had started getting invitations to deliver guest lectures at various forums and universities. This was frightening at first as he could only speak Tamil and Telugu.

"I made efforts to learn English...it is easier than learning Hindi, I say!"

Exposure and advice from well-wishers introduced Murugan to the concept of IPR (Intellectual Property Rights). With the help of the National Innovation Foundation (NIF) in Ahmedabad, he applied for a patent. He also received support from the NIF Micro Innovation Venture Fund to fine-tune his machine.

"I added a UV sterilisation unit, calibration for various pad sizes and increased the production rate to target 1000 pads per day."

However, the business model remained unchanged. Murugan refused to sell or license the technology to any large corporate. The low-cost napkin would be of, for and by women themselves.

Each machine is sold on turnkey basis directly to Self-Help Groups (SHGs) and female entrepreneurs. One day training

"I very much like the philosophy of Bhutan. It is the only country which measures the gross national happiness instead of gross domestic production."

and raw material is provided along with the machine itself. M S Swaminathan Research Foundation, All India Woman's Conference, DATA, Malabar Hospital, Community Centre-AAI Delhi, Mandal Mahila Samkiya and Sammilana were some of the early adopters. Companies like Jindal Steel and Moser Baer have taken up the project as a CSR activity in Orissa and Karnataka.

The napkins are sold under various trade names* like 'Easy Feel', 'Be Free', 'Feel Free' (inspired by the big brands) and vernacular ones (Saki, Nari Suraksa, Nalam, to name a few). Priced at ₹15 for a set of 10 pads, the entrepreneur make a profit of 50 paise per pad. Which adds up to ₹3000-5000 per month, depending on how many packets she produces.

"I remember how my mother struggled to earn money... This napkin business is a sustainable livelihood activity for each and every rural woman."

Murugan's goal is to create employment for one million (ten lakh) women. At the micro-level, Murugan's machines have given economic independence to many in need.

"See this lady is in Anantpur, her husband was shot by police, with my machine she can support herself."

Banks willingly provided loans to such women to buy the machine. The product has a regular, captive market and the equipment pays for itself in just 6 years.

By 2009, over 100 napkin machines had been installed in UP, Bihar, Andhra, Tamil Nadu and Haryana, catering to 2.5 lakh customers. But there was a 'bigger' picture in the inventor's head.

---

* A total of 742 brands names are in use in India and 7 other countries.

"In 1960s, Amul created white revolution. I want to create second white revolution using the federation model."

Towards this goal, Murugan has shifted his focus to working with state governments. It started with Uttarakhand, where the government-owned 'Uttarakhand Parvatiya Aajeevika Sanvardhan' bought and installed a machine in Barpur, a remote village in Tehri district.

"This place is 16 hours from Dehradun, you can see Ganga river below. There was no road, we had to take the machine on the back of a donkey!"

Women in this area began using sanitary napkins – for the very first time. Each micro-enterprise also provided employment to 7-8 women. This model was replicated across 22 villages in the area.

At the fifth national awards ceremony for Grassroots Technological Innovations in November 2009, Murugan was felicitated by President Pratibha Patil. The invention was noticed in government and IAS circles. Maharashtra, Gujarat and Chhattisgarh were the states which came forward with the most enthusiasm.

The idea of a 'Federation' model is that, like Mother Dairy and Amul, each state creates and markets its own unique brand. So, for example, all the women under the state scheme in Maharashtra use the brand name 'Nirmal' while in Gujarat, the napkins are sold as 'Sakhi'.

"Gujarat government is supporting very much and I think we will achieve 100% usage of sanitary napkin in this state very soon*. It will be a model for rest of India."

Yet, overall progress remains slow and steady with 947 machines installed by August 2013. Mostly because Murugan believes that means matter as much as the end result. When politicians approach him to order 100-200 machines at a time, he refuses.

"Maybe they give it like a free bicycle, free TV only to catch vote bank. But I don't believe in this 'free' policy. I am particular there must be an end-user."

* At the time of going to print, 55 machines had been installed in Gujarat.

Naxalite and tribal areas are Murugan's pet projects. Even when foundations come forward, he urges them to identify remote villages for his machines.

"Everywhere, ladies are making napkins and selling locally. This is not corporate model, it's national development."

However, there is interest not just from India but Bangladesh, Sri Lanka, Nepal, Mauritius and even distant South Africa, Kenya and Nigeria. The model works everywhere. Murugan is happy even if they buy one machine from him and replicate it in their own country, working with the same non-corporate principles.

Despite name and fame, Murugan remains humble and grounded.

"If you call my office I am only attending to phone. There is no secretary."

The machines are only assembled at the workshop, with 4 helpers. Manufacture of various parts has been outsourced to different suppliers, with specifications.

"Like how they do for Nano car," he grins.

Murugan's Jayashree Industries earns a small surplus on each machine sold*. It is more than enough, he says.

"I have some cost of production, over and above that some need. If I take more than that it becomes greed."

Murugan's logic is simple. The ultimate aim of human life, he believes, is 'enlightenment'. There are many, many rich people in the world, but only a handful of 'enlightened' souls. They renounced the world and its mundane pleasures, went to the distant Himalayas. But Murugan has no such plans.

"See, enlightenment does not come only by sitting in a remote forest…even in your business premises or in your home, you can become enlightened. It's just your mindset."

What do you need to be happy? As a child, you want a chocolate bar. As an adult, you want love, money, name, fame – the list is endless. Murugan needs nothing to be happy. He simply *is*.

"I am happy 24x7. Everything else is additional – this pen, this

---

* In 2013, the machine costs between ₹1.45 lakh to ₹2.5 lakh.

laptop. If I have someone to talk to I am happy, if I am alone I am happy."

A happy man, but with a clear purpose.

"Before my birth only 5 to 6% women in India are using napkin. I make a machine and after 10 to 15 to 20 years all women are using napkin. That's it, my life is over."

The question is, what are *you* going to leave behind? A house, a car, a bank account? Or, an idea that created a small ripple in this beautiful world.

ADVICE TO YOUNG ENTREPRENEURS

The problem with human beings is they are very much afraid for their survival. So nobody is bothered about how to develop, how to achieve. Just buying an apartment in Bangalore, marrying a beautiful girl, having two children, sending them to convent school...they feel it's an achievement. "I have settled down." No, it's actually just survival.

If I ask any student, "What are you studying?" They will tell MCA, MSc, BTech but these are all for namesake only. Finally, what they are going to do? Everybody is trying to make money.

I believe that engineers should try to innovate something in their field. Whatever is your field, you should create something in that.

If you are making a pen, make it very sincerely, better than any other pen. Automatically you get a name. Pen sells in Coimbatore, then adjacent state, then India, then Asia. The money will come as a by-product.

Think creative. What am I doing? I am not making machines, I am giving a solution to a small problem. Like this there are a lot of problems for human beings. You try to give a solution for one problem, that becomes your opportunity. You will stand out.

One last advice is that you must spend only what you earn. Do not go for bank loan, EMI etc, etc. Keep your life simple, your needs simple. You don't need anything to be happy 24x7. That is your birthright.

HIGHER LOVE

Dr Chandrasekhar Sankurathri – Srikiran Institute of Ophthalmology Kakinada (Andhra Pradesh)

Dr Chandrasekhar Sankurathri triumphed over tragedy, setting up the Srikiran Institute of Ophthalmology. Over the last 20 years, this charitable hospital has proven that Canada or Kakinada – excellence has no geography.

No meal in Andhra Pradesh is complete without curd-rice and pickle. The curd-rice is soothing while the pickle can set your mouth on fire.

Dr Chandrashekhar Sankurathri is something like that. He looks mild and avuncular. But inside, burns a fire seldom seen in this sleepy coastal town.

Lush green paddy fields whiz past as you drive down to Kakinada from Vishakhapatnam. The land is fertile, and blessed.

This is the land of Dr Chandrashekhar Sankurathri's birth. Growing up in a poor family with strong values prepared him for the hard knocks of life.

"I understand what poverty is, what suffering is – that is my asset."

Migrating to Canada in the late '60s brought Dr Chandra all other assets – a good job, beautiful house and family. But these blessings were taken away on 23 June 1985, when Dr Chandra's wife and two young children perished in the Kanishka aircrash.

A fire raged in his soul – stoked by bitterness and despair.

Was there even a reason to go on living?

The reason had to be something bigger than himself.

Dr Chandra returned to Kakinada in 1989. Under the auspices of the Manjari Sankurathri Memorial Foundation, he set up the Srikiran Institute of Opthalmology (named after his son) and Sarada Vidyalayam (named after his daughter). Over the last 20 years, these institutions have transformed thousands of lives.

A beautiful framed photograph of Manjari, Srikiran and Sarada adorns the entrance of the hospital. Their presence can still be felt.

Sarada – another name for Saraswati – spirit of the school.

Srikiran – ray of light – spirit of the eye hospital.

Manjari – name of a raga – spirit of this divine symphony.

A music that cannot be heard, but is felt by the heart.

HIGHER LOVE

Dr Chandrasekhar Sankurathri - Srikiran Institute of Ophthalmology Kakinada (Andhra Pradesh)

Chandrasekhar Sankurathri was born in Singarayakonda, in Prakasam district of Andhra Pradesh. But he grew up in the larger town of Rajahmundry.

"I am the youngest of 6 brothers and 2 sisters. My father was a stationmaster, we had very little money but all of us got a good education."

Chandra lost his mother when he was 5 years old and his father soon after. He attended the local municipal school but wasn't a very ambitious student. Neither did he have a sense of 'what will I become'.

"We had a mathematics teacher who bullied everybody. I used to hate him so much, I barely passed that exam. That's how I went to biology after Class 11."

Like all bio students, Chandra initially wanted to be a doctor. But he was just 15 when he completed Intermediate. The rule said you had to be at least 17 to enter medicine. So Chandra decided to do a BSc (Hons) in Zoology instead.

"I could have gone for medicine after BSc (Hons) but by then I didn't really care."

So Chandra stayed on at Andhra University, Waltair (Vishakhapatnam), and got an MSc in Zoology. It was his brothers and sisters who looked after him, helped him complete his education.

"I am very grateful to my family. Everything that I am today, I owe it to them."

While completing his Master's, Chandra was lucky enough to study under an excellent teacher – Dr K Hanumantha Rao. Inspired by Dr Rao, the young graduate decided that he too would enter the teaching profession. He applied for and secured a lecturer's job in Rajahmundry. Only to be quickly disillusioned.

"I wanted to teach many things but I could not find the receptive students."

Chandra resigned and joined the Central Institute of Fisheries Technology (CIFT) in Kakinada as a research assistant. The year was 1965. But soon enough the young man realised that his job consisted mostly of data collection – not research.

"I decided to apply for PhD to a foreign university where actual research was taking place."

One of Chandra's friends had joined Memorial University in Newfoundland, Canada, the previous year. He sent across the address and application form.

"That was the only university I applied to and, luckily, I got admission with scholarship."

Chandra's brothers bought him a one-way air ticket and some winter clothes. Armed with which he arrived in Canada on 29 September 1967.

Canada was very different from India – the food, the culture and, of course, the cold weather. But there was one big advantage of studying at Memorial University. The entire campus was connected by a series of heated underground tunnels.

"We rarely used to go out, so I wasn't much affected by the fog and cold."

After completing his Master's in 1969, Chandra was keen to do his PhD.

He was fascinated by the work of Dr John C Holmes at University of Alberta in Canada. Dr Holmes was an authority in the field of Parasite Ecology – a very hot subject in the late 1960s.

"I wanted to work with Dr Holmes but people thought I am mad to go to Edmonton."

The region is notorious for its extreme climate, with temperatures below zero for almost 6 months of the year. But not cold enough to deter a hot-headed young man.

"Nothing can stop me when I want to do something! Yes, it was 40 degrees below zero in January and February. But it was fantastic experience."

Working under Dr Holmes was a turning point in Chandra's life. Dr Holmes was a man of few words. He would stimulate you, point you in the right direction but never spell it all for you. You had to think and act on your own.

"I really didn't like him at first. But then I started enjoying his style of teaching."

Dr Holmes liked students to address him as 'John'. If you briefed John and he said 'okay', it meant everything is okay. If there is something missing, he would ask questions and in the process of cross-examination you would find out where you were lacking.

"I learnt how to think logically, this has been the most important learning of my life."

In 1974, Chandra completed his PhD. By this time, he had become a Canadian citizen. It had never been his intention to migrate permanently but he had no choice. He had applied for the prestigious National Research Council (NRC) scholarship.

"When I went for the interview, I was told that only Canadian nationals are eligible for National Research Council of Canada funding."

"In India, there is always somebody telling you what to do, how to do it. What I learnt in Canada was how to think for myself."

> **"When I saw those kids wanting to come to school even after working the whole day in the fields, it was a big eye-opener."**

So he did what was necessary and decided to settle down in Canada.

Chandra's first job was with the Pacific Biological Station in Nanaimo, a topnotch fisheries research centre near Vancouver. There were 2 renowned scientists already working on fish parasites. Chandra worked with them as a post-doctoral fellow for 2 years, supported by the NRC. But he didn't get a permanent job at Nanaimo.

In 1977, he shifted to Ottawa to take up a job with the Canadian Wildlife Service.

Meanwhile, Chandra had made a trip to India in 1985 and got married to Manjari, who hailed from Kakinada. Their son, Srikiran, was born in November 1978 and daughter, Sarada, in July 1981. The family led a peaceful existence in a spacious suburban house.

In 1984, Chandra became a Scientific Evaluator with the Bureau of Medical Devices (equivalent to the FDA in the United States). The following year, his wife and kids prepared to leave for India for their annual summer vacation.

"I promised to join them in August so that we could all return to Canada for the school reopening."

But that was never to be.

Dr Chandra dropped off Manjari, Srikiran and Sarada at Montreal airport and drove back home.

Air India flight 182 took off on 23 June 1985 at 00:15 GMT with 329 passengers. At 7:10 am, the plane was close to Ireland and due to reach London's Heathrow airport in an hour and a half.

At 7:14 am, the 'Emperor Kanishka' disappeared from the radar screen at Shannon Air Traffic Control. The plane, and all its passengers, had been blown out of the air by a bomb kept in a suitcase in the forward cargo hold.

There were no survivors.

Air India 182 or the 'Kanishka Bombing' as it came to be known, shocked the world. For Dr Chandrasekhar Sankurathri, there was no world left at all.

For 3 years, Chandra lived in a daze.

"I used to think that, you know, maybe there will be a miracle, maybe they will be found."

When the permanence of his loss became clear, Chandra beseeched God.

"Why me? Why my family? Why take them and leave me behind?"

God was silent.

But a voice from within said, "Go home."

Chandra quit his job, sold his house and returned to India. There was just one thought in his mind – to somehow help children.

"Starting an orphanage was the first thing that came to my mind."

After the aircrash, Chandra had worked as a volunteer with a Canadian organisation which runs an orphanage in India. But he had different ideas on how children should be raised.

"One day I realised, rather than convincing them, why don't I start my own orphanage!"

The place he chose was Kakinada, because that's where Manjari was from.

The first thing he did was to establish a registered charity in Canada in 1989 – the Manjari Sankurathri Memorial Foundation. Then Sankurathri Foundation was registered as a not-for-profit trust in India in 1989.

"Quality and precision are very important. Be it a teaching institution or a hospital, why can't we be the best in what we are doing?"

"You have to be empathetic towards patients, whether they pay money or not doesn't matter. Everybody needs good eyesight...not only the rich."

The next thing Chandra decided to do was build a house. But that wasn't as easy as it sounds. At that time, there were rules against foreign citizens owning property in India.

"I went all the way to Mumbai and met an official in the Reserve Bank. But he wasn't of much help."

Ultimately, he bought land in his sister's name and began construction. The house was completed in 1990 and Chandra moved in.

Right next door was the half-finished orphanage building and some paddy fields. Chandra used to wander around and often came across young children in the fields tending cattle.

He asked them "Why are you in the fields?"

The children replied, "My father brought me here to work."

Chandra asked, "Do you want to study?"

The children shot back, "How can we study? School is in the daytime – when we work."

Chandra said, "Okay, if the school is in the evening or nighttime – will you attend?"

The answer was an enthusiastic 'yes'.

That's how it all started. In January 1990, Chandra started an open-air 'school'. Kids came with a slate pencil and slate. There were no tables, chairs or books.

"I started teaching them Telugu alphabets and basic maths – addition, subtraction. Things they could use in day-to-day life."

The boys and girls were between 5 and 13 years of age. And what surprised Chandra was how eager they were to learn. They never ever missed a class.

"When I was a kid, I don't remember yearning to go to school like this!"

There was a government school close by – a typical setup with 2 classrooms, 2 teachers and 120 children in grades 1 to 5.

One day Chandra stopped a few kids and asked, "Which class are you studying in?"

The children replied, "Class 3/ 4/ 5."

"What is your name?"

"Rajesh."

"Write your name!"

They could not write their own names in their own tongue – Telugu.

Chandra said, "Okay…after school finishes at 3.30 pm, come and meet me."

Around 45 children started coming to Chandra's house every day after school. His sister, Hema, volunteered to teach them. Sitting under the mango tree, children of Class 4 and 5 learnt the basics all over again.

Some dropped out. After a few weeks, 20 children remained.

"Ultimately, they all learnt to read and write properly, became highly motivated to study further and did very well at school."

The impact of this small effort gave Chandra a glimmer of hope. If extra classes under a mango tree could create such an impact, what about an entire school!

Until then Chandra had been toying with the idea of setting up an orphanage. Now, Chandra saw a chance to raise the bar much higher.

"If I have an orphanage, I can help around 30 children in my lifetime but if I have a school I can help so many more."

"When you believe something, you have to put your foot down. You cannot compromise."

"I prefer to hire people just out of the school or college. They are not qualified but I train them and mould them to my mission and my vision."

The building Chandra was planning to use for his orphanage became a school instead. On 14 July 1992, the Sarada Vidyalayam was inaugurated with 25 children in Class 1, and 2 teachers.

"Subsequently we kept adding one grade every year."

Even as the school was shaping up, another issue caught Chandra's attention. An ophthalmologist friend based in the US, Dr V K Raju, used to talk about the large number of blind people in India. According to the World Health Organisation, 80% of these cases were curable.

"My friend used to come to India and hold charitable eye camps but it was very frustrating."

Dr Raju could only visit for a week or 10 days and the problem required much bigger intervention. Even the eye camps he conducted were in makeshift operation theatres, in rented school buildings.

Why couldn't rural Indian have a high-quality eye hospital? Many ask such questions but few provide the answers.

"I told Dr Raju that I was willing to build an eye hospital. Provided he was committed to lending his expertise and ensuring we give high-quality service."

Dr Raju readily agreed. On 21 January 1993, the Srikiran Institute of Ophthalmology started functioning in the same building as the Sarada School. While the school was housed on the ground floor, the hospital occupied the first floor.

"We had about 4,000 sq feet area in all."

The hospital had just 6 support staff and one young doctor – a recently qualified local lad. But word about the hospital quickly spread in Kakinada and neighbouring areas. Patients started coming in large numbers.

"I realised that the school and hospital cannot co-exist in the same building."

A small building near the gate was constructed to hold the classrooms. The old school building became a complete hospital. But beneath the brick and mortar lay the real foundation – of vision, values and principles.

"I was in Canada for 22 years and I wanted to incorporate all the best practices in the school and hospital. For that I needed to have the right people with me."

And get them to share that vision.

Chandra sent the young doctor he had recruited to the US for training. So that he could observe and imbibe the 'best' in the world.

Chandra himself visited Aravind Eye Hospital in Madurai and discussed his project with Dr Venkataswamy.

"He is one of the greatest persons, so very humble. Every time I had a problem here, I would just walk into his office and he would always guide me."

Srikiran Institute of Ophthalmology follows the Aravind Eye Hospital model of high-quality, affordable eye care. Like Aravind, Srikiran Institute adopted the practice of holding eye camps in rural areas, starting with a 50-100 km radius around Kakinada.

"We found that people were clueless. If they can't see they think it is normal – they don't know that they just need glasses."

Srikiran's mission was simple: to provide quality eye care with compassion. Still, for an outsider to come and suddenly win the trust of locals is not easy.

The strategy is to involve the community – first contact the *sarpanch* or a prominent leader and explain the purpose. Ask for a small school building and help in publicising the eye camp, which is always free of cost and open to all.

"On the day of the camp we see each and every person who is registered. Doesn't matter how many there are."

Those who need minor treatment get it on the spot. The rest are taken to Kakinada for further testing and surgery, if required.

"When I see the children, I forget all of it...(*the tragedy*)...that's why I just want to spend more time with them, see them in school, talk to them."

The first free eye camp was held on 20 January 1993 with 54 patients. Among them 18 people were identified with cataracts, but only 11 opted for surgery.

"The rest waited to see the outcome...are these people serious? Are they any good?"

The surgery patients were ferried to Kakinada in Dr Chandra's Maruti Gypsy and later dropped back. The vehicle could carry a maximum of 10 passengers, so often multiple trips had to be made. A bus would have been ideal, but it was expensive.

God answered Dr Chandra's silent appeal when a donation came in 1995 – from Jindal Aluminum. However, even this amount covered only 50% of the cost of a mini-bus.

"Still, we went ahead... I sold my Maruti Gypsy to raise the other 50%!"

Taking patients from their homes to the hospital was an unusual way to function. At that time, Rotary Clubs and Lions Clubs often organised eye camps and conducted operations in rented school buildings and community halls*.

"I felt that's not correct. If the patient has problems, where does he go? How does he know where to go?"

There is also higher risk of infection. Hence Srikiran Institute – despite pressure from many quarters – adopted the better practice. Surgery – only in Kakinada, in the fully equipped hospital.

Another unique practice Srikiran Institute adopted was post-operative follow-up. Even the best eye hospitals believe this is not necessary. If the patient has a problem – he will come back.

* It is illegal to conduct operations in this manner since 1998.

Dr Chandra begs to differ.

"In my observation, only 50% of the patients who have problem come back. What happens to the rest of the 50%? We don't know..."

Going to villages in a bus, collecting patients, examining them and taking them back home is an expensive proposition. But it is a necessary one.

"We wanted to follow up the patients up to the sixth week...this ensured higher degree of success."

The last but important difference was Dr Chandra's decision to provide IOL (intraocular lens implant) to all cataract patients. Even though – at that time – it was felt by many that, for poor patients, glasses were good enough.

"Our IOL implantation rate is 99.9%. The 0.01% is the patient who has some medical reason why we could not put the lens."

This is an astounding feat. In the '90s, the national average for IOL implantation was less than 40%. Even today it is not more than 60%.

So it was an ambitious – and expensive – project. The initial investment in land and building was borne wholly by Dr Chandra. For the first 4 years he also funded the operations.

"I never really planned a budget or worked out financials in great detail. Somehow God is great...we were small, my money was sufficient."

But as the number of patients grew, so did expenses. From ₹20 lakh per year, the budget went over ₹40 lakh. At this point Dr Chandra's well-wishers from Canada stepped in.

"People used to ask me, 'What are you doing?' I told them and I said – if you want to help you can give us small donations."

In 1997, Dr Chandra came across an organisation called 'Help the Aged Canada' which deals with the problems of elderly people. As cataract mainly affects old people, they agreed to fund a project with Srikiran Institute. That contribution of $200,000 CAD was a big boost for the young organisation.

"With this money, we could invest in medical equipment, training doctors and paramedical personnel. It made us strong and confident."

"My son was only 6 years old but he used to say when he grows older he wants to become an ophthalmologist for children... I don't know...why he said that."

For the next 9 years, Srikiran Institute received continuous support from Help the Aged Canada and CIDA (Canadian International Development Agency). The other major donors include Sensor Technology Limited, Canada, Eye care for the Adirondacks, USA and Infosys Foundation, India.

The reason Srikiran Institute needed so many donors or supporters was simple: 90% of the patients were treated free of cost*. And we are talking big numbers. From 475 surgeries in 1993, by 2002-2003 the operations reached a peak.

"We conducted 17,000 surgeries in that year with a team of 5 doctors and paramedical staff. In fact, we became the second biggest eye hospital in Andhra Pradesh."

The biggest hospital – L V Prasad Institute in Hyderabad – conducted around 25,000 surgeries but with a team of 80 doctors and a much larger infrastructure.

"That was our strength – taking very little resources and getting the maximum output!" beams Dr Chandra.

The secret was an assembly-line operation where paramedics handle all the pre and post-operative work. The actual surgery takes only 3 to 4 minutes, with the doctor making a small incision, removing the cataract and fitting the intraocular lens. But the workload is still huge.

"They are all very young doctors, you know, no one ever complained!"

Naturally, there were sceptics. Is it really possible to do thousands of surgeries in a small town in Andhra Pradesh?

Is this for real or some kind of scam?

---

* No other eye hospital in India conducts 90% operations free of cost.

The union health ministry sent a team from Hyderabad to investigate.

"In 2001 they came with a camera to see if we have a building, are we really doing operations?"

The investigators were stunned to find that every operation was documented, every action transparent. Each patient had an ID with his or her home address. All 17,000 surgeries had actually taken place.

This 'character certificate' was important for another reason. Under the National Program for Control of Blindness, Srikiran Institute was eligible to receive ₹750 for every free cataract surgery performed*.

"We were lucky to get the support of Canadian government, Rotary International and other aid organisations. But we were always spending more than we had."

The trouble was, this money refused to come in. A second team arrived from Delhi – senior accountant, junior accountant and an audit. They rifled through ledgers and knocked on patients' doors.

"Did you get operated at Srikiran Institute?" they asked.

"Yes."

"Did you pay them anything?" they pressed.

"Not a single paisa..."

"Did they treat well"?

"Yes, they treated us better than our family members treat us."

With not a speck of dirt to report, the team returned to Delhi. But still, the money was not released. The reason was quite simple.

"You have to grease palms to get the money. We were adamant about not doing that."

Finally, Dr Chandra made a trip to Delhi and took an appointment with Ms Sujatha Rao, chief secretary at the Union health ministry.

She called the people from the relevant department and said, "Dr

---

* The actual cost of a cataract surgery at Srikiran Institute is ₹2500 per patient.

"I want every young child in India to be a volunteer for making a better India."

Chandrasekhar is here – you can ask him anything you want."

There was pin drop silence.

One week later, Srikiran Institute's rightful dues of ₹70 lakh were released. The district collector of Kakinada signed the cheque himself and handed it to Dr Chandra.

"With that money, we started constructing this building," says Dr Chandra, gesturing to the four-storey modern structure currently in use.

Meanwhile, the first project – the Sarada Vidyalayam School – was also growing and thriving. By 2003, there were 140 students and 12 teachers. In the year 2008, a well-wisher in Vancouver raised $250,000 CAD which was used to construct a proper two-storey-high school building.

Compared to the ophthalmology institute, the budget for running the school was relatively small – around ₹4-5 lakh per year. But the impact it made on the community was huge.

60% of Sarada Vidyalayam's students are female. Children not only complete school but a few go on to study further – MSc, polytechnic diploma and even engineering.

Sarada pass-outs work with the hospital, as well. In the operation theatre, in admin and other support functions. The gardener's son is one such. The boy came to Dr Chandra after completing Class 10 and said, "I can't study any more…I need a job."

So he was assigned to the optical shop.

"He is a wonderful boy, when his own work is done he goes and helps somebody else!"

Patients from eye camps are brought to Kakinada on Sunday night. Every time a bus comes in, this young man volunteers to help in any way he can.

"I don't even tell him...he comes...that's the difference between our students and other young boys and girls!"

Volunteering is a way of life in North America. Something which Dr Chandra feels is missing in India.

"In Canada, every child will start volunteering since high school – in an old-age home or children's hospital. Over here, so many people, but they don't step forward."

In fact, Srikiran Institute attracts more donors and more volunteers from Canada than Kakinada. Resident doctors spend 3 weeks at Srikiran Institute, working without pay. The work itself is a reward – large numbers and complex cases rarely seen in the developed world.

"We are also working with University of Alberta to set up Tele-ophthalmology" program so that the patients from remote areas can be examined by the doctor at the base hospital."

The unsung story of an eye hospital in Kakinada came to the notice of CNN in 2008. Dr Chandra was nominated by the channel as a 'Real Hero' and the story broadcast on global television. In fact, he was the first one to be nominated from India. Only after that did the local Telugu newspaper *Eenadu* write an article on Sankurathri Foundation.

"On that Sunday my phone was ringing from morning to evening. It was nice to see people appreciating me...not that they should all give money."

More than personal recognition, it's the boost his staff receives that makes Dr Chandra happy. In 2010, when he was selected as a CNN-IBN Hero he dedicated the award to them.

"When I went to Mumbai to collect the award, they were all so happy. Openly I declared this award is for all of you, not for me. Let it inspire us to do much more work."

In 2010, Srikiran Institute was conducting 8000 free surgeries. The eye hospital's annual budget had jumped to ₹4 crore while the school budget stood at ₹18 lakh. Between the two organisations, there were over 130 employees.

"Since 2005, we are not getting international grants. Only individual donations, mostly from Canada which covers about 40% of our cost."

Srikiran Institute's own income is 30-35% (from paid operations, pharmacy and optical shop). On paper, 20% of the cost is covered by government subsidy. But the system refuses to release this money – the dues pile up.

Once again, Dr Chandra met Ms Sujatha Rao, who promised to do the needful. But even her intervention failed. As of March 2013, a sum of ₹50 lakh remains pending and Dr Chandra sees no future in working under this scheme.

"We are managing with our own resources in two districts... I am sure that nothing can change this system… it is rotten to the core."

Come hell or high water, Sankurathri Foundation will continue its work.

After more than 20 years in operation, Srikiran Institute of Ophthalmology now has a 'business plan'. The idea is to sustain the number of operations and also to increase services.

"We are thinking of starting a corpus fund. We will do same number of free operations, but we also want to attract more paid patients."

While 90% of Srikiran Institute's work is cataract surgery, the hospital and its doctors are well-equipped to do the most complex operations.

"We operated on an 8-month-old boy – he was born with corneal opacities which made him blind. We conducted corneal transplants of both eyes."

While other hospitals the family went to had quoted a fee of ₹2.5 lakh, Srikiran was able to do the operation completely free of cost to the family. The quality of care and precision of surgery is the same as any fancy hospital in a bigger city. Yet, the well-to-do hesitate to visit a 'poor people's hospital', thinking they can afford better.

"Only when patients come here and see our facilities, meet the doctors, they realise – no need to go to Hyderabad or anywhere else!"

When a patient comes in, he or she is met by a counselor who asks a number of questions. Based on their profile, poor patients are offered free treatment.

"I would say we have 97% success in identifying the poor patients. 3% who slip in claiming to be poor – it's too much to worry about them."

There is also a scheme of subsidised rates for the middle-income group while the rest pay full rates. The same surgery is performed for all patients. But those who pay can opt for the more expensive phaco and foldable lenses.

"The phaco lens surgery costs up to ₹1 lakh at other hospitals. Same procedure we charge just ₹20,000."

Dr Chandra believes that over time, the paid patients will bring in enough revenues to sustain the entire hospital.

"When the figure is 50:50 we can do same number of free operations without any outside donation."

At 70, Dr Chandra is as sprightly and active as ever, working 7 days a week. He wakes up at 4.30 am, does pranayama, checks emails and reads newspapers. Breakfast is idly/dosa/upma at 8 am. At 8.30 am he walks across from his house to the 'campus' next door.

He is either at the hospital or the school till 7 pm, with a small break for lunch.

"I seldom go out or attend social events," he adds.

But Dr Chandra never misses an opportunity to address school and college students. To talk about Sankurathri Foundation's work and inspire them to offer their services in their own community.

"I tell them – everybody thinks service means money. It's not just money but the thought itself."

For example, since 1994, the students of St Gregory's Catholic school in Ottawa, Canada, raise money for Sarada Vidyalayam through an annual bake sale. Over the years, they have contributed over $30,000 CAD.

"That kind of spirit is missing in our community…"

In 2010, Sankurathri Foundation initiated a voluntary service project with JNTU Kakinada. The students acted as 'foot soldiers', visiting all the villages within a 20 km radius. Giving them a taste of what service is all about. The students conducted camps in 19 villages in one month.

"They learnt what is team work and also had a sense of accomplishment."

Over the last 3 years, Dr Chandra has made more efforts to reach out to local residents, even holding a fund-raising event in Kakinada.

"I want to let people publicly know what we are doing. And that we need their need support."

And what happens – after Dr Chandra. Will the work continue as efficiently, as passionately? The optimist and rationalist believes it will. Dr Chandra's nephew, Dr Rajendra Sankurathri, has been associated with the Foundation since its initial days.

"He is the right person to take charge in the near future. That is our succession plan."

There are also systems and procedures, which put the day-to-day operations on auto-pilot.

"I go to Canada for almost 5-6 weeks a year and the show goes on," he smiles.

Leadership, after all, is the process of picking the right people and infecting them with a virus. The vision, mission and passion that you have.

It's not always smooth, or easy. Sometimes you will fail. Dr Chandra recalls the case of an early employee – the young doctor who was sent abroad for training. Initially, the doctor did a brilliant job.

"After 4 years he became extremely self-centred and was no longer a team player. I had to ask him to get out."

Sacking a senior doctor was difficult and bound to affect the young organisation. But Dr Chandra was clear about one thing.

"There are some things I never compromise in my life. If I have to fold it...I will fold it but I won't allow substandard work."

The other doctors and staff stood by Dr Chandra, supported him, kept the good work going.

"I have no regrets... One has to make tough decisions in the best interest of the organisation."

To sum up the past 20 years numerically – 1826 eye camps, 1,80,000 surgeries. To sum up emotionally – determination, perseverance and pure joy.

"When I see a blind man come to the hospital and leave with vision, I feel so happy. When I see the children at school, I see my children in them." (*Pauses*)

"It keeps my heart beating."

Every frustration, every struggle fades away.

And even that sense of personal loss.

"After all these years, I tell you, I have no grudge against God or even those terrorists… I am detached from all that. I enjoy peace of mind."

When you accept life as it is unfolding, and surrender yourself.

You will finally be free. And fully alive.

ADVICE TO YOUNG ENTREPRENEURS

It is up to the youth to have a vision for their country and a plan towards achieving that vision.

Act responsibly because the future of this country is on your shoulders.

In my opinion, progress is not Internet, smartphones, etc, but a decent living for every human being where they have access to clean water, sanitation facilities, education, health-care and the basic amenities to lead a good life.

All people must be empowered; otherwise the progress will be curtailed as the nation has to bear the cost of supporting them.

Basic human values seem to be diminishing in the society. The so-called progress or development should not be at the expense of our culture, values, humanism, ethics and family unity.

Money is not the only thing. If you are a student, you can tutor the next-door neighbour. Spend half an hour teaching maths. That's so easy. Whatever we can do, that's also a volunteer service.

Open up your mind. Be innovative, proactive and think out of the box.

Only then can we solve the many, many problems in front of us.

HUM HONGE KAMYAAB

(WE SHALL OVERCOME)

Dilafrose Qazi – SSM College of Engineering Parihaspora (Kashmir)

In 1988, Dilafrose Qazi set up a polytechnic for women in Srinagar. Facing every possible hurdle – including attacks by militants – this feisty lady went on to establish SSM College of Engineering, the first and only private engineering college in all of Kashmir.

"Agar dharti par kahin swarg hai, to yaheen hai yaheen hai, yaheen hai."

These words in my history textbook came alive when I visited Kashmir in the year 1986. Shalimar Bagh and Nishat Bagh were indeed Paradise.

I secretly ogled at the waiters in restaurants and actually saw apples on the cheeks of children on the street. What a wonderful place to live in, I thought.

I did not know then, what it was like to be an ordinary Kashmiri girl, struggling to find a job. The lives of Kashmiris beyond the tourist brochures, *shikaras* and shawls.

I read, with regret, the news of militancy in Kashmir. I did not understand the issue but I knew what it meant. No more tourists on LTC, no more Bollywood shootings. Kashmir became a 'no entry' zone for People Like Us.

And what of ordinary Kashmiri boys and girls? While I had a hundred colleges to choose from, in my own city and across the country, where would they study? Where would they find jobs? I never paused to think, for a moment.

Not about those handsome Kashmiri waiters, who no longer had customers. Or the apple-cheeked children picking up guns.

I cried while listening to Dilafrose Qazi, I cried as I wrote her story. These are our brothers and sisters, not statistics in a newspaper.

Garbage and hatred is clogging minds and hearts. But the lake can never stop being liquid. And we can never stop being human.

Searching for truth, longing for peace. Working for the greater common good.

One woman wears this conviction like a bullet-proof vest. A conviction that the pen is indeed mightier than the gun.

(This interview was conducted in Srinagar on the author's behalf by Aliya Bashir)

HUM HONGE KAMYAAB

(WE SHALL OVERCOME)

Dilafrose Qazi - SSM College of Engineering Parihaspora (Kashmir)

Dilafrose was born in Srinagar, in a lower middle class family.

"*Main belong karti hoon ek area called Chhataabal. Ek makaan mein paanch ghar rehte the, ek sehen share karte the.*" (I belong to an area called Chhataabal where we were 5 families staying in one house, with a common courtyard.)

Dilafrose was the eldest of 4 children, her father also bore the responsibility of his elderly parents and sisters. Although he tried his hand at many different kinds of businesses, there was always a shortage of money in the house.

"I went to the government school where the fees was ₹2 per month. But that too Papa would often delay paying for 6 months."

In those days, however, sending a girl to school itself was a big thing. The women in the neighbourhood gossiped and bitched but Dilafrose's family believed in the value of education.

"*Us mahaul mein reh kar bhi meri ma ki ek alag soch thi.*" (Even though we lived in such an atmosphere, my mother had a very different way of thinking.)

Unlike any other lady in the neighbourhood, she operated a *charkha* (spinning wheel). After school, Dilafrose would sit next to her mother and help her. The pashmina thread they wove supplemented the family's meagre income.

"*Woh ek inculcate ho gaya mere andar ki hamein Papa ki help karni hai, survive karna hai.*" (As a child I knew I have to work to help my father, we need money to survive.)

In 1981, Dilafrose joined the Government College for Girls in Nawakadal. Unlike the girls from well-to-do families, she did not have expensive clothes or shoes. Even her purse was a cheap one, made from PU foam. However, what Dilafrose had was good taste. And a way of carrying herself.

"*Shayad meri bol chaal cultured thi, woh mujhe help karta tha* (I spoke and acted in a cultured way). Girls from good families wanted to be my friends."

One such girl asked Dilafrose, "Where did you get this purse?"

Wanting to make a good impression, Dilafrose blurted, "I bought it in the bazaar for ₹250."

The friend immediately said, "*Arre*, please Dilafrose, get one for me!"

It was too late to reveal the truth. Dilafrose procured the purse from her father and made a 400% profit. In no time, she got more orders. In fact, the bags became a huge craze in the college.

"I am not exaggerating when I say I sold hundreds of those bags. I understood that I can do a business and I can make money."

Then, the fashion came to wear a 'firan'. Along with studies, Dilafrose learnt cutting and stitching. She then went to a shop in Lal Chowk and took a big order for jobwork. The shopkeeper supplied her with cloth and paid ₹7 per firan for stitching.

"This is how I was earning while I was studying!"

Dilafrose was a mediocre student but she was an all-rounder. Apart from business, she participated in numerous extra-curricular activities. In fact, she won several awards including 'best sportsperson', 'best dancer' and 'best NCC cadet'.

NCC, in particular, gave her a lot of exposure. One year, she travelled to Jammu for an NCC camp. Her father scraped together some money for her pocket expenses but she returned the entire amount to him without spending a penny.

"I knew that he must have borrowed from somewhere."

In fact, even the money Dilafrose earned from stitching, she never spent on herself. A long time ago her grandfather had taken a loan of ₹5000 from the bank, which he could not repay. The principal amount, along with interest, was now over ₹20,000.

"When I was small, officers from the bank used to come to our house and threaten us... I used to be scared."

The young girl dreamt of the day when the family would be free of this *karza* (debt). Armed with a degree in law, she began looking for a government job – the dream of every educated person in Kashmir. But it was not at all easy.

Dilafrose applied for the post of sub-inspector, for which the interview was in Jammu. Somehow, her father arranged for ₹300 for her travel expenses. The minimum height requirement was 5 ft 2 inches. Being half an inch shorter, Dilafrose was disqualified.

In many other interviews, merits of the candidate did not matter as much as how much she was willing to 'compromise'.

"*Mere andar ghairat hai bahut zyada. Main kuch jhuk nahin sakti hoon, zyada bol nahin sakti hoon.*" (I have a very high sense of honour. I cannot bend or ingratiate myself.)

On one occasion, Dilafrose applied to J K Tourism for the post of a receptionist and received an interview call. There were hundreds waiting, but the first 2 candidates who went inside were selected. The rest of the interviews were cancelled. Everyone else went away quietly but Dilafrose was livid.

"*Mujhse bardasht hi nahin hua ki – aisa kyun? Pata chala ki director tourism ne apni beti ko job de diya hai.*" (I could not tolerate this injustice. I found out that the director tourism had given his daughter the job.)

Armed with her certificates, Dilafrose and her father went to the house of the chief minister – Farooq Abdullah. As always, there was a sea of people waiting to see him. Unable to push herself through the crowd, she did not get an audience.

However, one of Farooq Abdullah's security guards was from their neighbourhood. He directed her father, "Send your daughter quickly, *sahib* is coming towards his car."

"My parents were not educated in a school but they were cultured. *Exposure tha paison ki kami thi.*" (We had the exposure, only we did not have money.)

Dilafrose ran up to Farooq Abdullah, tears streaming down her face. She narrated what had happened and showed her own credentials.

The Chief Minister said, "*Beta,* get into the car."

When they reached the tourism department, Farooq Abdullah strode in and demanded, "Where is the list?"

There was pin-drop silence.

"Her name should be on top of the list!" he ordered.

A new list was hastily typed out. The director (tourism) was out of station, hence his signature could not be taken. The date was 1 July 1984.

The next morning, Farooq Abdullah's government was toppled. The list went up in smoke, the dream shattered.

"*Dekho Allah ka karna tha* (it was Allah's doing), I was not meant for that job…something bigger was in store for me!"

The search continued. Dilafrose applied to the industrial department to open a unit in garment technology, since she had some experience in that field. Every day, she would visit the Baug-e-Ali-Mardakhan where the office was located. But, the clerk would not register her name, he would simply make her wait.

"*Achha lagta tha koi khubsoorat ladki baithi hai saamne, filhaal hum nazara karein…*" (He liked to have an attractive girl sitting there, so he could stare…)

Dilafrose could not tolerate this – she dropped the project. Being a law graduate, she thought about practicing in court. But she soon realised the atmosphere there was not conducive to girls. Time was ticking away, no job in sight…

"I was 25 years old, everyone was saying – get her married. But I was adamant. I did not want to become a housewife."

Finally, lady luck smiled. Dilafrose applied for a job at the Oberoi Palace Hotel as a guest relations officer. The girls called for the interview were mostly from army background and spoke very good English. Dilafrose felt unsure, out of place. She went inside with no hope of getting selected.

The interviewer asked, "Where have you done your schooling?"

Dilafrose softly replied, "Gorment School."

The interviewer heard 'convent school' and selected her. The position was for 3 months, during peak season.

"Entire time I thought, if they see my certificate they will throw me out but it did not happen."

Instead, it was a wonderful learning experience. Many well-heeled Indian and foreign guests stayed at the hotel. Talking with them, Dilafrose quickly improved her English language and communication skills.

"I got lot of confidence that I can do something on my own."

So once the job ended, Dilafrose decided to start a small business of her own. The idea was simple – a training institute for girls. Wealthy Kashmiris did not allow their daughters to work after completing college, but they wanted the girls to keep busy with some hobby courses before marriage.

"I thought I can teach girls how to do cutting-stitching or typing shorthand."

The first thing you need for a good business is a good location. Dilafrose decided to start her institute in Rajbagh, a posh area of Srinagar. She located a house which was available on rent.

"*Mere andar bahut zyada shauk tha koi bhi kaam seekhne ka.*"(I had a lot of interest in learning any kind of work.)

"*Main kitni bhi fighter ho sakti hoon par ek aurat ki jo nazaakat hai,* I want to maintain that." (I am a fighter but always, I maintain the dignity of being a woman.)

The landlord said, "I will give you the property for ₹5000 per month but you have to give me 5 months' rent in advance."

It was a huge sum at that time – where would she get the money? Dilafrose took a bold step. Her grandfather had kept ₹22,000 to buy gold ornaments for her, at the time of marriage.

"I took this money and gave it to Mr Baig – the landlord. Of course, *ghar par sab paagal ho gaye* (everyone at home was horrified)."

An uncle tried to make her see reason. *Isko business karne ka itna bhoot hai* (she is keen to do a business), let her buy an auto for ₹7000.

"I will buy 3 autos for you," he said. "Every evening they will come and pay you... *tumhe to kuch karna hi nahin* (you won't have to exert yourself)."

But he had underestimated the fire inside her belly, to *do* something.

"I want to have a work and to create a work for others."

The first job at hand was to find students. Dilafrose knew a girl from a very rich family, whose parents did not let her go to university.

"Rukhsana, why don't you join my institute?"

Rukhsana was interested but not in any hurry.

Dilafrose pursued her, prodded her, pleaded with her.

"*Yaar, admission le le.*" (Please take admission, my friend.)

When Rukhsana went to her nani's house in Karan Nagar, Dilafrose followed her all the way there – to collect the fees. A princely sum of ₹100.

Once Rukhsana joined, 3 of her friends also joined. The institute began functioning in March 1988. Within a month, there were 9 girls in all.

Dilafrose was the 'principal' of the institute, as well as the principal teacher. While she taught cutting and stitching, an elderly *sardarni* who lived nearby took flower-arrangement classes.

"I used to call her as 'aunty' and she never charged any money."

However, Dilafrose had to buy sewing machines. An uncle arranged 4 machines on an installment basis. The infrastructure was basic but the air was infected with the enthusiasm of youth.

"Creative and innovative ideas used to keep coming to my mind. Like that, one day I told the girls – let us hold a funfair."

200 entry tickets priced at ₹5 each were printed and the girls went out to sell them. They were all so pretty and well-spoken that the tickets sold out in no time. A second lot was printed and that too went like hotcakes. So now the focus shifted – what to do at the funfair?

The students came up with various ideas. Masooda got some *matkas* and set up a stall of *'matka phodo'* (break the pots). Seher put up a tambola stall. Simran got her music system and played the latest English songs.

Dilafrose was at the cash counter, selling tickets for games and there was not a moment of rest. On popular demand, the funfair was extended by a day.

A catty neighbour remarked, "*Jumma jumma aath din bhi nahin hue, yeh kaun sa funfair hai*!" (They started just a month ago, what is this funfair already!)

But Dilafrose could not be bothered. At the end of two days, the cash collection was close to ₹1.5 lakh. After paying the *shamianawala*, *bandookwala* and various other suppliers, there was a net profit of ₹25,000. The exact amount which Dilafrose had taken, to give to her the landlord.

"Initially, I did not have such a big dream *ki* university *kholni hai*. I thought I will teach some small courses which will help girls to become independent."

"Faith is an investment. Once someone puts faith in you, you try your best to live up to their expectations."

"I returned the money and from that day I have not looked back. I started taking risk upon risk, risk upon risk..."

Nobody had thought a group of girls would pull off such a big event. There was new respect in their eyes.

In October 1988, Dilafrose agreed to an arranged marriage with Qazi Shabir Ahmad, a teacher of English at the sainik school and a commissioned officer there. While he did not object to Dilafrose running her institute, her mother-in-law was convinced it was a waste of time.

"She used to send messages to my parents *ki isko job kara do* (let her take up a job). In any case she has only 5-10 students."

By January 1989, militancy had increased to such an extent that all colleges in the state were shut down. Dilafrose kept herself busy at home, by spinning the *charkha*.

She had no intention of sitting idle and gossiping with the neighbours. The situation in the valley improved and she was able to restart classes.

"I kept paying rent all those months because I knew, this has to continue."

A 3-month shorthand typing course had been introduced and it was attracting students. At the end of the course, the girls wanted a certificate. Dilafrose printed a letterhead in the name of 'Srinagar School of Management Trust' and wrote: 'This is to certify that so and so student has done a 3-month course in shorthand.'

But the trust was registered, the course was not recognised. Parents objected, saying that the certificate would not carry any weight with employers.

Dilafrose approached the technical board to get recognition for her course.

"In the board there was one director Mr Salaam Butt – *Allah unko jannat naseeb de* – he guided me."

Mr Butt said, "Dilafrose, technical board and AICTE only approve polytechnic courses of 2 years for secretarial practice."

There was also a 3-year course for architectural assistantship. Dilafrose applied to start both these courses. Even as she was waiting to get the recognition, Mr G M Shaikh, Principal of Kashmir Government Polytechnic sought admission for his daughter. That girl became the first student in the secretarial practice course.

"Maybe Shaikh saab had a confidence in me. I don't know – I never met him. But his decision helped a lot."

People thought it must be recognised, it must be a good institute. In the first year itself, there were 22 admissions, from as far as Baramullah. AICTE granted recognition and the course got underway.

"I stopped doing 3-month courses and got teachers for theory subjects like accountancy."

Since students paid fees at the time of joining, there was some money to hire staff. But not enough to buy drawing boards required for the architecture course.

"Shaikh saab lent me some boards and survey equipment from his polytechnic until I got my own. This helped me a lot."

Another big help were her own younger brothers, Bilal and Inteqaab, and sister, Arifa. They worked in the administrative positions, working without salary.

"Our college became the main aim for everyone, they left their own higher studies in order to work for it."

"*Mujhe dar nahin hai – maine apne bachche apni sister ke hawale kare hain, ki kabhi mujhe kuch ho jaye toh inko dekh lena.*" (I am not afraid, I have given the responsibility of my children to my sister – in case something ever happens to me.)

"I have created thousands of engineers who will be our future generation. That is my contribution."

It was not planned, it happened naturally. By this time their father was ill and had shut down his own business.

The success of SSM Polytechnic spawned competitors. In 1992, an institute called 'Kite Polytech' opened in Rajbagh. Being a co-ed college, it started attracting a larger number of students.

"I realised that parents spend more on educating boys and, to survive, we would have to change ourselves."

The SSM Women's Polytechnic became a co-educational institute. While Kite Polytech faded out, SSM Polytech continued going from strength to strength.

Apart from the usual teething troubles, Dilafrose had to face some very tough situations. A situation caused by militants.

A girl from Kupwara came to SSM Polytech with a recommendation from the chief of the Hizbul Mujahideen. She wanted a passing certificate without attending any classes. To complicate matters, the local Hizbul commander was against the girl's admission. And Dilafrose was caught in the crossfire.

"I don't want to remember those bad days… I have seen the worst possible things…"

One morning, her brother was kidnapped from Pampor. The militants demanded a ransom of ₹50,000. Dilafrose went to their camp, to secure his release. As she walked in, young boys with long beards and Kalashnikov rifles made rattling noises with their guns.

"*Par mere andar khauff bilkul nahin tha* (I was not scared). I am very strong inside."

When Dilafrose met the commander, she said, *"Bhai, main aapki behen hoon…"* (Brother, I am your sister.)

The matter was settled with a payment of ₹5000.

Meanwhile, another organisation in Dal Gate heard that a ransom had been paid. So they kidnapped her husband and demanded ₹50,000.

"*Pehle group ne rehem kiya magar yeh log nahin maane. Unhone college mein aakar tod-phod ki.*" (The first group showed mercy, the second did not. When we said we have no money, they came to the college and broke our equipment.)

Despite all this, Dilafrose never considered shutting down. The college continued to flourish and by 1995 it had a large number of students. By this time, AICTE had changed its rules. A college could no longer operate from rented premises – it had to have its own land and building.

The search for property began. Land was available quite cheap in a place called Parihaspora, 20 km outside Srinagar. Dilafrose purchased 10 'kanals' for ₹25,000 per kanal*. When an architect was hired, she enquired about the budget.

"*Zameen khareedne ke baad mere paas sirf bees hazaar the.*" (After purchasing the land I had only ₹20,000 left.)

She said, "You need at least ₹2 crore. At the very least you should have ₹20 lakh!"

Since there was no money, the initial buildings were small – made of mud and stone.

Students cribbed about the poor infrastructure but they had no cause for complaint when it came to studies. The focus on academics remained strong and sincere.

Equally sincere was the manner in which Dilafrose managed every aspect of the college. To fund the construction and expansion of SSM, she had to raise funds. And people agreed to lend to her because they knew, here is a woman who keeps her word.

"If I borrow money, I return it as per my promise. *Kashmiri mein isko parteet kehte hain.*" (This is known as 'parteet' in Kashmiri.)

There are some problems which can be solved, with passion and perseverance. And others, which rattle your very being, test your character and your courage. For SSM College of Engineering, this

---

* 1 kanal = 505 sq metres

"*Mujhe gussa aa gaya, dekhte hain...kaun mujhe maarega!*" (I was angry, I said let me see who will dare to kill me.)

test came in the form of Iftikhar Husain Ansari. Leader of the Shias in the Pattan belt.

Ansari had one clear objective: "*Main yahan college nahin chalne doonga*." (I will not allow a college to function in my area.)

This was a powerful man, with the police on his side. And a dangerous one too.

Everyone advised *ki Dilafrose, yahan se nikal jao* (leave this place).

"Even my husband had surrendered. But the college was doing so well, how could I leave?"

Somehow, Dilafrose bore the brunt of it. Verbal threats, mental harassment and physical bullying.

"*Shayad main lady thi to survive kar payi...*" (Perhaps I survived, because I am a lady.)

Several times, the police entered the college premises to break down under-construction buildings. Acting at the behest of Ansari.

"*Main saamne aati thi, toh lady ke upar kuch kar nahi paate the*." (I would stand in front of the building and they could not lay a hand on me.)

On 8 May 1995, Dilafrose was supervising the laying of a slab for a new building. Her husband had gone to the bank to withdraw some money.

That day Ansari came out himself, with *goondas* on tractors. All of them had big wooden sticks. A truck was on its way to the college carrying stones. Ansari and gang set it on fire, some distance from SSM.

Gunmen told the people on that truck, "*Jao, madam ko lao*." (Go and fetch madam.)

Meanwhile, villagers had come and warned Dilafrose that she was in grave danger.

"*Aap abhi iss waqt niklo yahan se, kyunki aapko maarne ka aaj pura plan hai*." (Please leave immediately from here, today they are out to kill you.)

Everyone was in a panic and streamed out of the campus. Everyone, except Dilafrose.

"*Mujhe gussa aa gaya, dekhte hain...kaun mujhe maarega*!" (I was angry, I said let me see who will dare to kill me.)

However, as the campus became desolate, Dilafrose felt a sliver of fear. She scribbled a cryptic message on her visiting card: "Please come to my rescue as I have been cordoned by some gunmen."

The card was carried to the SHO (Station House Officer) in Pattan by a *mazdoor*. The officer did not take the SOS seriously. In any case, he neither had a vehicle nor any order from above. Why interfere in an ongoing dispute and incur Ansari's wrath?

However, an Additional Superintendent of Police happened to be travelling from Sopore towards Srinagar in a 7-Ton (all-terrain military vehicle). The SHO mentioned to him, "*Janaab, woh madam ne yeh likha hai ki usko koi trouble hai*." (Sir, that madam has written a note seeking our help.)

The SP immediately said, "Let us go there!"

On the way, they saw the truck in flames and the road leading to SSM completely deserted. Something was definitely very wrong. Arriving at SSM, they quickly bundled Dilafrose into the bulletproof car. As they drove back, past the burning truck, firing began from all sides.

"*Main un donon ke beech, chooee-mooee si, machine gun chal rahi mere kandhon pe*." (I was crouched in between, the machine gun was being fired from over my shoulder.)

"I am not thinking this college is 'my property'. If tomorrow it shuts down who will lose? The society will lose."

"*Mujhe abhi bhi satisfaction nahi hain*...I don't feel I have done anything. That I am 'somebody'."

Somehow, the vehicle left the firing zone and reached the station headquarters. The SP noted that for the first time in 10 years tackling militancy, the police had fired 900 rounds. The gun battle had been so fierce, it was a miracle they had survived.

Even after this incident, Dilafrose remained adamant. Because in a fight of good against evil – there is no ground for surrender.

Still, SSP Munir Khan tried to work out a compromise. He invited both Dilafrose and Ansari to his office for a dialogue. Ansari did not come himself, he sent his brother Abid.

"*Madam, aapko kya chahiye?* (Madam, what do you want?)," asked the SSP.

Dilafrose said, "Ok, I am ready to leave but I need compensation for my land and buildings."

The land cost was ₹9 lakh (for 30 kanals at ₹30,000 each) and buildings ₹16 lakh – a total of ₹25 lakh.

Abid Ansari consulted his brother and then declared, "This *khasra* No 506 (Deed No 506) is a cow-grazing pasture – it cannot be owned by you."

Dilafrose protested that his own people had sold this very same land, and given her a legal document for it. Abid took a more aggressive stance, claiming that even the land she had bought legally was not worth more than ₹3000 per kanal.

"*Iske paas haram ke paise hain* (The Devil has given her money)," he concluded. "I will pay ₹2 lakh only."

This was just not acceptable. A loss of ₹5 lakh or even ₹10 lakh Dilafrose was prepared to bear. But this offer was no offer at all. She would be left with nothing – no land, no money to start the college at another location.

"I became strong... *Allah pak ki kasam kha kar, mere andar ek ajeeb kism ki energy aa rahi thi."* (I took Allah's name and a new energy came into me.)

Dilafrose refused to compromise, refused to leave. Ultimately, the fight was not for land. It was for human values. The right to education is a fundamental right, but one which many seek to deny others.

"*Unko laga ki agar yahan ke log padhenge likhenge, aware ho jayenge to usko manenge nahin, vote nahin denge.*" (He realised that if the people get educated and aware they won't listen to him blindly and vote for him.)

It was the people of Parihaspora who called the maulvi's bluff.

"*Jo uske apne mureed, apne log the, unhone mera saath de diya* (His own people spoke in my favour). That was the biggest plus point and support."

The college has survived and thrived, proving that the *kalam* (pen) is indeed more powerful than the Kalashnikov.

In 2013, SSM College of Engineering had 4000 students on its rolls across 10 streams. Despite growing demand for quality education, it remains the only private engineering college in Kashmir. Because the valley is still a volatile place, where people hesitate to invest.

"We have many engineers in Kashmir, they have a lot of money and land. So why God gave this work of starting an engineering college to me?!"

Because more than money or technical know-how, it requires conviction. A sense of purpose, a mission.

"*Chahe koi bhi mulk bane par mere students jo hain, yeh woh log hain jo is mulk ko behtar mulk banayenge.*" (Whatever Kashmir may decide about its future, my students are those citizens who will make their region a better place to live in.)

And the moulding of those citizens is an important task in which Dilafrose takes personal interest. Even though it is not required of her, as vice chairperson.

"*Main apne college mein ek ek bachche se milna chahti hoon.* (I

"I went to Pakistan for a peace conference and said to Mr Musharraf, '*Agar aapko hamdardi hai Kashmir se toh aap pen ki jagah gun nahin pakda dete... Musalman ladkon ko, chhote chhote bachchon ko.*" (If you truly feel for Kashmir, you would not put guns into the hands of little children.)

would like to meet each and every student of my college). I want to know what are their problems."

One issue she wants to work on is mental health. According to a recent survey, 20% of Kashmiris below the age of 16 are suffering from depression.

"*Jin bachchon ke hasne khelne ke din hain woh kyun depression mein hain? Kyunki unhone kabhi hasi dekhi nahin, unhone sirf goliyon ki ganganahat suni.*" (Why are our children depressed? Because they have not heard laughter, they have grown up hearing the sound of guns.)

Children should live in freedom, in peace. And though she steers clear of both religion and politics, Dilafrose never hesitates to reinforce basic human values.

A young boy refused to look at her, saying the *hadees shareef* prohibits eye contact with any woman who is not a mother or a sister.

Dilafrose replied, "*Kya ma sirf wahi hoti hai jiske kokh se ham janam lete hai? Ma woh nahin hoti jo padaati hai, likhaati hai jo aapko insaan banaati hai*?" (Is only the woman who gave birth to you your mother and not the one who teaches you and makes you a good human being?)

Respect for elders, for teachers is a universal principle. The boy understood.

"*Usne sar ooncha kiya aur aankh se aankh mila kar baat karne laga.*" (He lifted his head and looked me in the eye.)

Equally important are academic standards and discipline. One time, Dilafrose slapped a girl who had bunked all her classes and even the exams.

"I felt personally responsible. Because her father was in London and had said, '*Main apni beti aapke hawaale kar raha hoon.*'" (I am entrusting my daughter in your care.)

However, the incident made her realise that tact and dialogue were better ways to get through to the young people of today. Such as the issue of how boys and girls should interact with each other – a very sensitive one in Kashmir.

3 girls came up to Dilafrose and asked, "Ma'am, why are teachers saying that we should not sit with the boys to discuss our projects?"

Dilafrose simply talked to them about freedom and responsibility.

"*Maine ma ki tarah bola, ki dekho, idhar aapko free mahaul milta hai. Badkismati se kuch bachche uska najaayaz fayda uthate hain. To aap batao ki hum kya karein?*" (I spoke to them, like a mother, saying here you have all the freedom. But some students take undue advantage of it. You tell me – what should we do?)

And they all promised, to uphold the decorum. So that no parent or politician can raise a finger about the conduct of SSM students. But even if an incident should come up, Dilafrose no longer acts in a dictatorial fashion.

"Now I call the student, talk, see his or her problems, performance… I don't just get angry now, I know other tactics."

Tactics are also needed to cope with the many hurdles SSM faces from the academic establishment in Kashmir. As a private college, it must be recognised by AICTE, the J & K state government and affiliated with the University of Kashmir. That affiliation took 7 long years and is yet to come for new courses.

"Last year, I wanted to start an MSc in Physics and Mathematics for which we put up a building and got equipment."

The college got approval from the J & K government but not the University. And Dilafrose is not one to beg, or to pull strings.

"They see *Dilafrose itna zyada kar rahi hain. Issko aur courses dein? Yeh nahin soch rahe Dilafrose kis ke liye kar rahi hai.*" (They

> ***"Jin bachchon ke hasne khelne ke din hain woh kyun depression mein hain? Kyunki, unhone sirf goliyon ki ganganahat sun hai."*** **(Why are our children depressed? Because they have have grown up hearing only the sound of guns.)**

are jealous that Dilafrose is doing so much, so why give her more courses. But they don't think who am I doing it for.)

Knocking on the same door only bruises your knuckles. It's more productive to find another door. In 2009, SSM opened a sister college for MBA and BBA in Haryana. A state which is far more welcoming to entrepreneurs.

"If you follow the procedure, fulfil the criteria, getting NOC and recognition is easy."

The Srinagar School of Management and Technology (SSMT) in Gudhrana (Hodal district), Haryana, now has 800 students, all from Kashmir. The location may be out of the state but the aim remains the same – to train Kashmiri youth. To ignite a passion within them – to 'do something' in life.

One such young man came to meet her some months ago. He had returned from London, where he was working in a coffee shop.

He said, "I can make a good coffee shop in Srinagar, better than Café Coffee Day or Barista, and much cheaper."

Dilafrose sensed a fire within him. She gave him ₹1 lakh and an invitation to open a coffee shop in her college.

"Why? Because if Butt saab, Shaikh saab had not given me a chance, where would I be today? They trusted me."

There is no contractual agreement, no rent or advance. When he starts making money, he will come on his own and start paying back.

Paying back her own debt to society, Dilafrose has also given vocational training as well as loans to hundreds of women in rural

Kashmir. Apart from that, twice a year, she distributes 2 quintals of rice, namkeen, chai and sugar to those in need.

"There is so much poverty, I feel I must do something... Because of my childhood I can empathise with them. *Yeh meri zeheniyat hai*." (That's my mentality.)

It is in that spirit that Dilafrose reached out to 30 survivors of rape in Kupwara, to help in their rehabilitation. For all these efforts – and more – Dilafrose Qazi was one of the 1000 women from around the world working for peace, collectively nominated for the Nobel Peace Prize in 2005*.

"When I received their letter I was blank... *sham ko thodi khushi hui* (later I did feel happy) but I don't get excited by certificates and awards. These are political things."

The recognition Dilafrose truly craves for is from her own people. Her students, her alumni, her peers. A professor once compared her to a princess who has brought back glory to Parihaspora – the ancient capital of Kashmir.

"Coming from a Kashmiri, those words gave me so much inspiration!"

But the biggest inspiration and support is her family. Husband, Shabir Qazi, has been by her side through thick and thin, offering support and encouragement. Whenever she faced criticism he would simply say, "No one ever kicks a dead dog!"

Since 1989, Shabir is also a part of the institution and, at present, chairperson of the SSM College of Engineering.

Her parents have also played a very big role in making this dream possible.

"I have been extraordinarily lucky to have them with me so the children have never felt my absence."

In fact, even her siblings live in the same compound, so in the evenings the whole family gathers. They choose one topic to speak on, or sing a variety of songs.

---

* Nobel Peace Prize in 2005 was ultimately won by International Atomic Energy Agency (IAEA) and Mohammed El Baradei.

"Singing is one thing which relieves you of your tensions. I also enjoy gardening and swimming."

While elder daughters, Insiya and Sana, are studying outside Srinagar, Haya is still in school. They know their mother is busy, and they understand.

"I try to make time for small pleasures. Like, suddenly, we will go for a drive, eat an icecream. I discuss what happened in the college that day – was I wrong or right?"

The girls are her 'judges', her critics and best friends. They tease her when she shuns *wazwan* and goes for simple rice and egg curry.

"*Mom aap kis liye kamate ho, aapko to khana pasand hi nahin hai!*"(Mom what is the point of earning money when you don't enjoy good food!)

Neither does she like to spend on jewellery or expensive shawls. There is one exception and that is, a trip abroad every year. Not as an indulgence but in the spirit of exploration and adventure. In that spirit, Dilafrose recently took out her Fortuner and drove down to the Gurez valley with her daughters.

"There is so much to explore in our own state…but I don't like this word 'my' state, I think the whole globe is mine."

Let people mingle freely, learn from each other, love and accept each other. This is Kashmiriyat, this is *insaniyat.*

"An NGO wanted me to be chief guest but they are saying, throw out all the outsiders from Kashmir. I don't agree with them."

And this has nothing to do with nationalism or patriotism.

"Khuda ne pura jahan khubsurat banaya hai...kisi jagah pahaad rakha, kisi jagah samundar rakha. Kisi jagah orange ugaya, kisi jagah apple ugaya." (God created a beautiful world. Somewhere he created a mountain, somewhere an ocean.)

The mountain dweller longs for the sea, while the one on the coast dreams of the hills. That is the way of nature. It is *we* who create barriers.

"*I say to the Almighty – tumhara hai, tumhare hawale. Mere to hai nahin kuch.*" (Everything is God's, it is His to protect. Nothing is mine.)

You come into this world alone and you leave alone.

You leave behind only the fragrance of your being and depth of feeling, in the hearts of others.

ADVICE TO YOUNG ENTREPRENEURS

If women want to be entrepreneurs they can be very successful. Why? Because women are very meticulous. Once they take up something, they do it religiously. We see China – women are doing so much work there and that's why that country is making so much progress.

Only problem is women give up very easily, they don't have so much stamina to fight. Let me clarify here that you don't have to be a fighter for the sake of being a fighter, you have to be very tactful instead of taking up cudgels. Because important thing is to reach your destination.

Have patience but strive for your goal. You have to be consistent.

If someone closes one door for me, I try to find the alternative – can I go from the window. There is nothing in the world which has no alternative.

Always plan ahead. If you see my diary, the first 2 pages are what is my plan this year.

Sijo Kuruvilla George

Sanjay Vijaykumar

Pranav Suresh

LET'S GET THIS PARTY STARTED

Sanjay Vijaykumar, Sijo Kuruvilla George & Pranav Suresh – Startup Village Kochi (Kerala)

Kerala's first campus startup is on a new mission – to spread the startup virus in colleges across Kerala. Their outlandish dream is to incubate 1000 product startups, and create a 'Silicon Coast' – the Silicon Valley of India.

To any young man from a 'middle class' background, the world of business looks like an elite club. You can peer over the hedge and observe the party.

But you know, you will never get invited.

There is only way to join the party – gatecrash it. That's exactly what Sanjay Vijaykumar did. As a second year student of engineering at the College of Engineering, Trivandrum, he and his friends started a business to make some extra pocket money. It was a runaway success.

Inspired by the success of this venture and by the likes of Steve Jobs, Sanjay roped in 7 of his classmates and formed a company.

"We were the first student-initiative to be incubated at TBI (Technology Business Internet) in Trivandrum. That was in August 2005."

At the same time, the boys had a much bigger idea. They called it the 'Dream of a Silicon Coast' – a Silicon Valley-like culture in Kerala. Which encouraged and supported young entrepreneurs.

"We used to share this idea with any important person we met. But we were kids at that time – no one took us seriously!"

7 years later, MobME is a Rs 25 crore mobile internet company and a certified success story. The government has now joined hands with the 'dudes' to turn the dream of a 'Silicon Coast' into a reality.

Startup Village in Kochi is the first-ever Public-Private-Partnership (PPP) model Technology Business Incubator (TBI) in the country. Bursting with raw passion, energy and ideas.

The corridors are overflowing with inspirational quotes and coders creating inspired apps. But they need a market, they need investors and, most of all, they just need someone who says, "I understand. Keep doing more of this!"

"We were lucky to have great guides and mentors, every startup needs that to succeed."

It's about dreaming big – for your state, for your country, for the *idea* of entrepreneurship.

You gatecrashed the party, now unlock the entrance.

Let in new people and new ideas – start a whole new celebration.

LET'S GET THIS PARTY STARTED

Sanjay Vijaykumar, Sijo Kuruvilla George, Pranav Suresh – Startup Village Kochi (Kerala)

Sanjay Vijaykumar was born in Trivandrum.

"If you are born in Kerala, you have to be an engineer or a doctor. But for some crazy reason I never wanted to do what everybody was doing."

Sanjay's dream was to be a basketball player. In Class 9 and 10, he played the sport at the national level and was, in fact, selected by the Sports Authority of India for further training.

But when he went to his father and said, "*Acha*, I am done with this studying thing, I want to play basketball."

His father said, "Unless you are like a Sachin in cricket, you don't make money."

The only job prospect for a basketball player in Kerala is with the State Electricity Board – as a clerk.

Sanjay gave up basketball and, instead, appeared for entrance exams in both engineering and architecture. With an all-India rank of 22, he secured a seat at the School of Planning & Architecture in Delhi and was all set to join. A big adventure for a small-town boy who had never been beyond Ooty or Kodaikanal.

But then Sanjay's brother – who was already a second year student at the College of Engineering, Trivandrum – said something which made sense.

"Why do you want to go to Delhi where you don't know anyone? Kerala has a great college basketball circuit – stay here!"

That, and the lure of mom's home-cooked food, made Sanjay change his plans. He joined College of Engineering, Trivandrum (CET), in the industrial engineering department. But his mind was still whirring, the *keeda* to do 'something different' remained.

Hanging out at the 'Sallap' coffee house near the college gate, Sanjay and his friends would bounce about ideas. Mobile phones had just entered college campuses, it was the new 'in' thing. Sanjay realised he could make some extra pocket money by selling recharge coupons on campus.

"We soon realised the phone companies have many special schemes, but none of them make sense for students."

In 2005, Sanjay and his friend, Vivek Francis, walked into the BPL Mobile office in Trivandrum and asked to see the head of sales. Quite cockily, they declared that the company did not have a presence on campus, because it did not understand the college crowd.

"So what should we do?" asked the Regional Sales Head.

He agreed to create a special 'talk-time plan' for students by making a few software changes. The scheme was 'pay for 6 months, get 6 months free' with special rates to friends within the same network.

"We can't pay cash but if you give us 100 SIM cards on credit, we can sell them to our friends," said Sanjay.

The company obliged. Sanjay got a few CET batchmates and friends from colleges across the state, to join in the effort. The target was to sell 1000 SIM cards over the next year. But in just 3 months, they sold over 14,000 SIM cards, making a cool Rs 8 lakh.

"In the next one month we ended up spending Rs 4 lakh. We took the hottest girls in college for fancy dinners...we went to Bangalore and bought bikes and high-end mobile phones."

Once the craze for spending subsided, the boys decided to do something 'productive'.

"We were very inspired by Steve Jobs and so many others in Silicon Valley and we thought, 'Why don't we start our own company?' "

Sanjay and Vivek formed a partnership firm called 'Torque Technology Solutions', along with 5 other CET batchmates (Sony Joy, Pranav Suresh, Anil Antony, Vishnu Gopal and Jose Luke). All 4 were literally 'chuddie-buddies' since their KG class days at Loyola school in Trivandrum.

So far, so good – but what was this new company to do? The boys hit upon the idea of creating ringtones and wallpapers to promote Malayalam movies. It was quite common in the Hindi film industry but nobody had done it in Kerala.

"We decided to meet Mammootty and sell the idea to him."

But how does a bunch of college students meet the 'Amitabh Bachchan of Kerala'? They land up in Cochin and go from studio to studio in search of him. The superstar was finally located and Sanjay & team managed to get a face-to-face meeting. This ability to 'barge in' anywhere proved to be very useful.

"Basically, we told people things they didn't know but which they realised could be of value – so they sent us straight to the top."

Being a technology and gadget freak, the superstar was game to try 'something new' for his upcoming film *Rajamanikyam*. When the movie was a runaway super-hit, a stream of movie producers lined up – all wanting the 'same thing'.

"We got the rights for all major artists in Kerala so we became like a '*hungama*' or '*mauj*' of the Malayalam film industry."

MobME soon had tie-ups with all the biggies in the content business, from Onmobile to Indiatimes. The team also went back to BPL Mobile with a 'zillion ideas', one of which was setting up voice servers for 'out-dialler' services.

"The funny thing is, we had never seen the inside of a server room or how a server looked like."

When they called IBM and asked for a server, the sales rep wanted to know 'specifications'.

"We just said, 'Send a machine that cost Rs 2 lakh'. We figured that being an expensive machine, it would take the load and do what we wanted it to do!"

In this unorthodox way, the team found its way forward. The boys were soon spending more time outside the classroom than inside

An entrepreneur must work like a bull and live like a nomad.

it. But they were not whiling away time – it was all about practice, not theory. Being on the ground, getting things to work.

In the fifth semester of college, August 2005, the team decided to get 'serious' about their business. A news item about an entrepreneurship seminar in Trivandrum caught their attention.

"We cut short our industrial visit to Bangalore and went to Technopark which was this amazing hi-tech place with glass buildings..."

The Technopark Technology Consultant, Mr R C Dutt, had no idea what to do with a bunch of engineering college students with no business plan and no money. But, he liked the spirit and sensed an opportunity. He became the first mentor to the company.

Using Torque as a 'test case', Technopark applied to the Department of Science and Technology (DST) to start an incubator. The Technology Business Incubator (TBI) came into being in August 2006. What's more, Sanjay was put on its board and allowed to frame policies.

"They told me that anything you want, you must write as a policy so that the startups that come after you get it as well."

Take the example of rental. At that time, the rent for a 4-seater space at the facility was Rs 14,000 per month. The rate was reduced to Rs 4000 per month but even that was too high for Torque.

"Our engineering fees for an entire semester were Rs 5000!"

Ultimately, Technopark TBI waived off the entire rent for a period of 12 months. The young entrepreneurs began working with telecom operators and TV channels to provide many different services.

"Our teammate, Vishnu Gopal, was a programming whiz – the rest of us just learnt stuff along the way!"

A third year CET student, Vishnu had spent his summer developing a platform which could flash exam results on mobiles. He led the team of 7 at MobME which developed a content aggregation platform called 'Fastcode'. (The company also sent bulk SMS for mobile operators in Kerala.

Of course, juggling coursework with client commitments was not easy. Luckily, by mid-2007, a senior at CET – Sijo Kuruvilla George – had graduated. He chucked his job with Infosys and joined the venture full-time.

During these heady early days, the young team was also lucky to find a set of 'believers'. Mammootty had introduced them to his chartered accountant, Sanil Kumar.

"The CA played a most critical role in our success...we got our first investor through him."

Knowing Sanil Kumar was like having a LinkedIn network. He introduced the MobME team to Jose Pattara, a Malayali entrepreneur who'd made it big in the Gulf. Although he did not follow the details of the 'pitch' made to him, he was taken in by the team's passion and youthful enthusiasm.

Pattara agreed to invest Rs 80 lakh in the venture on 12 December 2006.

Another individual who made a 'huge difference' was Kris Gopalakrishnan of Infosys. Sanjay had sent him a 'cold call' email which read: "I am very inspired that a bunch of middle class engineers could build a world-class enterprise. I want to meet you, the next time you visit Trivandrum."

Not only did Kris agree to meet, he actually came to the company's tiny 4-seater office in Technopark.

Looking around, he remarked, "We started Infosys in a room this big."

Since that day, Kris Gopalakrishnan has been a mentor and guide to the young team.

By the end of 2006, the partnership firm 'Torque' was converted into 'MobME Wireless Solutions' Private Ltd. In July 2007,

A mentor does not give you a solution, a good mentor can give you context – this is what I did in a similar situation.

MobME got a second angel investor in the form of George Brody, a Keralite who was a Silicon Valley veteran. Brody also became the Chairman of the MobME board.

"If you want to succeed, you need a lot of people around you who also want to see you succeed. We were fortunate that we had a lot of people like that."

This included their professors, HOD and Principal at CET – in particular, Dr B Anil (Staff Advisor) and Prof Meera Kumari (Staff Representative to the College Union). In the final year of college, Sanjay had 0% attendance yet he was granted '90% attendance' and allowed to write the university exams.

In the midst of it all, the team had written a concept note titled 'Dream of a Silicon Coast' – an innovation hub like Silicon Valley situated in Kerala.

"This was before YCombinator* and the idea of 'incubation' became popular," recalls Pranav Suresh. "We thought of it as a 'hack space' where students can hang out and get inspired to start something."

But how do you get such a Big Idea off the ground? Whenever the team had a chance to meet an important personality, they would share a copy of the concept note. One such personality was Dr A P J Abdul Kalam.

The meeting took place in April 2007 at Rashtrapati Bhavan. In the 45 minutes he spent with the group, Dr Kalam was extremely supportive.

"Youth are future of this nation," said Kalaamsaab. "You should also think of giving back to society!"

* YCombinator is a very successful Silicon Valley incubator which has funded over 550 digital startups including Dropbox, Reddit and Airbnb.

However, the 'Silicon Coast' was an idea ahead of its time – it found no takers. The team had enough on its plate and had to prove itself.

2007 was also a decisive year for MobME, with the core team graduating from college. Not all stayed on with the company. Of the original team members, Sanjay, Vivek, Sony, Pranav and Sijo continued. They had raised an additional Rs 2.4 crore in funding. The challenge was how to grow further.

The office shifted to Cochin, to be closer to telecom operators. When MobME was selected for the Lockheed Martin DST 'India Innovation Growth' program some team members shifted to Delhi.

"We were doing work for Airtel and CNN-IBN 'Citizen Journalist', so we set up a 'marketing office' in an apartment in Gurgaon."

At that time, the team came up with an application called 'Mobshare' which allowed users to share photos and videos from their phones. 'MobME' was featured as one of the 'top 10 IT Innovators' in the country. By the end of 2008, MobME had 30 employees and revenues of Rs 1.74 crore.

However, by this time, the core team had shrunk. Sanjay and Sony stayed on while others took up jobs or entered MBA programs.

"The company did not need all of us, it made sense to go out and do a PG program and see the world," says Pranav. "And maybe come back some day!"

While Pranav joined IIM Kolkata (batch of 2008-10), Sijo opted for the one-year program at Great Lakes Institute of Management in Chennai. Both accepted campus placements. Sijo worked with PWC and Deloitte for a couple of years before taking a 'complete break' in 2010.

"I came to Cochin, read some books and was comfortably sitting, doing nothing at all for a year!" he says.

Towards the end of this period, he reconnected with Sanjay. The 'innovation hub' they had proposed in 2007 had been noticed by a gentleman called H K Mittal, advisor to the Government of India. Dr Mittal realised that the existing schemes for entrepreneurs were

This is an open space – we don't deny any opportunity, reject any idea...

not working*. There was a need to scale up beyond IITs and IIMs and move into smaller towns.

He was the first expert who said, "We need to have PPP (public-private-partnership) in incubation."

Dr Mittal painstakingly took the proposal through various committees in the government. This process took almost 2 years. Meanwhile Sanjay requested Kris to come onboard as 'Chief Mentor'.

"You put fire in my belly," said Sanjay. "Now I need you to put fire in a thousand bellies!"

A mission was thus formulated: to spread the entrepreneurship virus in colleges across Kerala. And incubate 1000 Internet and mobile product startups over the next 10 years.

The approval came in November 2011, with the Kerala Government and Technopark also pledging support. While Sanjay was Chairman of the Board, Sijo joined in December as CEO.

"I was the 'employee no 1', at Startup Village, which is a non-profit society entirely independent of MobME."

The 'telecom innovation hub' as it was referred to in the proposal, had a funding requirement of Rs 5 crore. With 50% of the capital coming from government and 50% from the private sector. The private partner is responsible for the infrastructure as well as operations of the incubator.

KINFRA (the Kerala state industrial park promoter) had set up a biotech park in Kochi, which was lying unutilised. The agency came on board as a partner and agreed to give Startup Village

---

* DST has over 60 incubators functioning since the 1980s but very few 'success stories'.

5000 sq feet of temporary space in this park. At a very low cost of Rs 2 per sq ft.

"Actually there was a water tank on top of the building, supported by stilts. We said – give it to us and we'll see what we can do with it!"

The Malayali network once again came handy as Sijo requested builder Jose Thomas to help with the construction. Known for putting up a 40-storey building in record time, Thomas put his team on the job. In this manner, a 4-floor building was constructed in just 7 days.

Startup Village officially 'started up' on 15 April 2012.

Getting incubates was the next task, which proved to be surprisingly easy.

"People saw MobME and thought – their parents had government jobs but they started a company. So can I!"

Through campus connections and some outreach programs, Startup Village was able to quickly attract its first batch of 12 companies. By the end of 2012, over 400 applications had been received and 150 incubatees accepted. But to scale up further, Startup Village would need more hands on deck.

At this point, Sanjay reconnected with Pranav – it didn't take much to convince him. Pranav quit his corporate job and joined Startup Village as COO.

"To scale up, we need 4 elements – more infrastructure, more mentors, seed-stage capital and policy support. We had work cut out for us, on all fronts!"

By December 2013, that number had swelled to 494 incubatees, of which 173 are 'student startups', with team members still in college.

"When we hold sessions in colleges we don't even use the word 'entrepreneurship'. We just say, start doing some stuff you are interested in!"

There is no strict 'evaluation' or screening process. An idea may come in one form, morph into another.

Nidal, Nijil and Sreekumar came to Startup Village a year ago, fresh out of Cochin University, with the idea of an e-publishing

The idea of a 'Silicon Coast' is a dream, it is not a business plan.

tool. What they actually built is a cool hardware product called the 'Mashinga' – a multi-touch table using IR sensors.

In just 8 months, the team built a prototype, raised some angel funding and secured its first order. That's the magic of an 'ecosystem'. The Startup Village team knows what it takes to keep a 'crazy idea' alive in the initial phase.

"In Silicon Valley, it's easy to raise the first $1,00,000, but not in India."

This is where Startup Village steps in. It channels funds from existing schemes under DST and the state government to young companies in need of seed capital. Such schemes provide anywhere between Rs 2-5 lakh without collateral or interest.

At the next stage, it connects entrepreneurs with angel investors. On a single 2-day event called 'Weekend' at Startup Village in late July, 40 companies made pitches to investors – 5 of them received term sheets the following week.

"We also help startups who need to buy expensive equipment, so they can work better."

'Backbench Studio' is an incubatee working on a 2-D animation series called 'Little Holmes'. The company needed to put together a video for a potential investor in the impossible time-frame of one month. Startup Village extended a soft loan for a Rs 3 lakh device which allows you to draw directly on screen.

But the things you can quantify, it's the freedom to just 'be' which makes Startup Village special. The misfits, the nerds, the creative thinkers – everyone is welcome. They come from unsung colleges like 'Toc H' and 'Adi Shankara Institute' but here, no one cares. It's what you are *doing* that matters.

The focus is on product startups – here's one team to a table, no cubicle culture.

"We have a lot of mentors from outside but there's 'peer mentoring' as well. Beyond a certain point it's all about people talking to each other."

At the end of one year, the National Advisory Committee of DST reviewed the performance of Startup Village. They concluded that the incubator had completed its commitments for 5 years in the first year itself. Therefore, DST would be happy to consider an 'expansion proposal'.

But the dreamers at Startup Village are thinking much bigger.

In the summer of 2013, Sijo, Sanjay and Deepak Ravindran* were selected as 'Rajeev Circle' fellows in Silicon Valley. The fellowship has been instituted by Asha Jadeja Motwani in memory of her late husband, Rajeev Motwani, an early mentor to Google's Larry and Sergey Brin.

The fellows got huge access into the Valley – meeting the likes of Jack Dorsey (Twitter), Marc Andreesen (Netscape), Ram Shriram (Sherpalo Ventures) and many other legends.

"This experience helped us realise that it's *possible* to create a billion-dollar company in India. This is an opportunity not just for us, but for the 600 million Indians who are 26 years and below."

The stairwells and corridors of the Startup Village buildings are lined with inspiring quotes from Silicon Valley geeks. Somewhere in front of a blinking computer, sits the guy who doesn't think 'this can't be done in India'.

"These kids can get a job but they are putting prime years of life into a cause they believe in. Our challenge is how to support all of them!"

How will it happen? By expanding the mentor network to a 1000 entrepreneurs and CXOs. Setting up mini-incubators and 'innovation zones' in 500 colleges across Kerala. And creating 1000 professional app developers, in a one-year time frame.

Startup Village now has SEBI approval to put together its own $10 million dollar angel fund. A new 1,00,000 sq foot facility is also 'under construction' so that more startups can be physically

* The second campus startup incubated at Technopark was Deepak Ravindran's Innoz. He is also on the board of Startup Village.

incubated (right now 48 are on campus, in two separate buildings, the rest are mentored remotely).

"Our dream is to have 1,00,000 sq ft of space where people can come and go anytime. They should have beanbags and good quality Internet…the rest they will figure out!"

The way the MobME team did. In March 2013, the company started by third year engineering students crossed Rs 25 crore in revenue, with Rs 10 crore in profit, Rs 100 crore in 'market value'. But at 29 years of age, the founders have got their funda in life completely clear.

"The kind mentors we had always told us, it's never about how much money you make."

You all have to die someday and you can't take that money with you.

"What you need to have is a purpose in life, a mission, a philosophy…"

By simply doing what they wanted to do, what they believed in, MobME paved the way for so many others. Inspiring sons and daughters of government servants, to think beyond a 'secure job'. The Technopark TBI* and Startup Village have together incubated over 500 young entrepreneurs.

So much so that the Kerala government is the only state in the country to come out with an official 'student entrepreneurship policy'.

4% grace marks and 20% attendance relaxation will be provided to any college student running a company which is part of a business incubator. The state government has also earmarked 1% of its budget (Rs 500 crore) for young entrepreneurs.

The idea of creating more startups has caught the imagination of the public. And, it has had support from leaders across the political spectrum, regardless of who is in power – something rarely seen in India!"

"The reason it happened is because we were kind of fighting the

* From 2006-12, more than 150 companies were incubated at Technopark TBI, creating over 4500 jobs and Rs 180-200 crore in revenue.

'system'...we are a new generation with our own dreams and aspirations."

And when a whole lot of people come together and believe in a dream, it becomes a shared dream. A dream so big, it belongs to everyone.

"Our dream is, there will be a day when the sun sets in the dusk in Silicon Valley and it rises in the Silicon Coast in India..."

The first rays of that brilliant sun can be seen over the horizon.

A 'tryst with destiny' for the next generation, a new kind of freedom.

ADVICE TO YOUNG ENTREPRENEURS

Sanjay

We live in a world where people fear failure more than they fear death. Every small mistake is magnified so much more than it needs to be. I think if you have courage in your heart and the will to conquer fear, there is absolutely no limit to where you can reach.

We didn't know anything – we were completely self-learnt entrepreneurs but we had some great people guiding us. They never gave us any easy 'solution' but it's so important to have a guide because even if you are Michael Jordan, you need a coach like Phil Jackson.

Without a coach you can win games, but you can't win championships.

Colleges must support students who want to start a business. At least, treat entrepreneurs at par with sports and NCC and give them some 'grace marks' and attendance.

Sijo

It is difficult to turn in amazing work until and unless you absolutely love what you are doing.

Before you jump into entrepreneurship you truly need to understand why you want to jump into it.

It is not easy and it is hard work.

But then if you love a challenge and you love what you will be doing as an entrepreneur, then it will be a lot of fun.

Do it for the learning, the experience, the journey.

Don't do it for the money – money may or may not happen but you will be that much richer for the experience.

Pranav

Start young, really young. College is the best time to start up. Absolutely no societal pressures or fear of failure.

It gives one all the time in the world to experiment and fail.

The trick lies in not taking any of it to heart and persisting.

The best time to start up is yesterday and if you have an idea whose time has come jump right in.

The rest you will figure out if you truly want to do it.

There are enough and more good people in this world who want to help you and who will help you. All you need to do is seek them out and ask.

START UP RESOURCE

If you would like to contact any of the entrepreneurs featured in this book for help/advice, here are their email ids. Do try and be specific in your queries and a little patient in getting a response!

1. **Chandubhai Virani** – *contact@balajiwafers.com*
2. **Nand Kishore Chaudhary** – *nkc@jaipurrugsco.com*
3. **Vivek Deshpande** – *vivek@spacewood.in*
   Kirit Joshi – *kirit@spacewood.in*
4. **C V Jacob** – *c/o georgepaul@synthite.com*
5. **Parakramsinh Jadeja** – *ceo@jyoti.co.in*
6. **Jagjit Singh Kapoor (c/o)** – *kapl.ritu@gmail.com*
7. **Mukhtarul Amin** – *mamin@superhousegroup.com*
8. **Bahadur Ali** – *c/o drjaiswal@ibgroup.co.in*
9. **Deepak Dadhoti** – *deepak@servocontrolsindia.com*
10. **Rohith Bhat** – *rohith@robosoftin.com*
11. **Sriram Subramanya** – *sriram.subramanya@integra.co.in*
12. **Sandeep Kapoor** – *sandeep@yorktransnational.com*
13. **Virat Khutal** – *vkhutal@gmail.com*
14. **Abhijit Barooah** – *premiercryo@sify.com*
15. **Vibhor Agrawal** – *info@multimax.in*
16. **Srikumar Misra** – *srikumar.misra@milkmantra.com*
17. **A Muruganantham** – *muruganantham_in@yahoo.com*
18. **Dr Chandrasekhar Sankurathri – chandra@srikiran.org**
19. **Dilafrose Qazi** – *qdilafrose@gmail.com*
20. **Sanjay Vijaykumar** – *sanjay@mobme.in*
    Sijo Kuruvilla – *ceo@startupvillage.in*

INCUBATORS ACROSS INDIA

This is a partial list which includes some of the most active incubators located in the smaller towns of India

1) Startup Village, Kochi

A unique public-private partnership enterprise that offers a platform for student-led startups aiming to invent pathbreaking technology in the telecommunications industry. They offer support through funding, tax incentives, consulting, etc.

http://www.startupvillage.in

2) Deshpande Foundation India — Hubli Sandbox

Through a bottom-up approach, the foundation located in Hubli, Karnataka lends a hand to startups involved in the areas such as social enterprise, health, environment in order to create scalable and sustainable models of development.

http://deshpandefoundationindia.org email: infodcse@dfmail.org

3) National Institute of Technology (NITC)

Technology Business Incubator—National Institute of Technology, Calicut (TBI—NITC)

In partnership with the National Science and Technology Entrepreneurship Board (NSTEBD) and the Department of Science & Technology of the Government of India, NITC's incubator supports young startups by providing technical support, infrastructure, training and funding.

http://www.nitc.ac.in/index.php/?url=content/index/175/2/145/145

Email: tbi@nitc.ac.in

4) Tiruchirappalli Regional Engineering College—Science and Technology Entrepreneurs Park (TREC—STEP)

TREC—STEP fosters young entrepreneurs by providing them with general-purpose machines for production (thus, reducing investment in capital), training, infrastructure, technology research labs and libraries.

http://www.trecstep.com

Email of Executive Director R. M. P. Jawahar: jawa_ts@yahoo.com

5) Business Incubators at the IITs

TBI at IIT Kharagpur

http://www.step-iit.org

Email: mdstep@hijli.iitkgp.ernet.in

Technology Incubation Centre at IIT Guwahati

www.iitg.ernet.in/tic Email: tic@iitg.ernet.in

Sidbi Innovation and Incubation Centre, IIT Kanpur

http://www.iitk.ac.in/siic/index.html Email: siic@iitk.in

6) Technopark—Technology Business Incubator, Trivandrum

A joint effort by Technopark, Trivandrum and the Department of Science and Technology, Government of India, T—TBI helps technology startups gain access to funding through banks and venture capitalists, and infrastructure. They also provide mentoring and counselling.

www.technoparktbi.or

7) Vellore Institute of Technology—Technology Business Incubator

In partnership with the Department of Science & Technology, young entrepreneurs at VIT—TBI can get access to VIT's technical resources, infrastructure and faculty expertise. Entrepreneurs can also connect with VIT's network of bankers, academicians, venture capitalists and businessmen who could support the startup.

Learn the art of writing with Rashmi Bansal
(All workshops held on Zoom, on weekends)

For dates visit: https://rashmibansal.in/workshops

Short Story Writing Workshop (3 hours)

If you want to start telling your stories, register for this hands-on workshop. The goal is to have a complete story written by you at the end of just 3 hours. The best stories from the workshop get published on my website

Deep Dive Non- Fiction Workshop (2 days/3 hours each day)
This workshop is designed for anyone who is keen on writing an impactful non-fiction book. The workshop is practical in nature and features hands-on exercises as well as Q & A. I also cover 'how to get published' and provide a review for 3 chapters of your book.

Personal Story Telling Workshop (3 hours)
Whether you are a CEO, or a junior manager, stories will help you energise your team and build your personal brand. Learn how to tell your personal story with confidence and flair.

All workshop attendees also become part of a virtual writing community.

Discover the Power of Storytelling

Customised workshops for schools and colleges
Team building and leadership workshops for organisations
Coaching CEOs in the Art of Storytelling.

If you want Rashmi Bansal to conduct a hands-on worksho write to: enquiry@rashmibansal.in with your requirement.